Stefan Roigk

de—COMPOSED

» Sound as a *mark* to place ephemeral splinters in the surroundings — Sound as a *gesture* to draw with invisible lines and pervasions — Sound as a *color* to paint environments with transparent atmospheres — Sound as a *volume* to determine or fill space in time

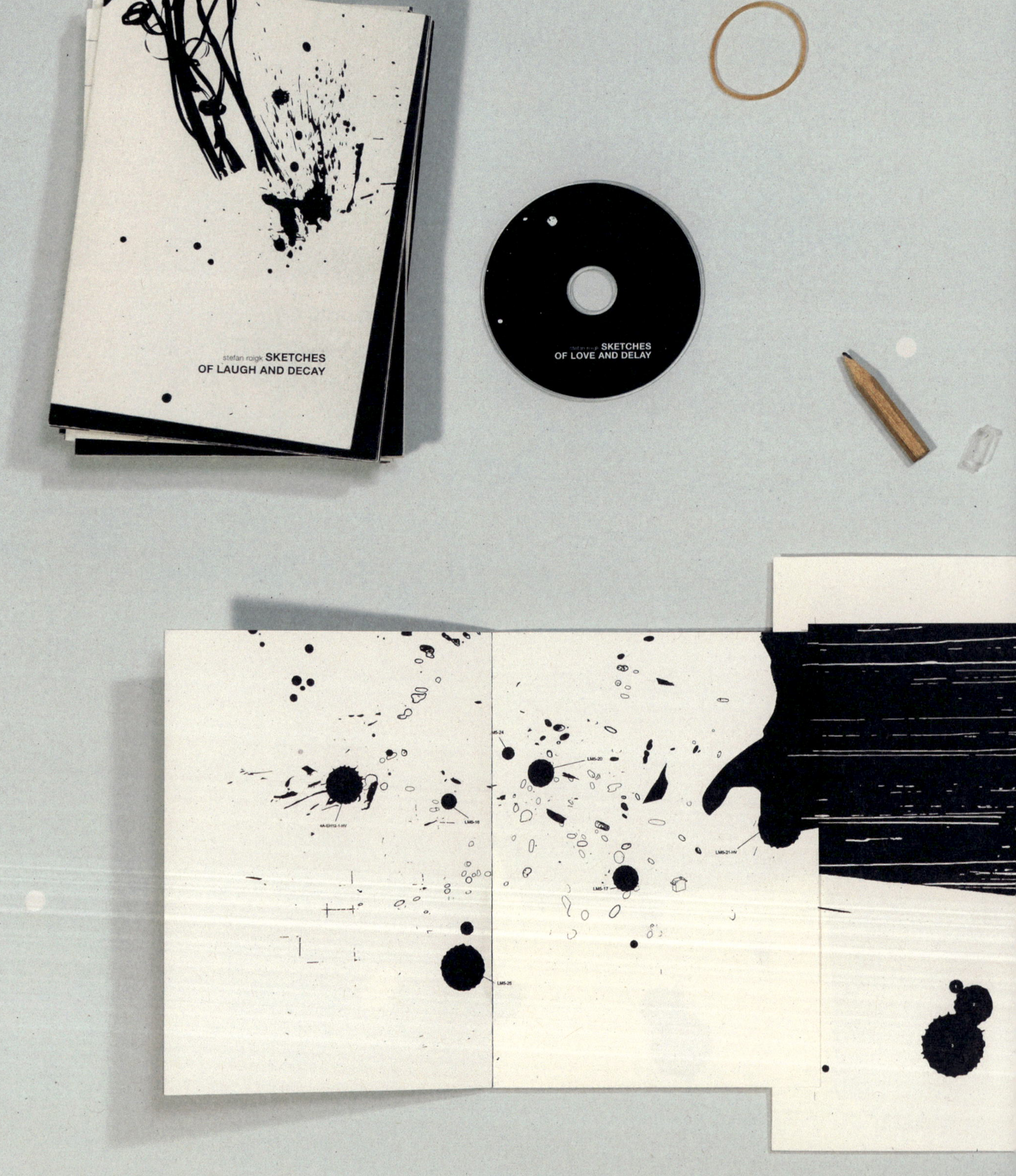
stefan roigk SKETCHES
OF LAUGH AND DECAY
SKETCHES
OF LOVE AND DELAY

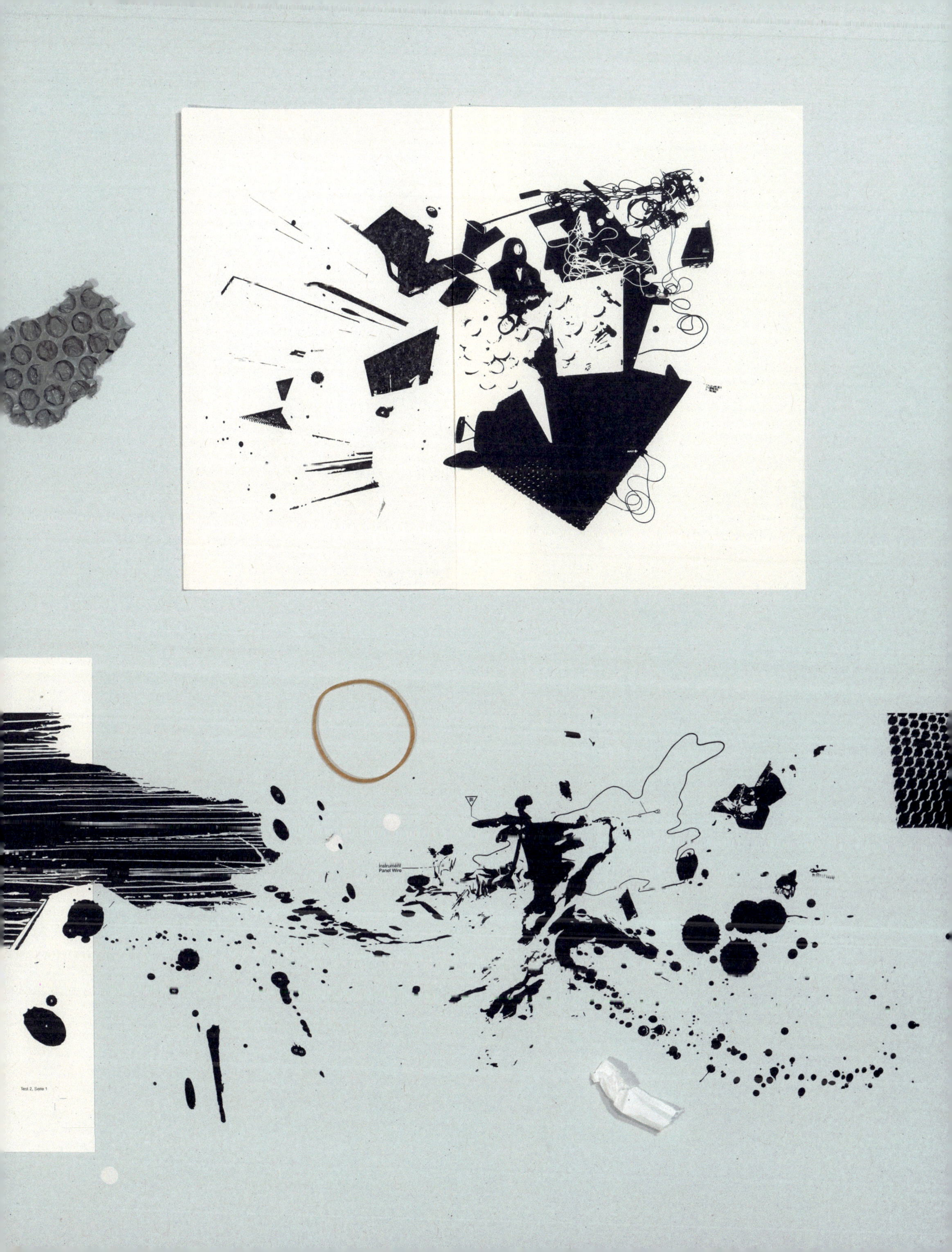

Instrument
Panel Wire
Test 2, Serie 1

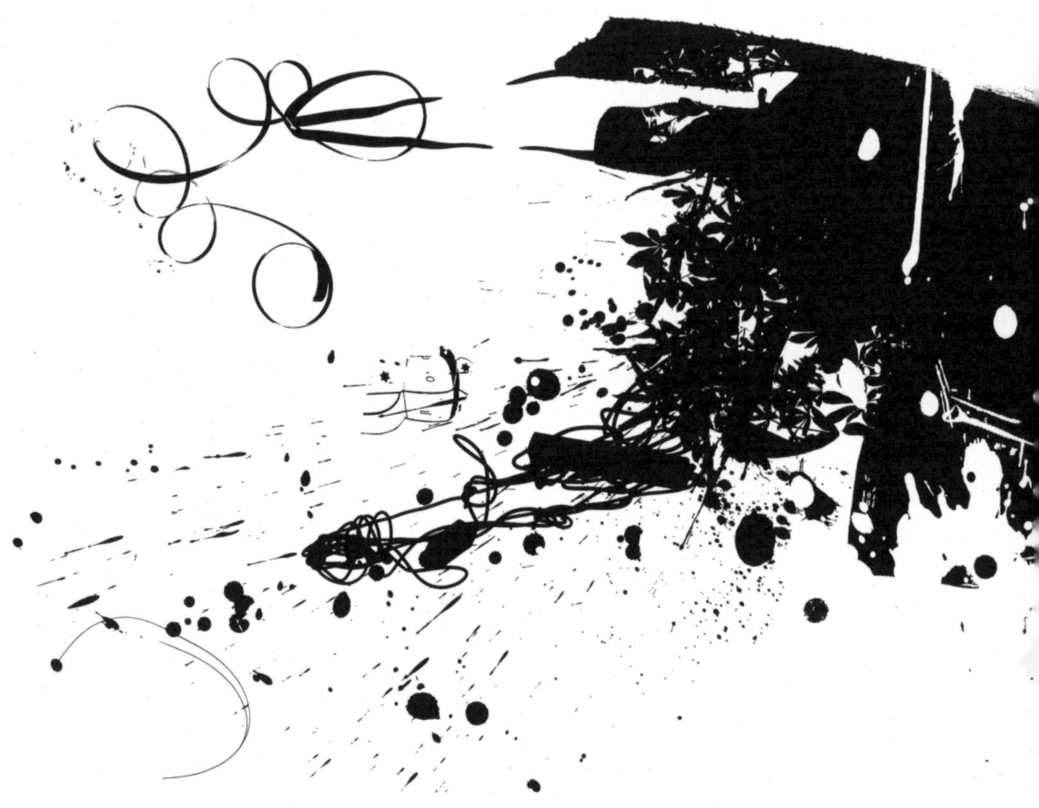

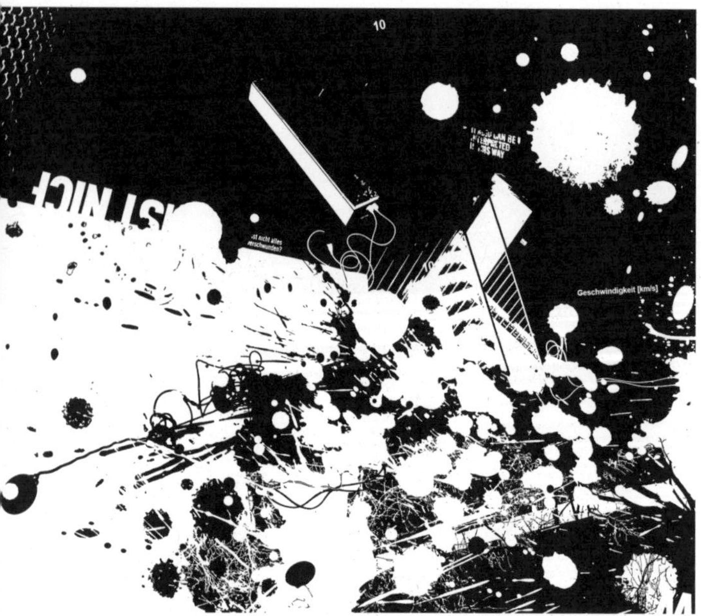

Sketches of Laugh and Decay (Book) + Sketches of Love and Delay (CD)

2009

musical graphics and audio CD

» An Emotional Dungeon of Sonic Short Stories – Inspired by a Walk Through the Woods to Get Handcrafted Ice Cream

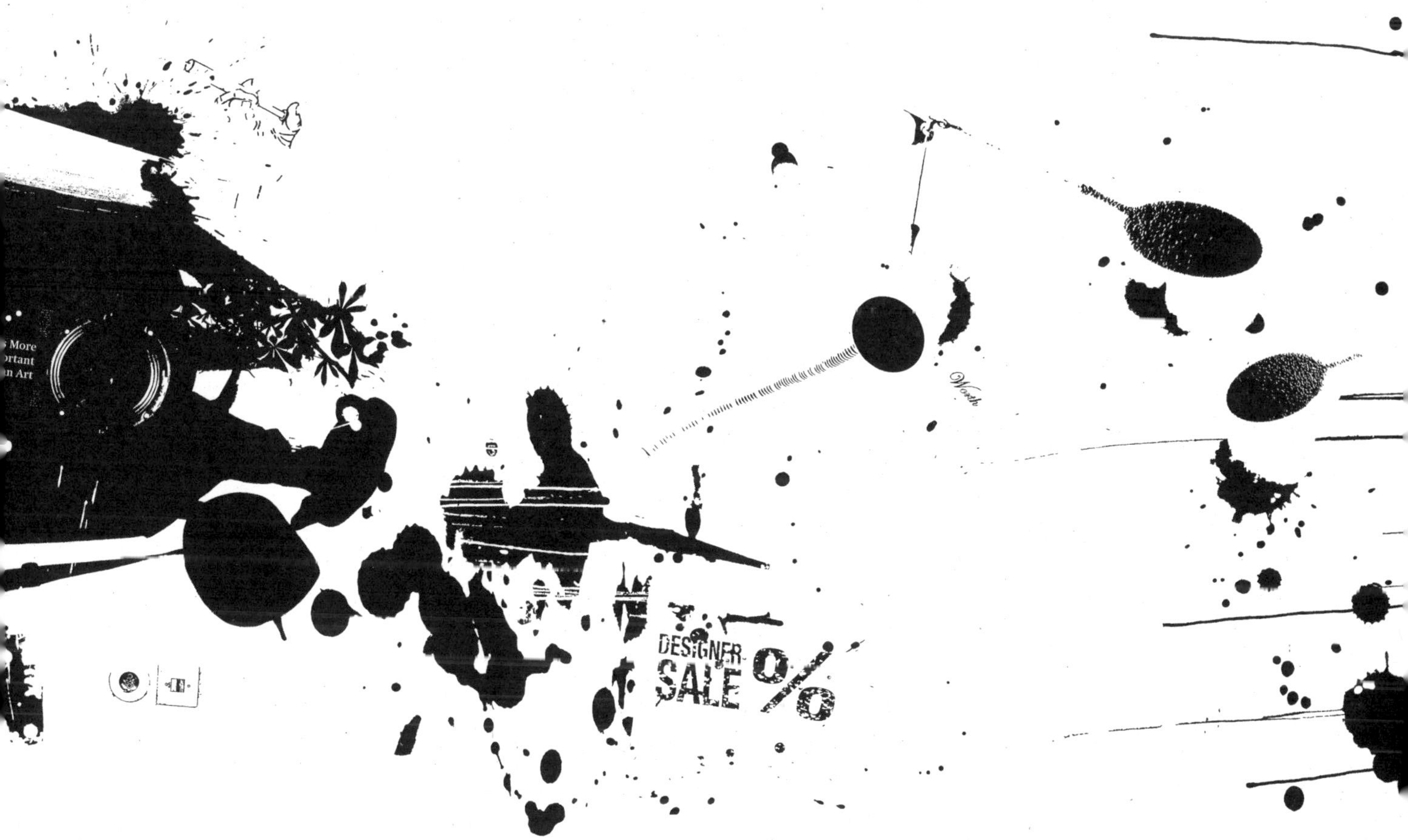

the multifaceted dynamic
illustrations of the book
"Sketches of Laugh and Decay"
are expanded upon in the
Musique concrète composition
"Sketches of Love and Delay",
featured on an accompanying
audio CD, and make clear the
connections between musical
graphics and sound collage

Book :
Art and Theory, Volume 10 /
published by Bernd Milla
(ed.) in co-operation with
Künstlerhäuser Worpswede
+ Argobooks /
black-and-white print /
42 pages / 16 x 12 cm

Audio CD :
acousmatic sound collage /
3" CD / 13 tracks / 20:38 /
CD 2 – track 2

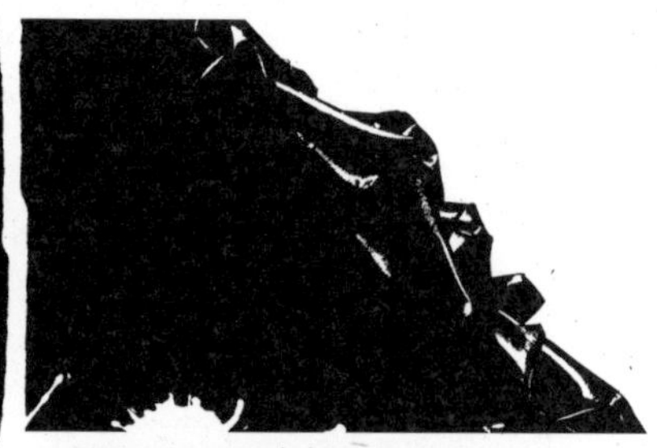

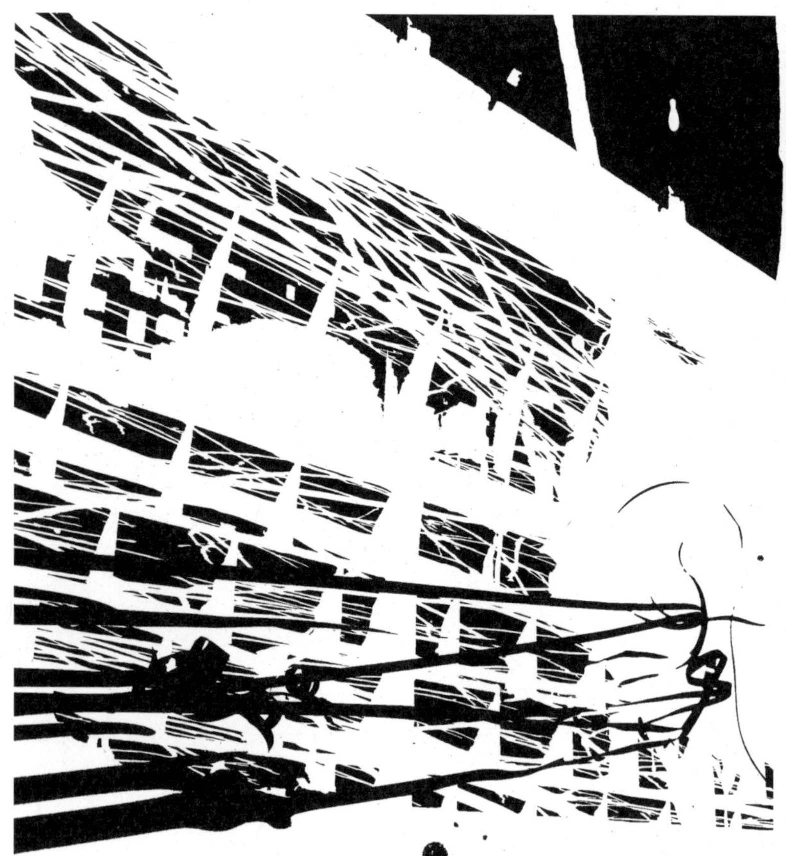

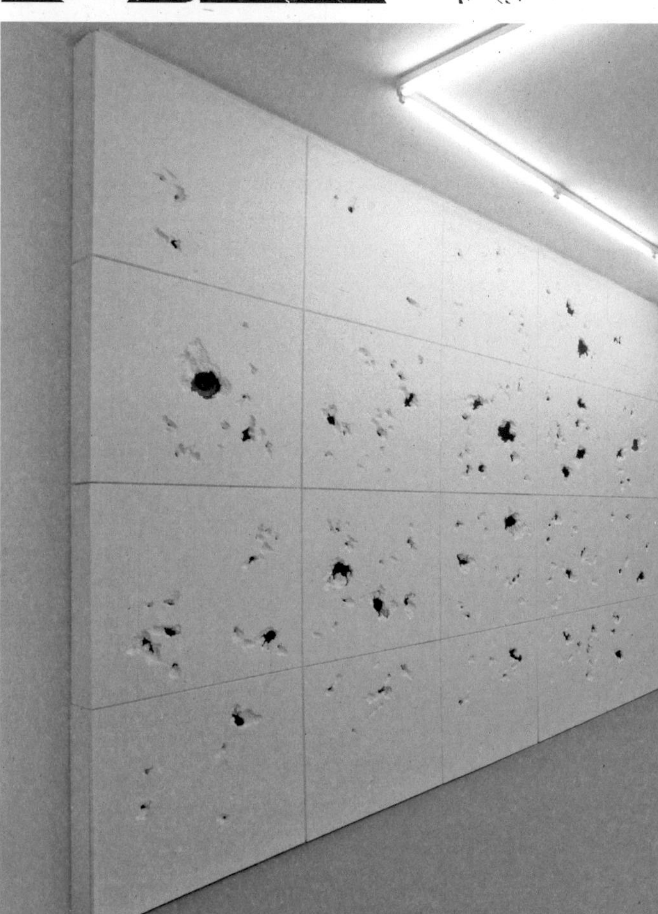

Swarm

2009 ——————————

mixed-media sound installation

**» Polyphonic Invasion of
Swarming Holes**

Objects : black convoluted acoustic foam, polystyrene, wood, full-range loudspeakers, playback equipment / 500 x 500 x 400 cm

Sound : 4-channel composition / dense field of heavily modified ringtones and noise interference / dynamic sound movements / loop (35:30) / CD 1 – track 5

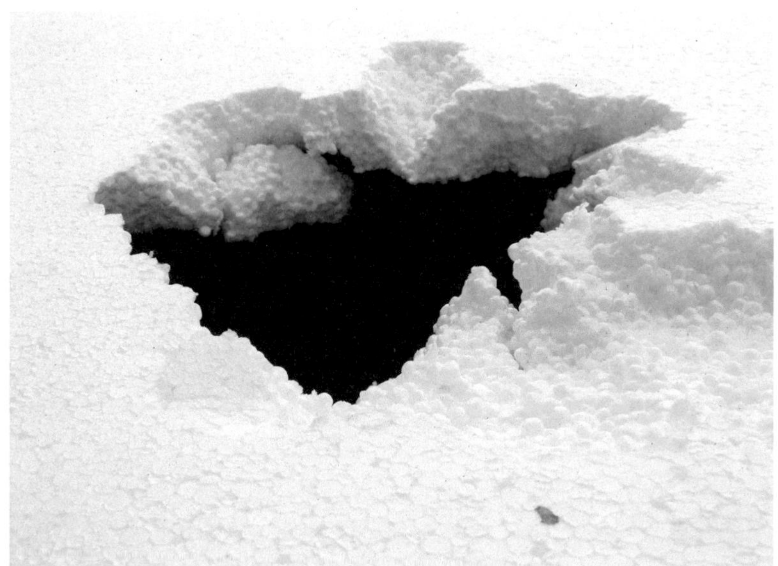

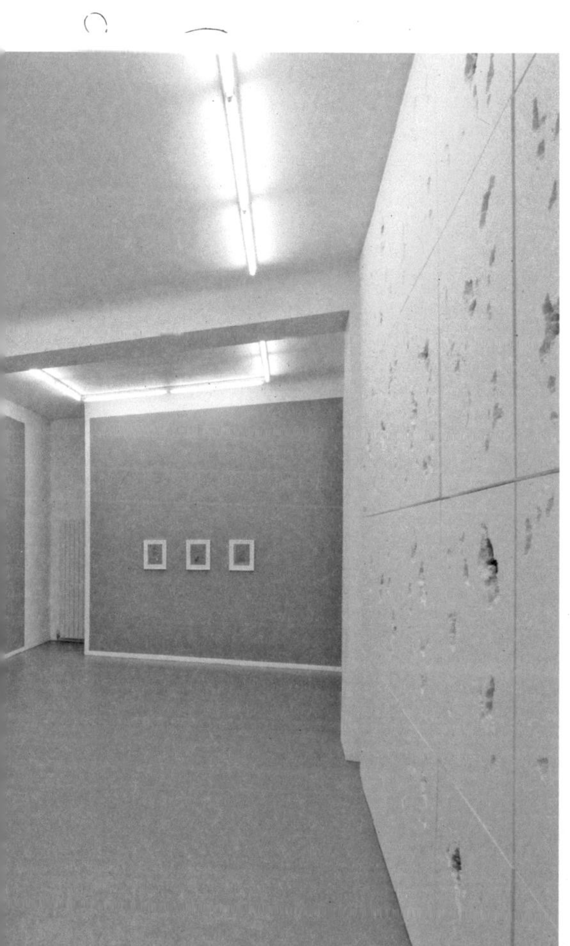

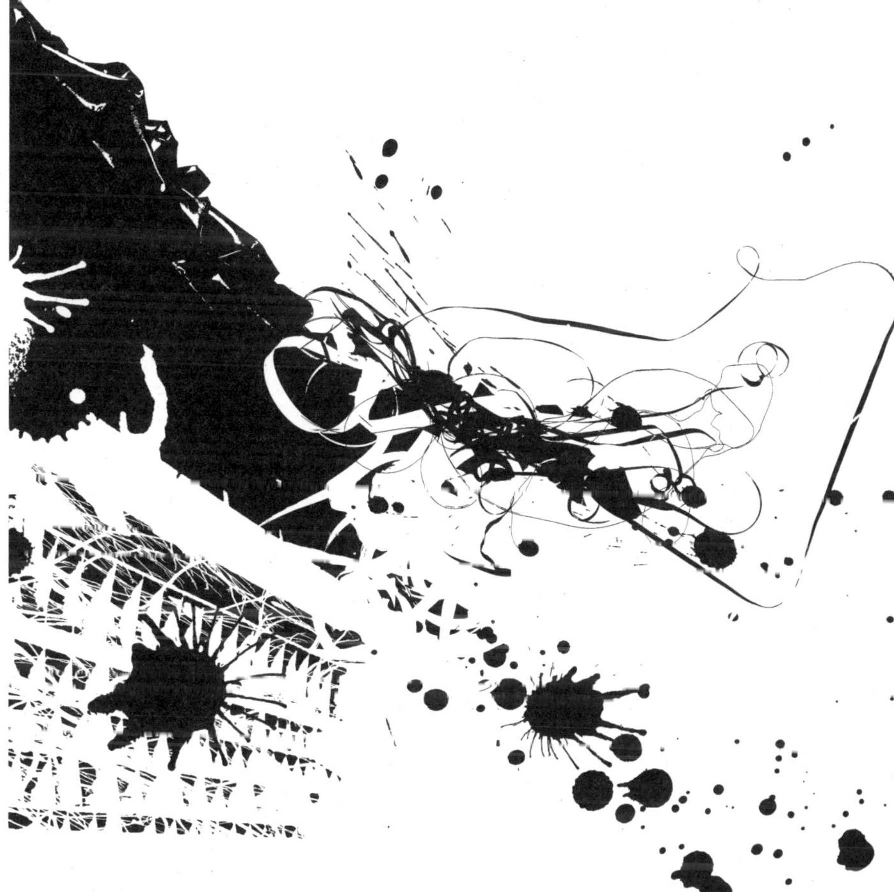

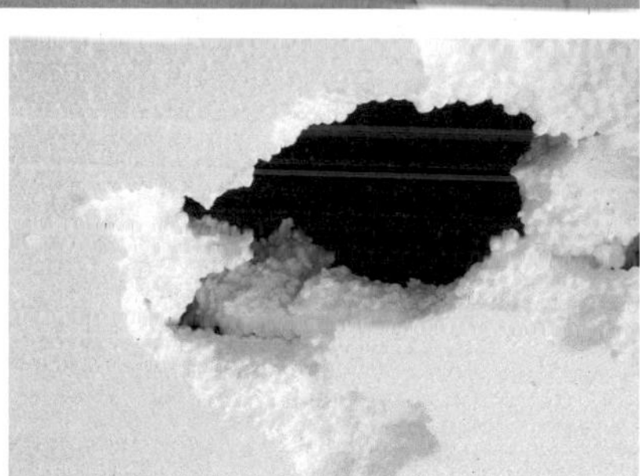

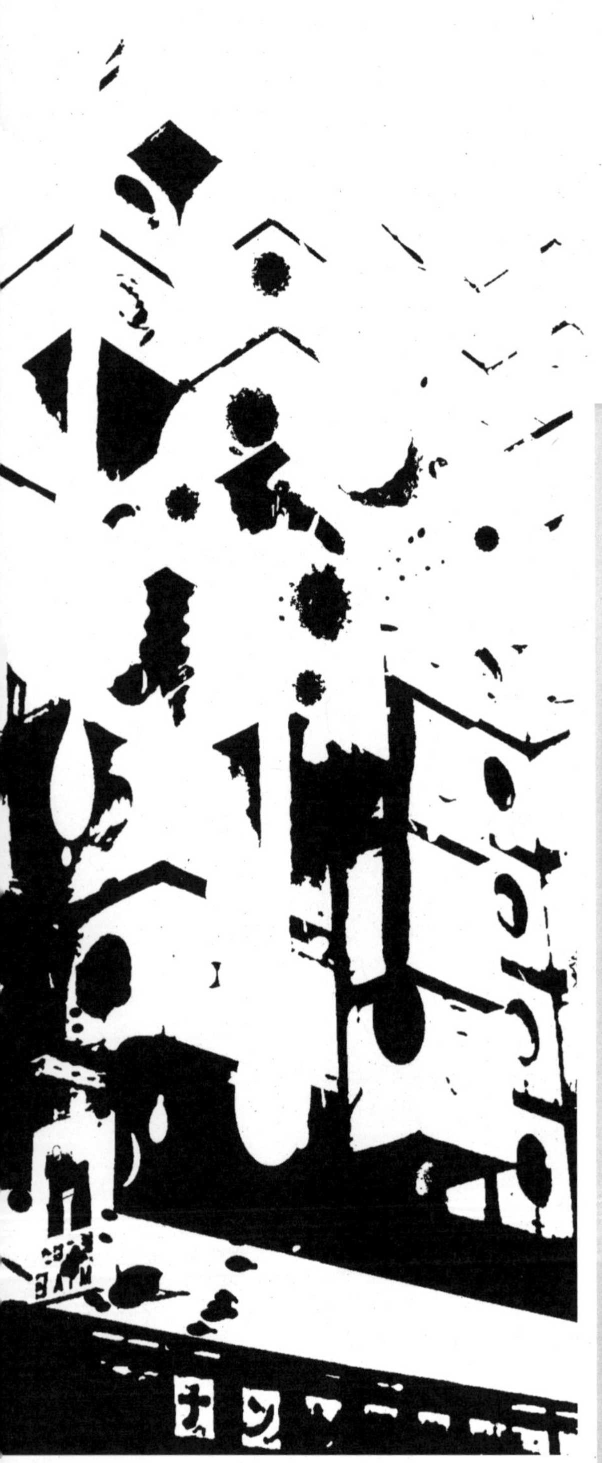

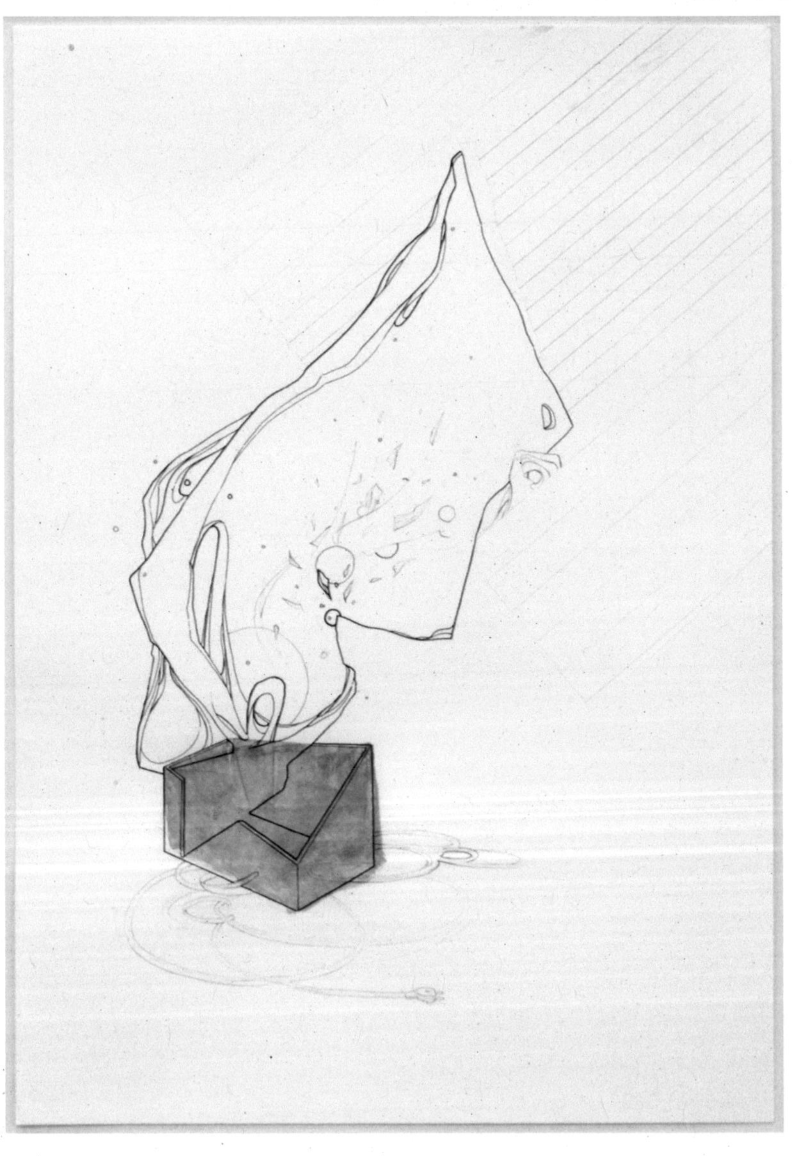

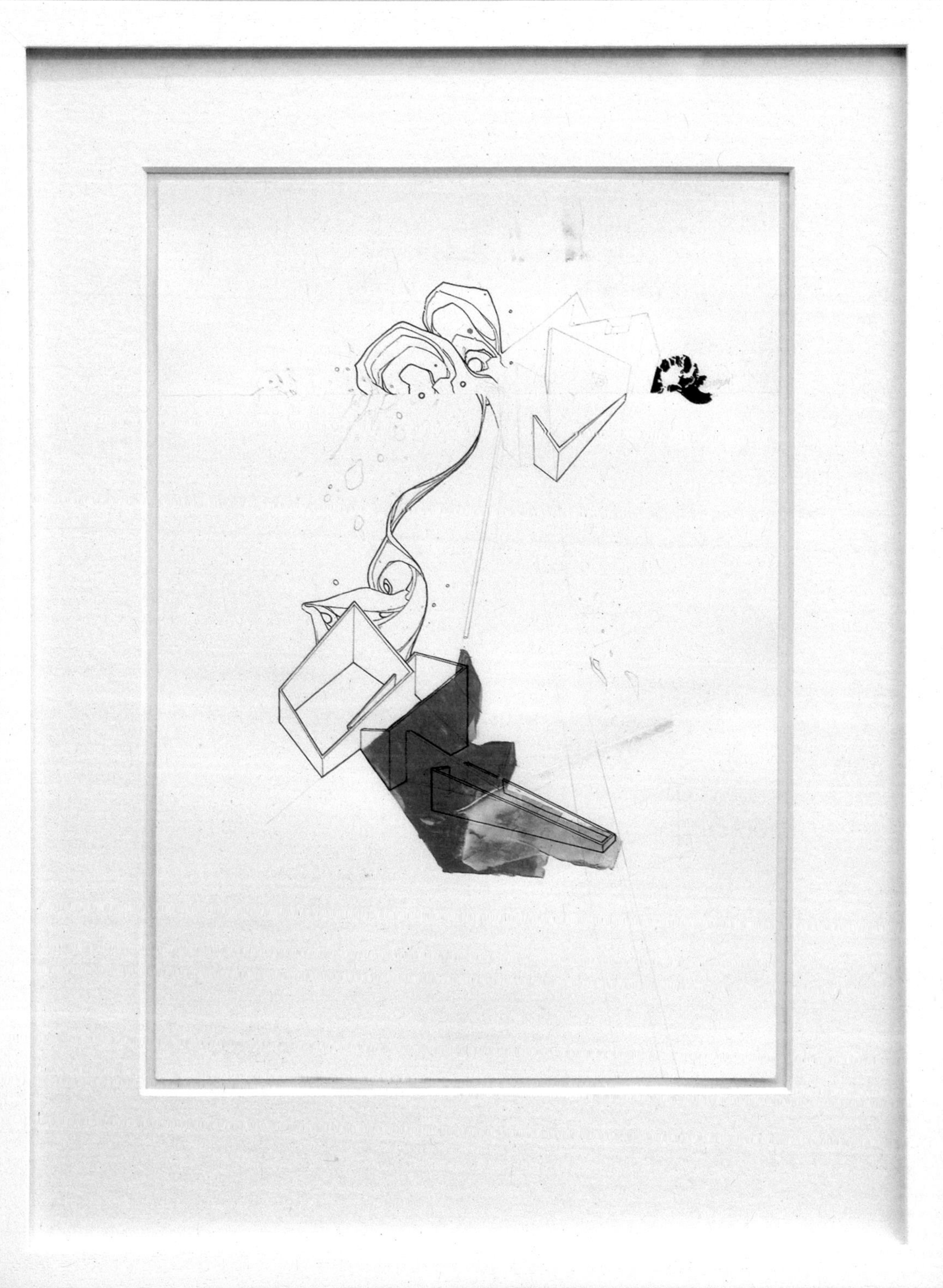

Campink

2009

mixed-media sound installation
» a Sonic Opera – an Italian Love Story, a Drama Queen and the Male Star with Make Up

Objects :
black vinyl adhesive foil, grey paint substrate, power outlets, plugs, cables, full-range loudspeakers, playback equipment **/** 1000 x 500 x 400 cm (set-up variable)

Sound :
4-channel composition **/** dense sound field composed of manipulated opera recordings, augmented with noises from aluminum foil, cardboard, sheet metal, ping-pong balls, glass, plastic lids and voices **/** loop (43:21) **/** CD 1 – track 16

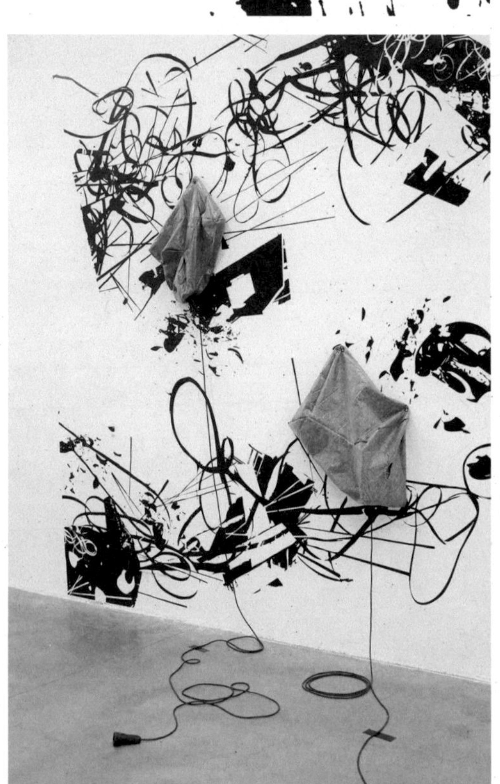

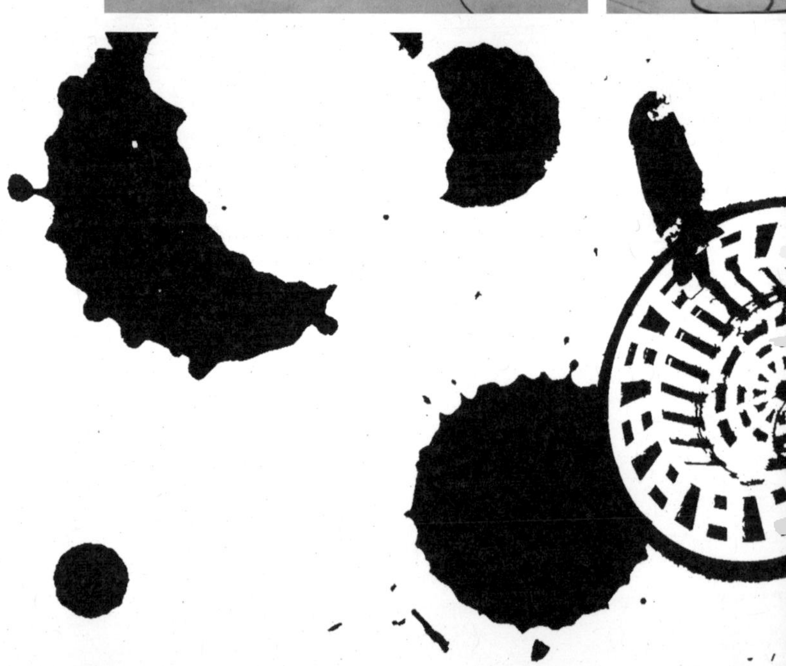

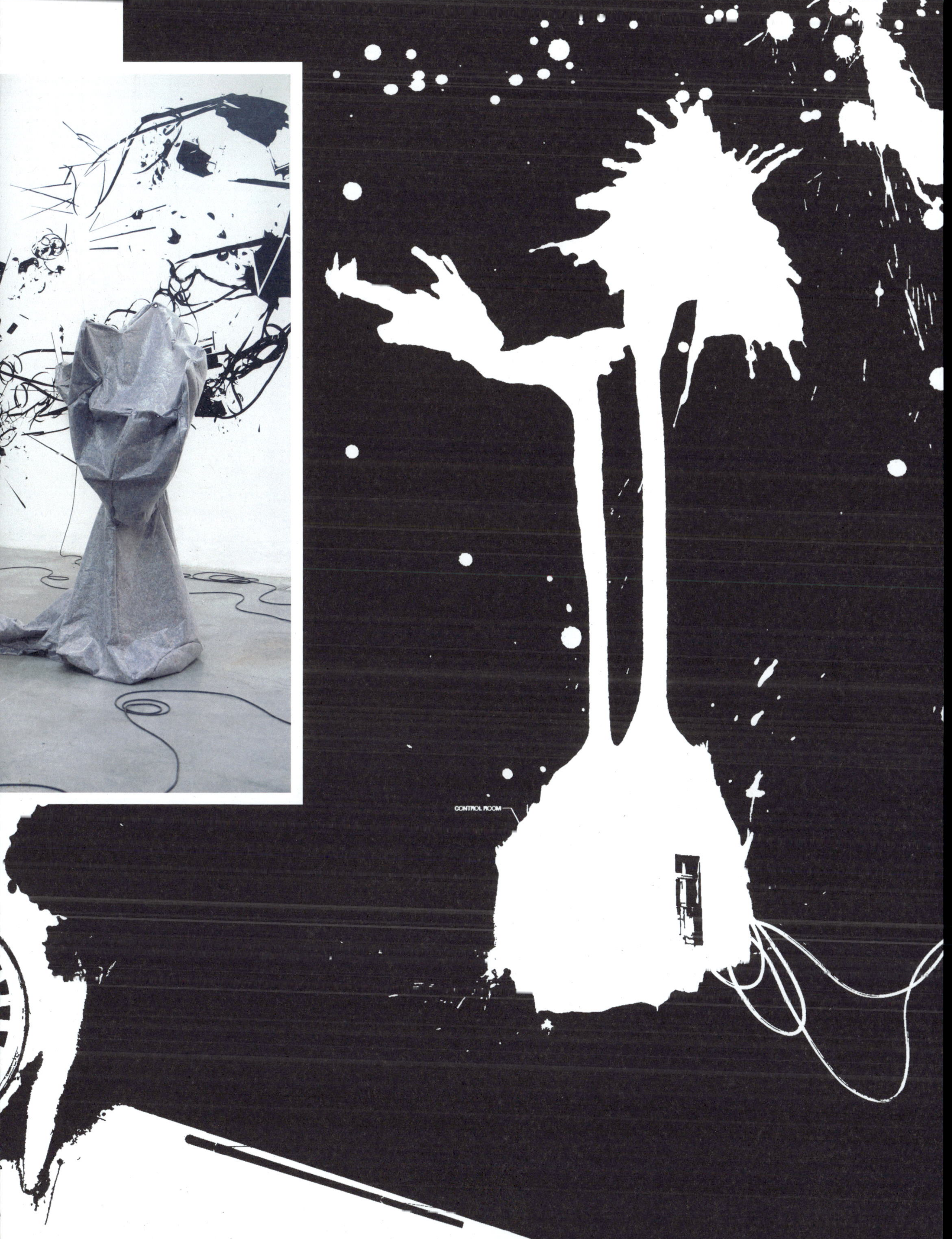
CONTROL ROOM

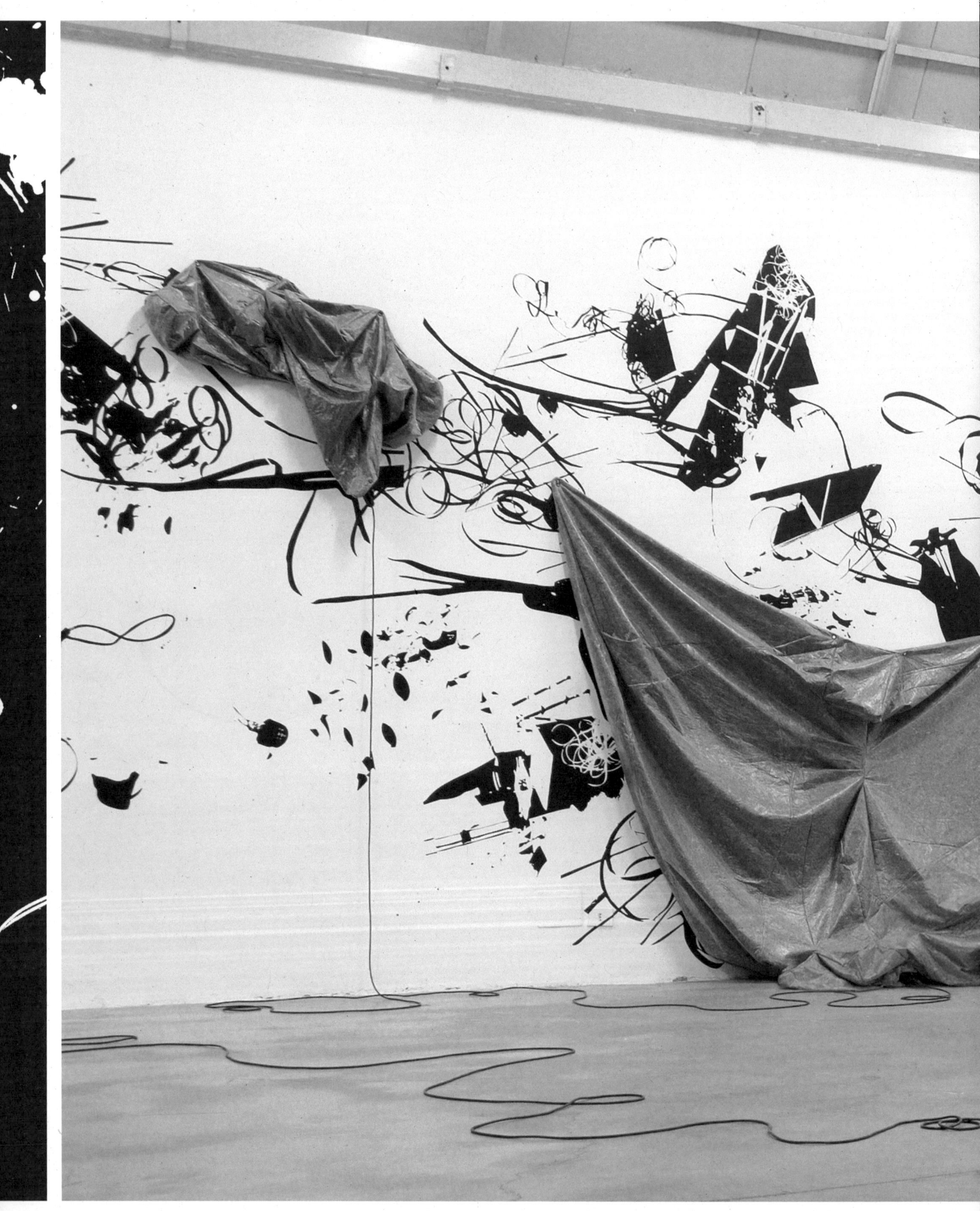

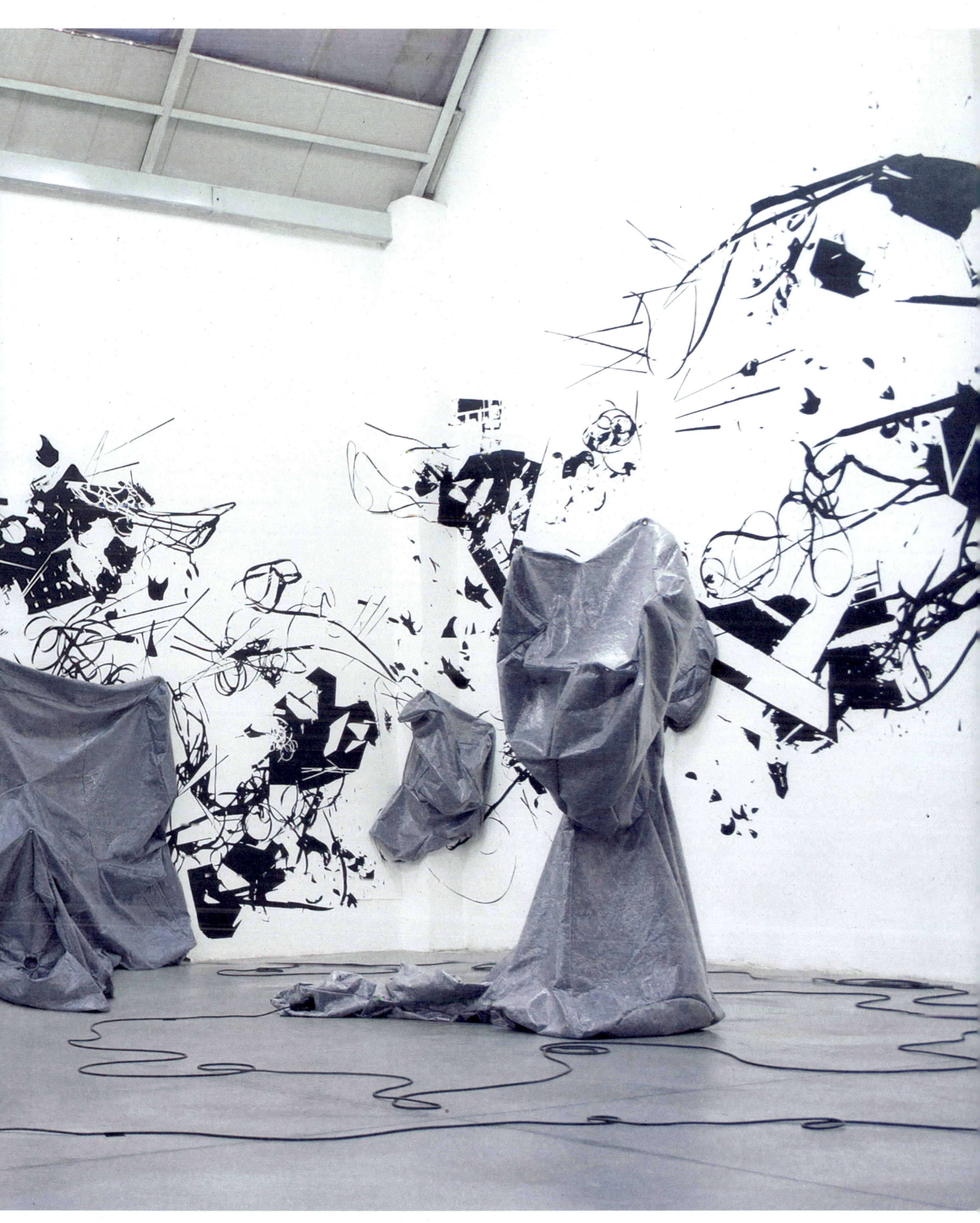

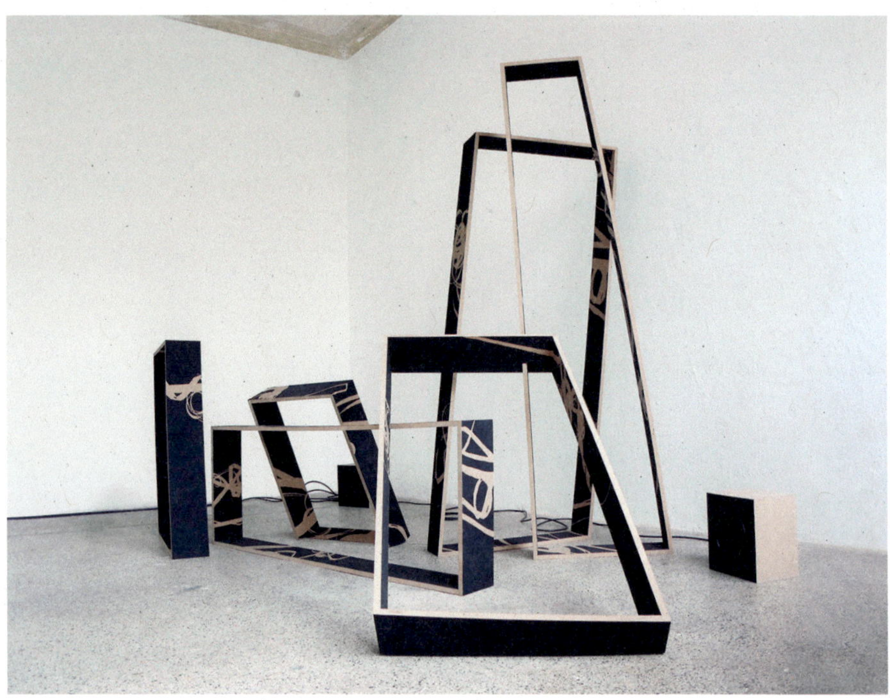

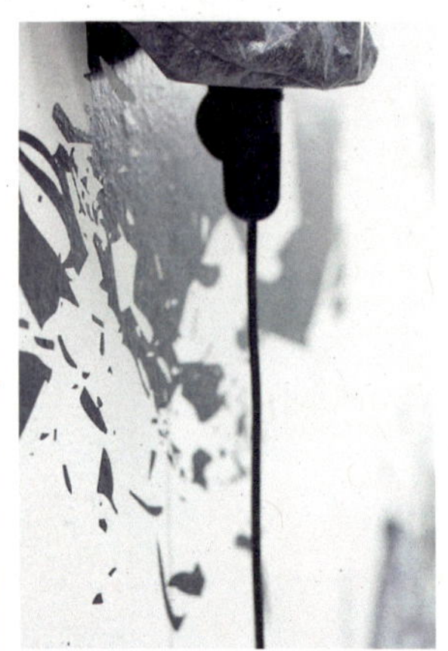

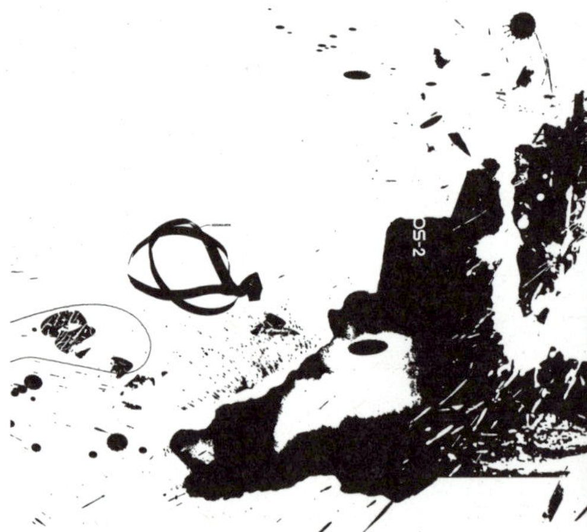

The Line Between

2010 ——————————

mixed-media sound installation
» Duet for Two Rooms

Objects :
acrylic paint, full-range
loudspeakers, cables,
medium-density fiberboard,
playback equipment **/**
500 x 200 cm (drawing) **+**
400 x 200 x 220 cm
(installation)

Sound :
4-channel composition **/**
dense field composed of
distortion, the vibration of
a knife blade on wood,
beating wet towels and
spinning wooden picks
on a concrete floor **/**
2 loops (11:42 + 11:44) **/**
CD 1 – track 15

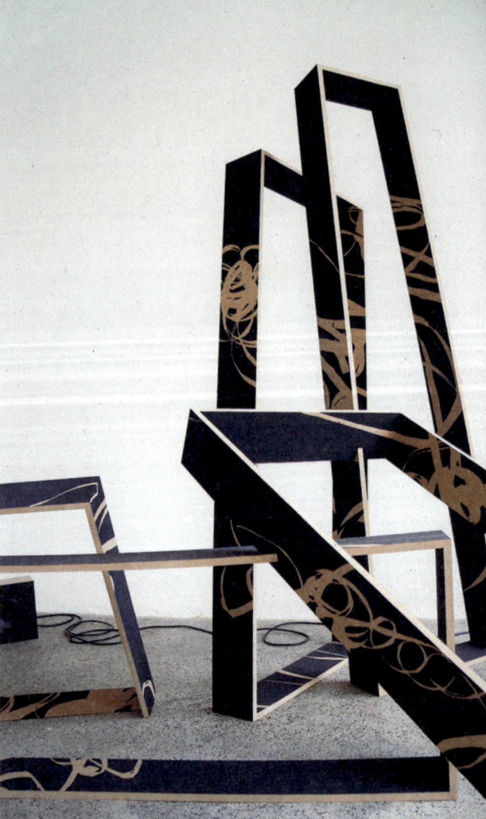

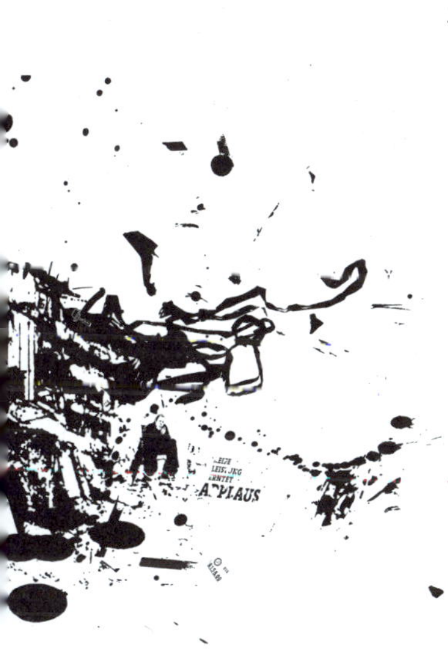

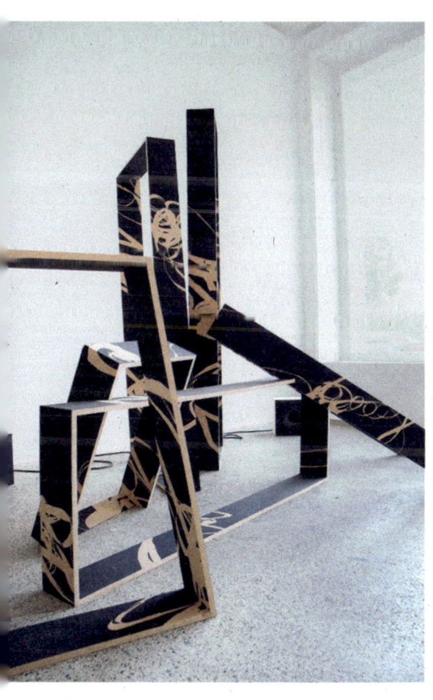

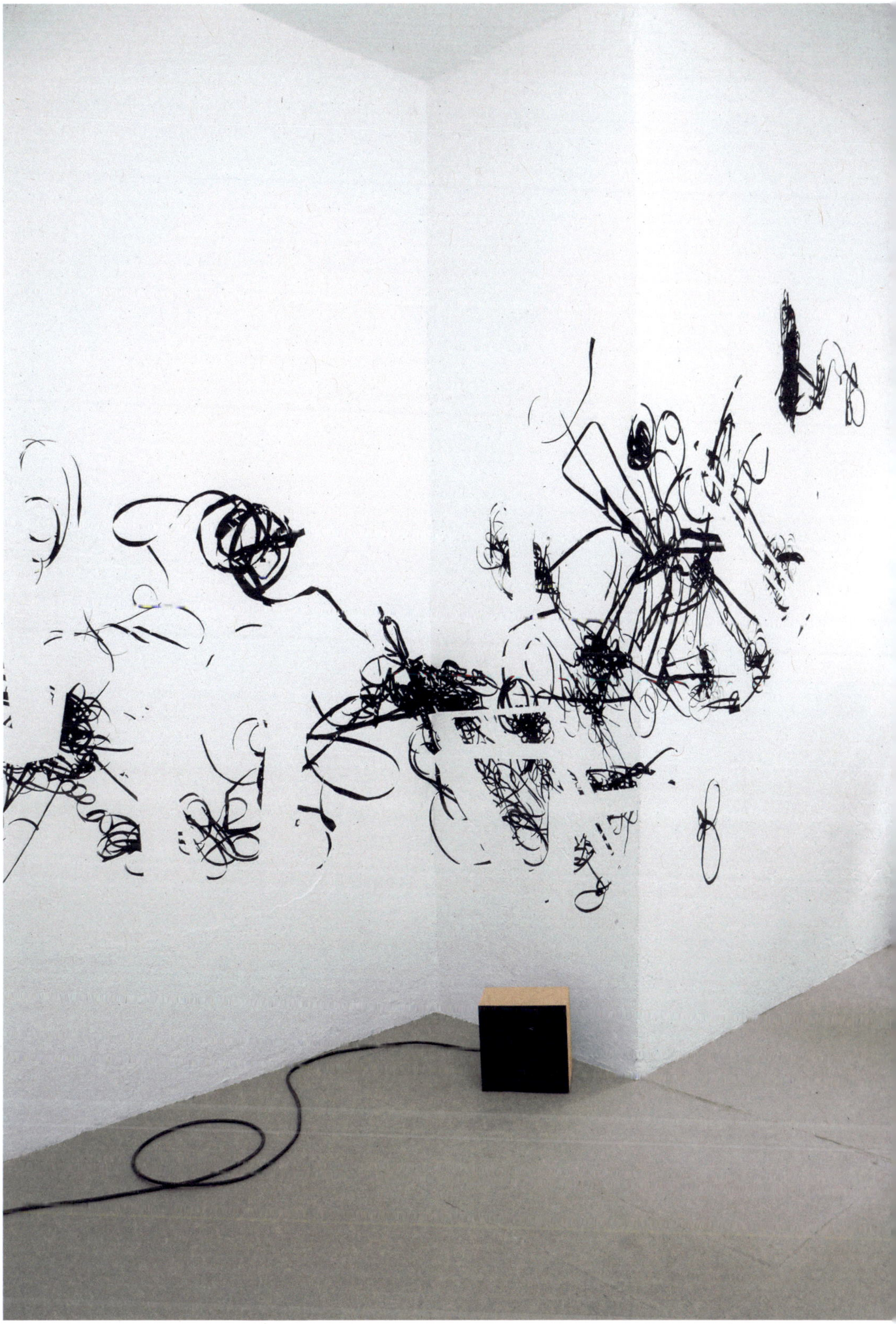

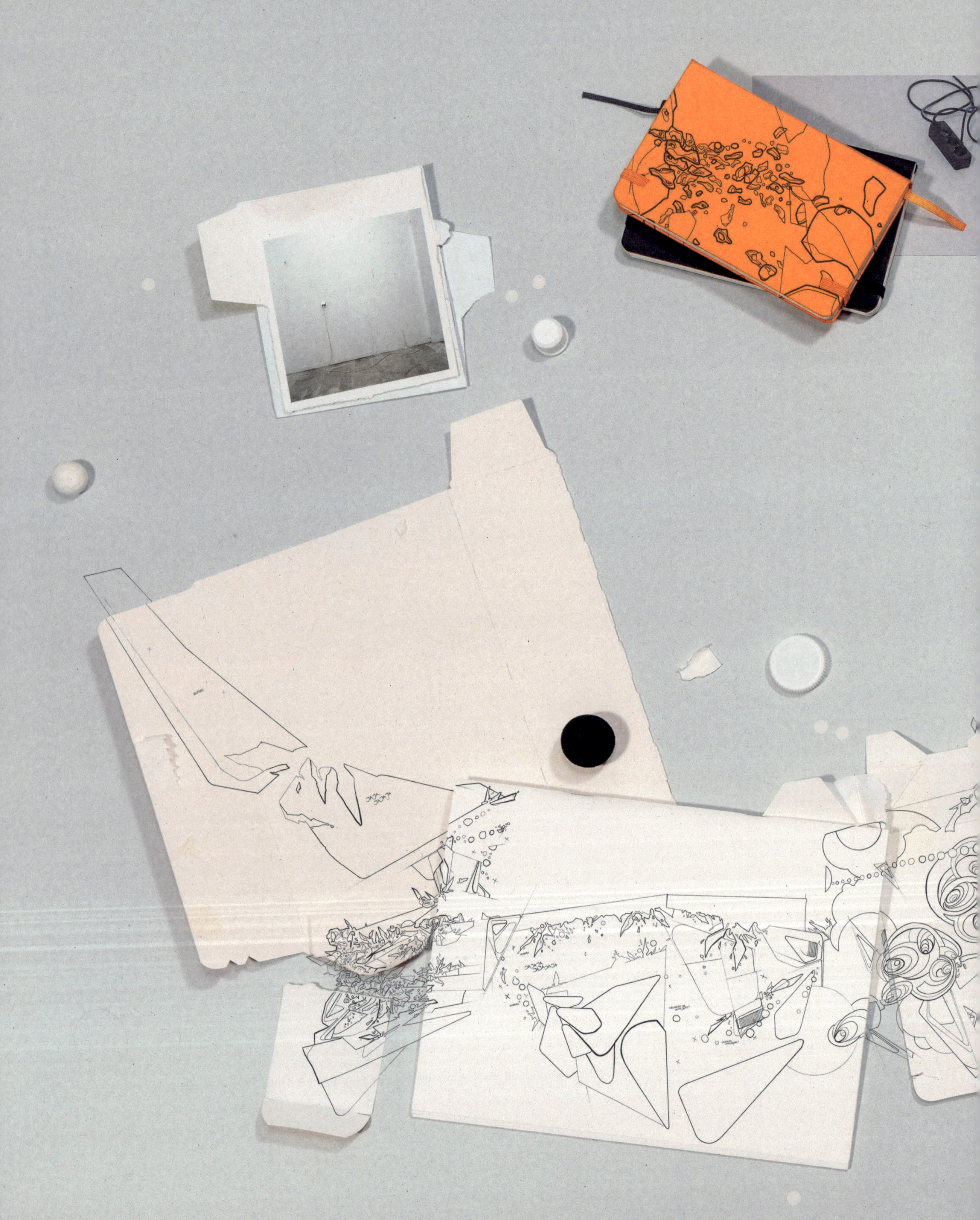

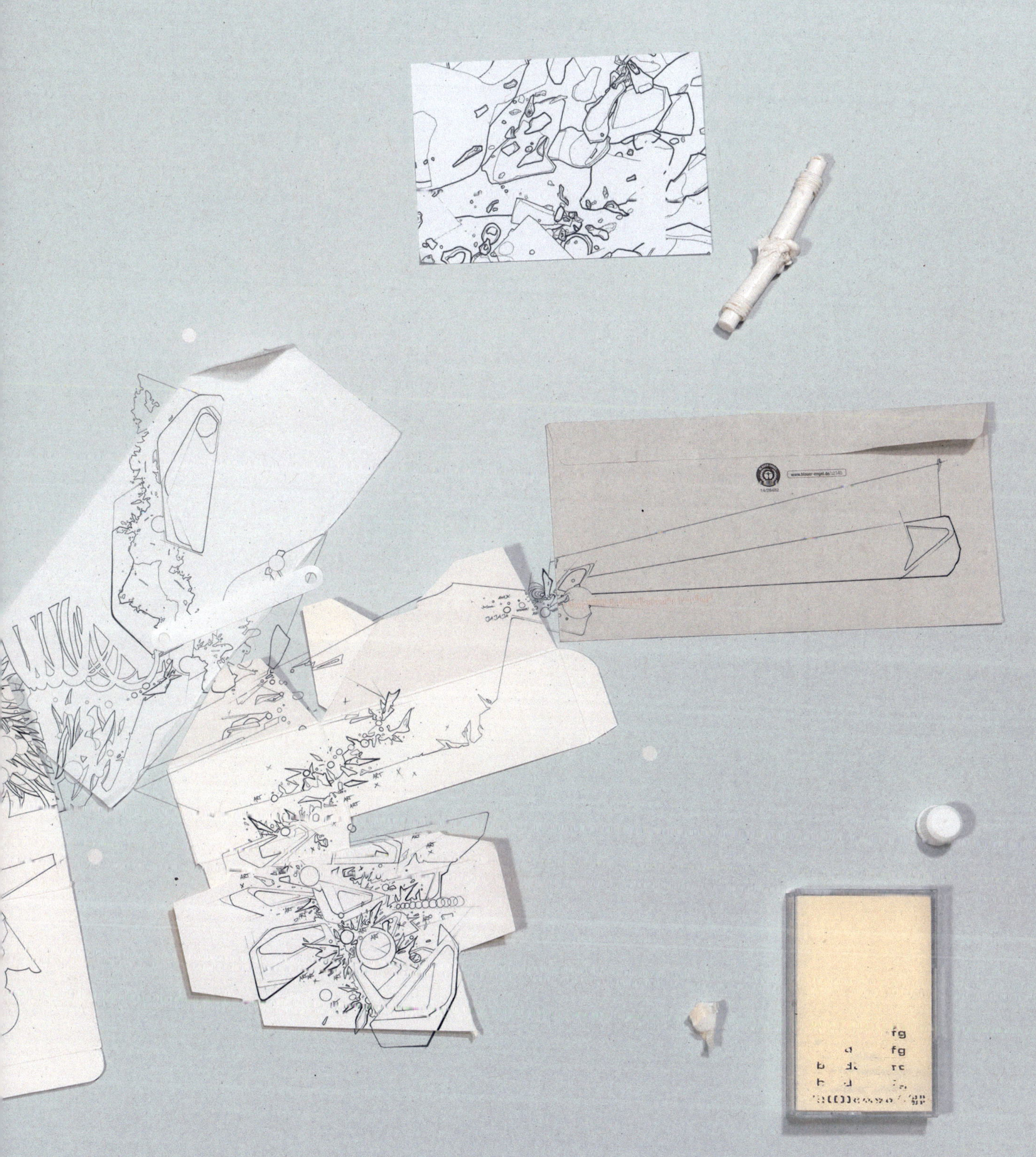

Bilder meiner Ausstellung

2007

Eight Ephemeral Audio Sketches of Sound
Interventions and Installations in an Imaginary
Museum Made of Real, Existing Art Spaces

PART 1 **JOURNEY THROUGH THE LOBBY**
(0:00—1:37)

The deep organic sound of a big and nearly empty
museum creeps subtly to the fore(ground).
Quiet conversations animate the background
and a bunch of time goes by. Suddenly three
harsh paper shreds tear the room into pieces.
Popular Joseph sings his line before the big and
empty hall comes slowly back in style.
The sound of wooden footsteps leaves the room
and passes by several times. At the same time,
crackles swell to an ocean of cooking grease,
and strange thuds and rumblings mold a nearly
concrete scenery.

PART 2 **IMAGINARY LAMPSHAKES**
(1:37—2:49)

Just at the moment a slurp is peeling from left
to right, a wall of sound enters the place.
A broad range of low babbling voices, snatches,
dramatic rattlings and chaotic fidgets spin
around and take place in every part of the room.
After the trashing retreats for a pause in the
background, it returns directly with a deep
organic squeak and disrupts everything into
small scraps. The hubbub rotates massively in
panorama while a peeling slurp decomposes
the fading room.

PART 3 **INVOCATION OF MY
BEARING OTHER**
(2:49—4:24)

A deep organic noise opens the scene which
quickly becomes a frosty purr. The crowd waits
eagerly and there is always Joseph's music in
the air. When the performance starts, deep
horns take command with a boggy field of
warm outpourings. Screeching vocal treat-
ments, staccato-like, ensnare the wide panning
horn figures while cracklings and burbles release
the concert with a highlight. A discontinuity
makes room for the clueless audience as another
horn enters from the rearmost part of the room
to the foreground. Two piercing sounds abruptly
rule the board with panicked strain. Vocal treat-
ments rise for a last peak before they fade away
in the endless catacombs of the museum.
The audience has left the building.

PART 4 **UNTITLED JET**
(4:24—5:56)

An undertow gathers the brightness of slides
and the lights go on with a deep buzzing on the
right side. Hippy chants explore the universe
while a deep bass-pounding pumps up from a
great distance. Razor-thin phase modulations
open the surrounding so that the deep buzzing
can stream in the whole panorama. The cruising
of vacuum cleaners brings the tubby rhythm
to the foreground, and the warm hippy chants
return with undulated stretches.

PART 5 THE LEGEND OF AIR
(5:56—6:35)

The bursting of fine glass splinters puts an end to this psychedelic drone of freedom and throws the focus onto a cold blackness. No daylight falls on this background composed of subtle drippings and thick murmur. Flogging strokes and intense bass convulsions form a field of proliferating jungle-like rhythmical structures. A stumbling sine-wave modulation soon craves attention and fades away that organic coil of polyrhythmic plateaux.

PART 6 HOMAGE TO CELLE
(6:35—7:15)

A whirring drone comes closer as a loud bang illustrates the clean stage by its tiled reverb. Small high-frequency crunches crack cluster bomb-like out of the blue. Their spatiality and shape are squeezed and scrunched by a deep organic drone which ends with a click and liberates the scene from its density. The crackling dissolves in the entrance of the adjacent gallery.

PART 7 THE UNASKED ANSWER
(7:15-8:30)

The subluminal rush of the showroom is terminated by a fax machine from the back of the stage. After a small pause, clangs interconnect with recurring walking sounds and build a swinging blue note-like rhythm cluster. Yapping and whining of the word art expand the yet minimal figure which is completed by sharp and stretched chimings of a cooking top. The funk, groovy till now, becomes an aggressive sharp-edged braiding, while the barking drafts its desire and relapses into silence.

PART 8 WALKING THROUGH THE WHITE ROOM
(8:30—14:12)

Where we are from an artist sings a pretty song and there is always a young and nice trainee who comforts an important collector on the phone. Meanwhile someone leaves the gallery. The air conditioner starts unnoticed, and now it seems to run statically until the end of time.

"Bilder meiner Ausstellung" consists of an acousmatic composition, a poetic description of the sounds and a musical graphic (previous page : "up.grade" / 2007) / the composition was published in 2007 on the one-sided vinyl record "up.rising" by Tochnit Aleph / 14:12 / CD 2 – track 10

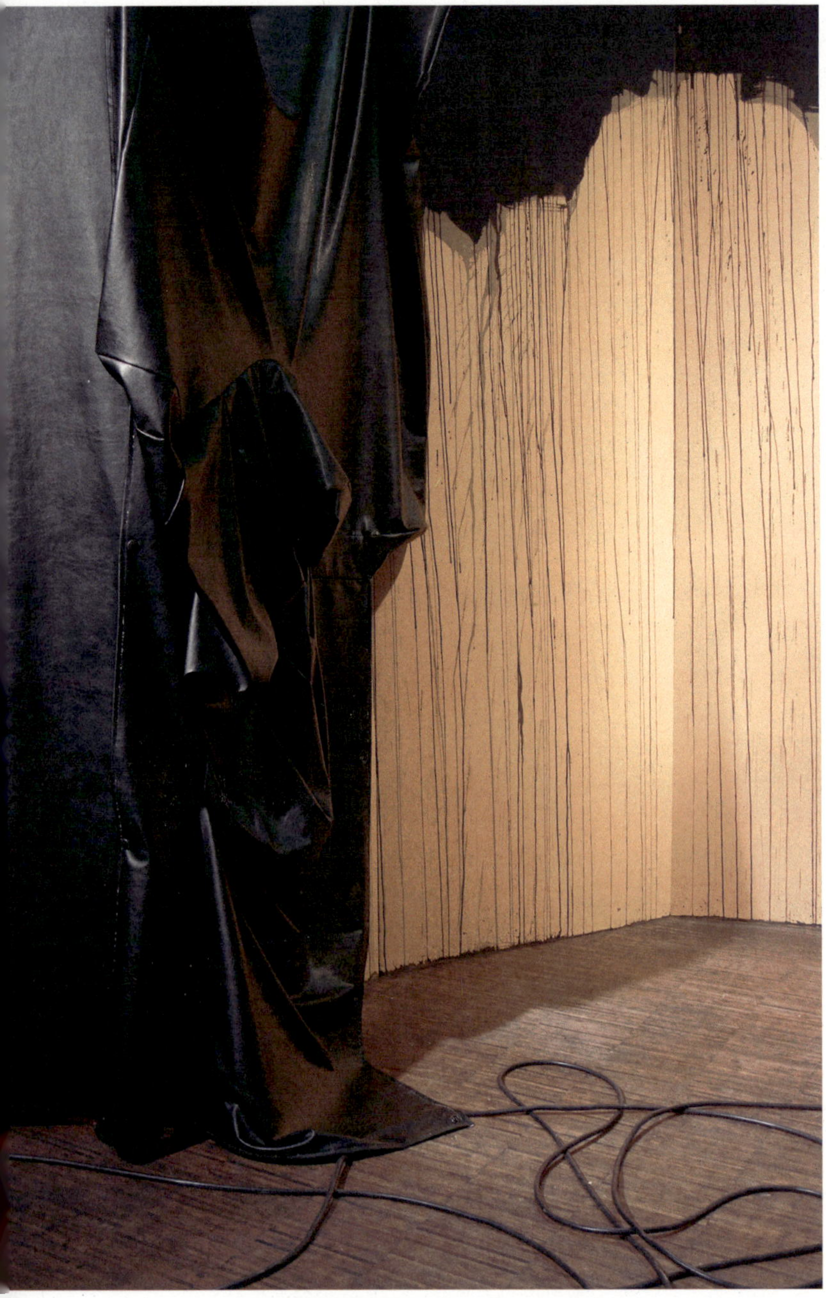

Objects :
leatherette, medium-density
fiberboard, foam rubber,
acrylic paint, full-range
loudspeakers, backdrop hinges,
power outlets, plugs, cables,
playback equipment **/**
500 x 700 x 250 cm
(set-up variable)

Sound :
8-channel acousmatic
composition **/** organically
slow-moving sound mesh:
deformation and fragmentation
of a spoken text, detonations,
bodily noises, field recordings,
static and simultaneously
running alarm clocks (including
winding and chiming) **/**
loop (18:15) **/** CD 2 – track 7

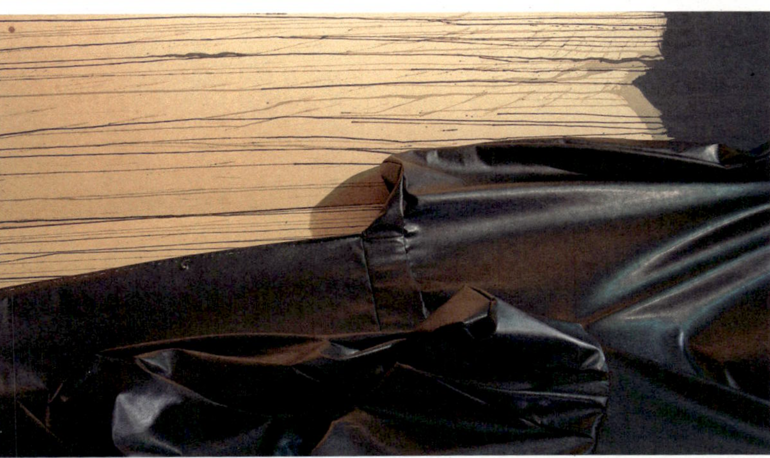

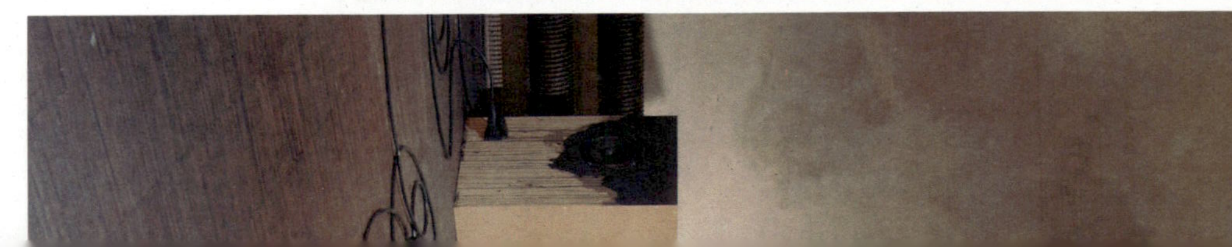

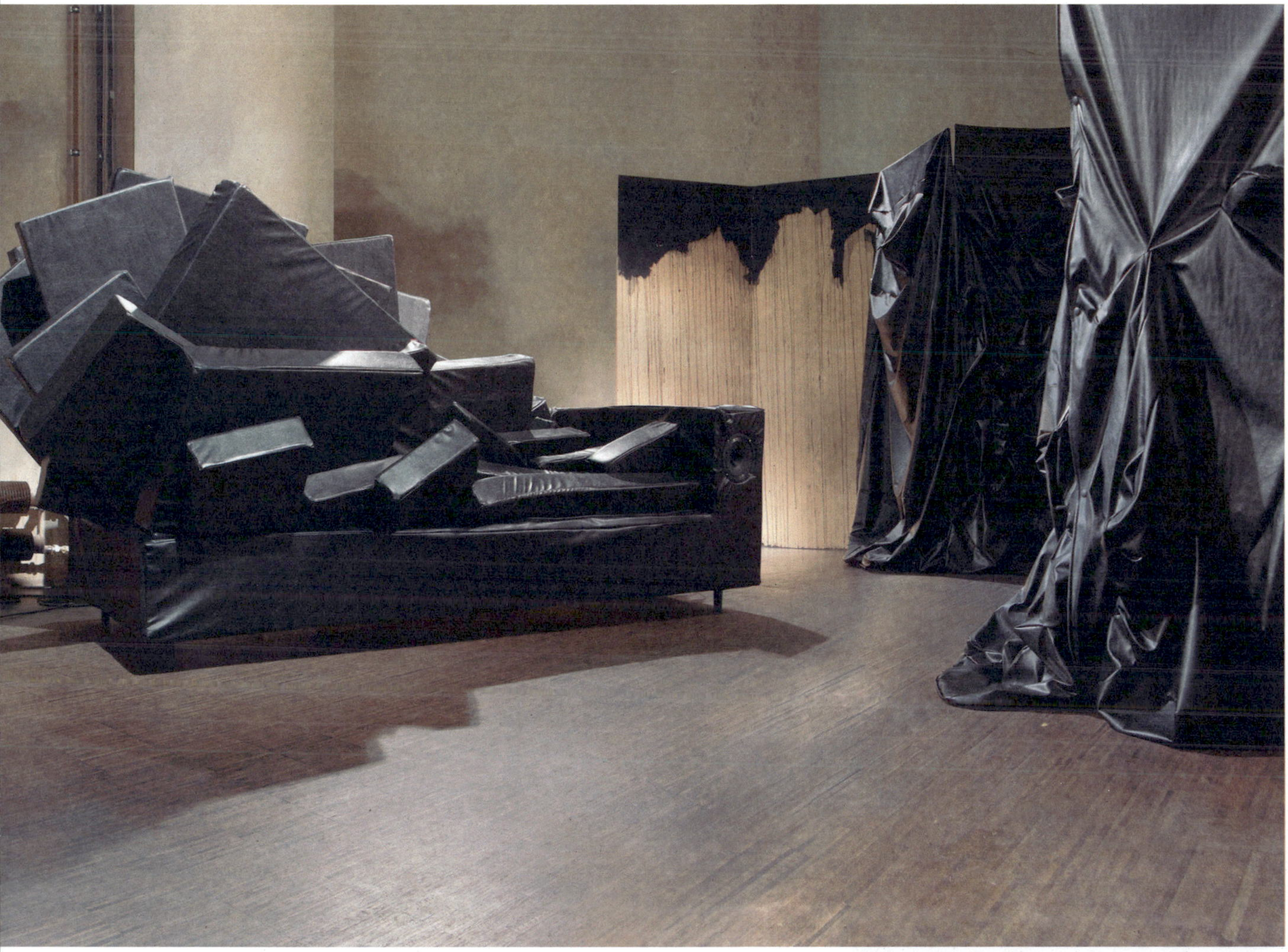

Hanging Garden

2008

mixed-media sound installation

» Where the Sofa Transforms Into a Sea of Ice, the Cold of Society Has Already Penetrated the Retreat of One's Own Four Walls

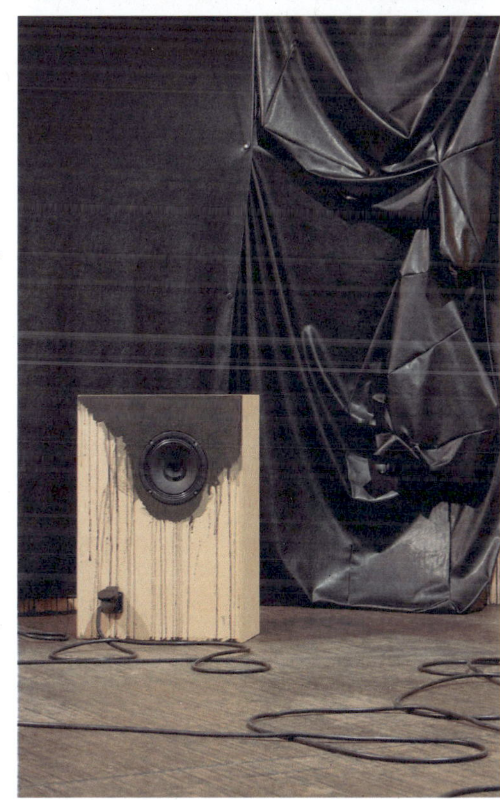

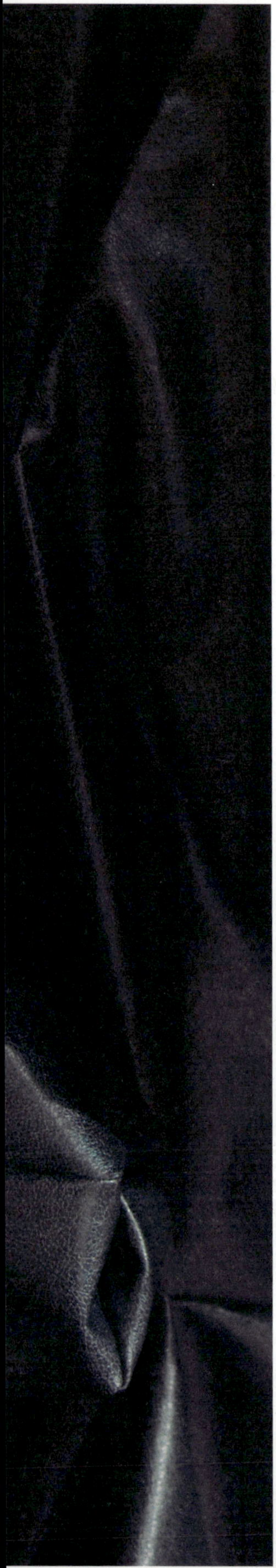

Black Murmur

2007

mixed-media sound installation
**» Floor Mats as the Primer of an
Endlessly Permutating Sound Pattern**

Objects :
black leatherette, foam
rubber, medium-density
fiberboard, blackboard paint,
plugs, power outlets, cables,
full-range loudspeakers,
playback equipment **/**
450 x 350 x 170 cm

Sound :
2-channel composition **/**
dense field of digitally
modified noises of droplets
falling on a hotplate
and whistling of a soda
syphon subjected to overly
high pressure **/**
2 loops (1:20 + 9:05) **/**
CD 2 – track 8

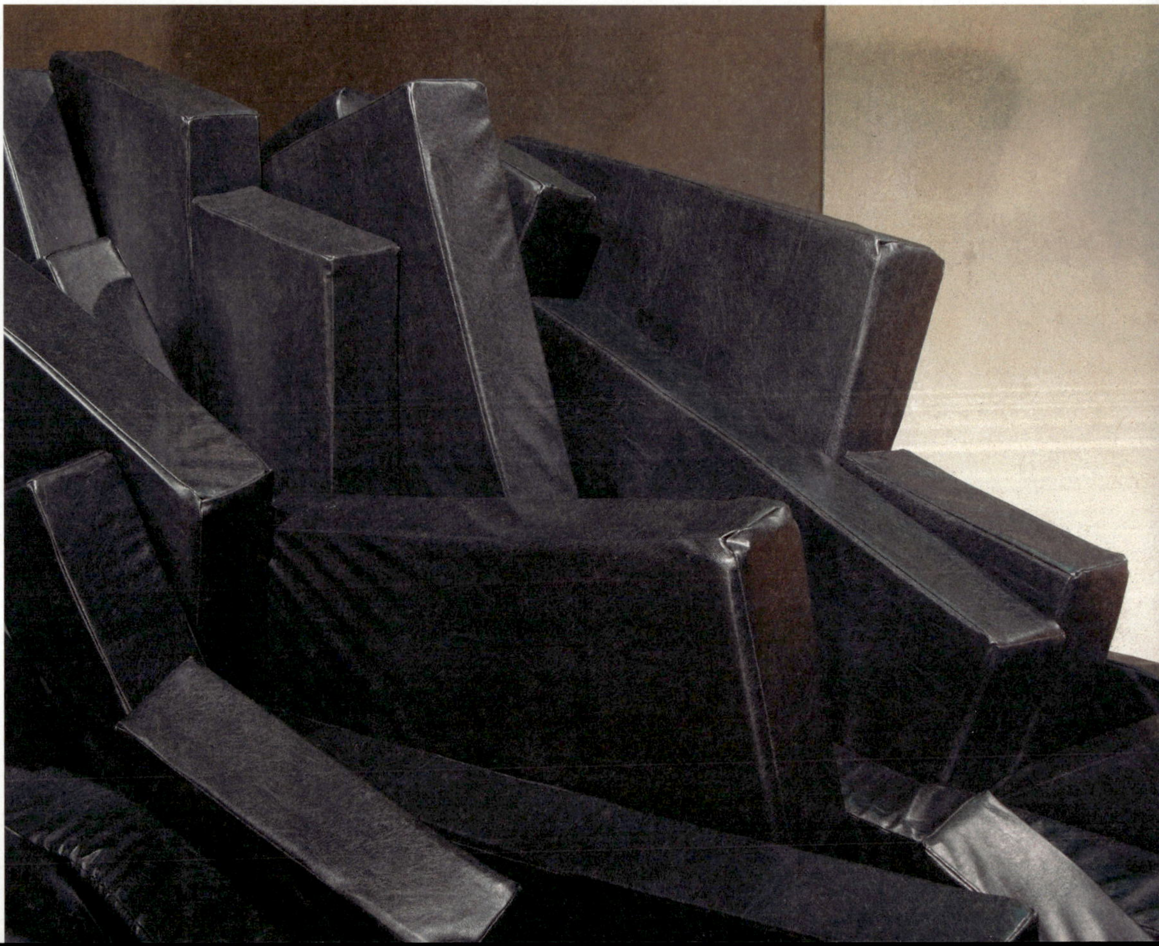

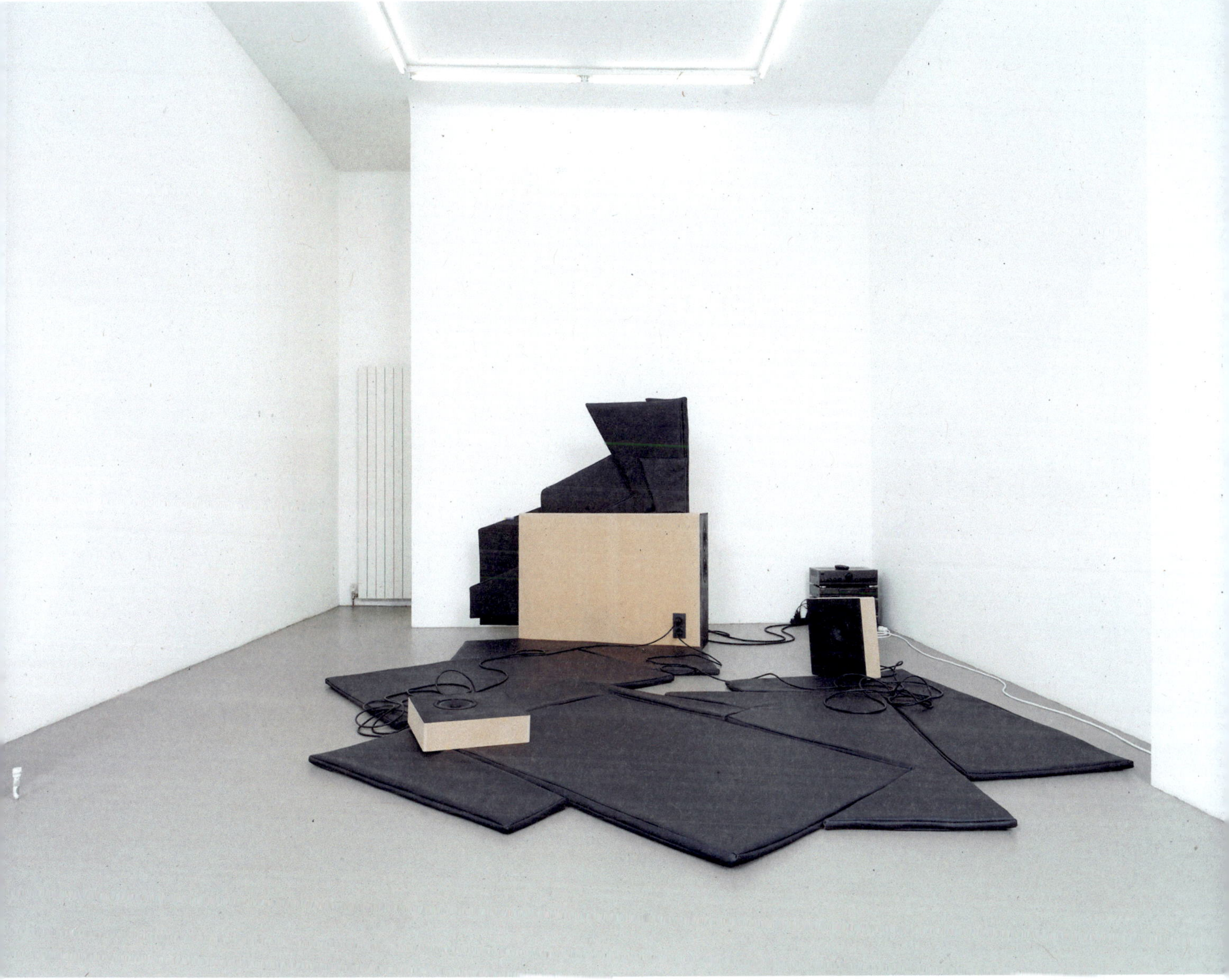

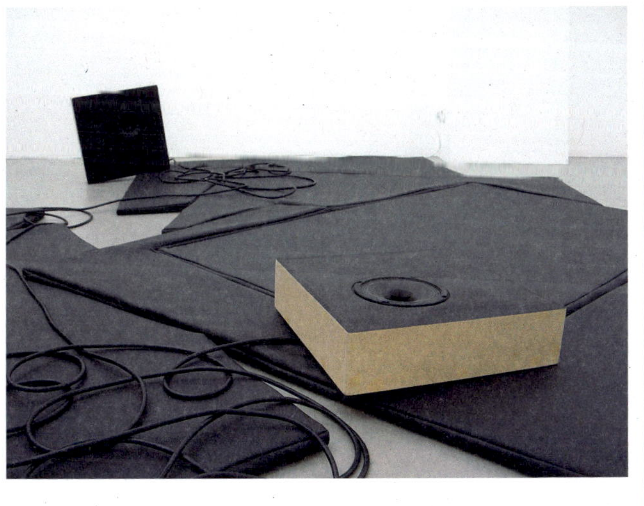

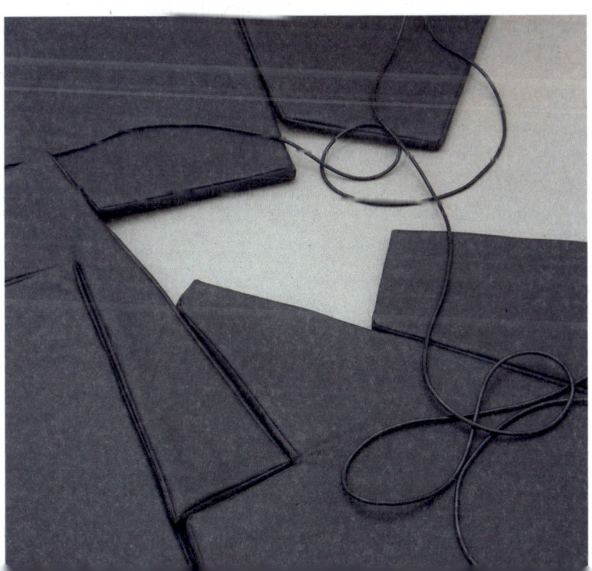

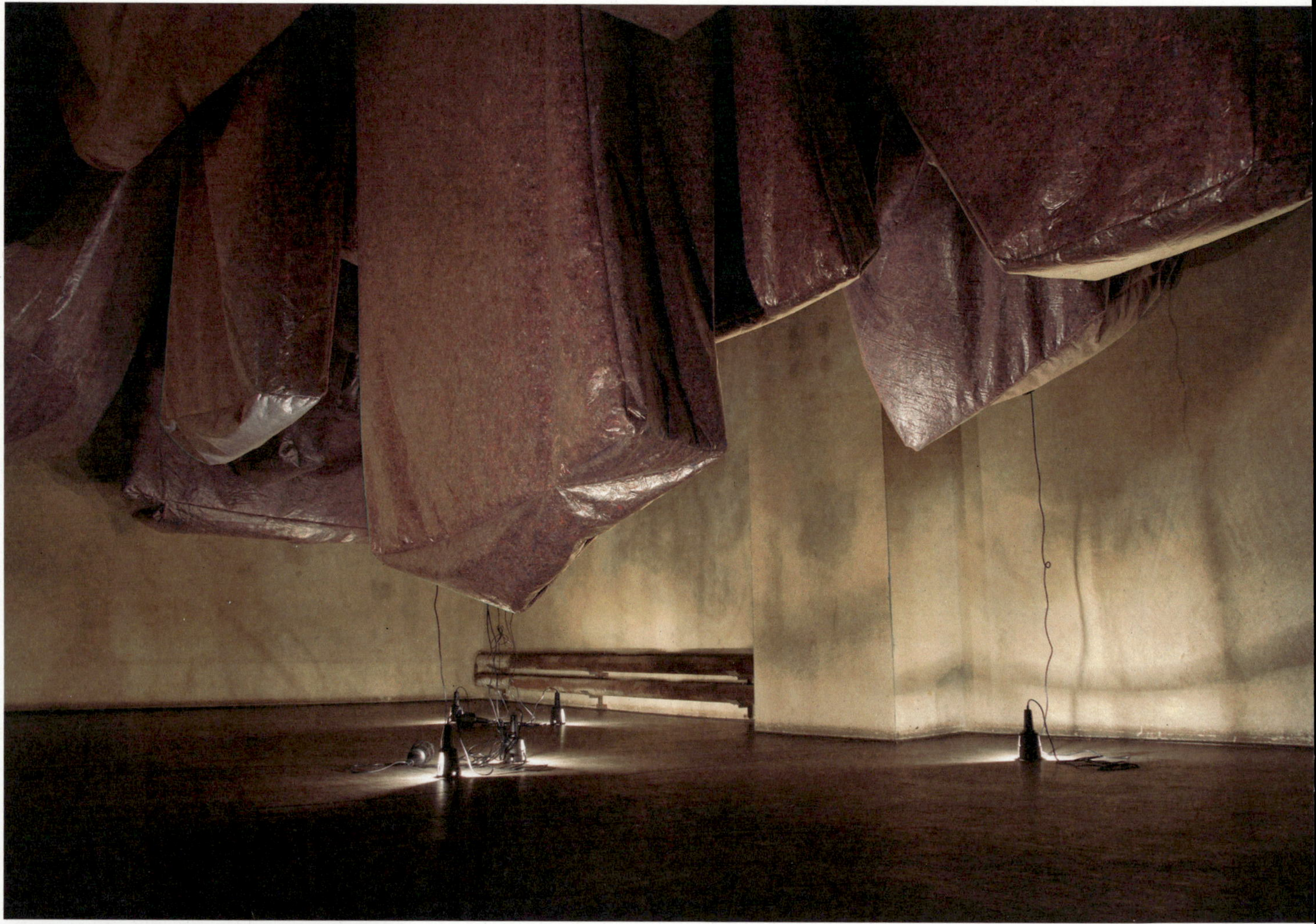

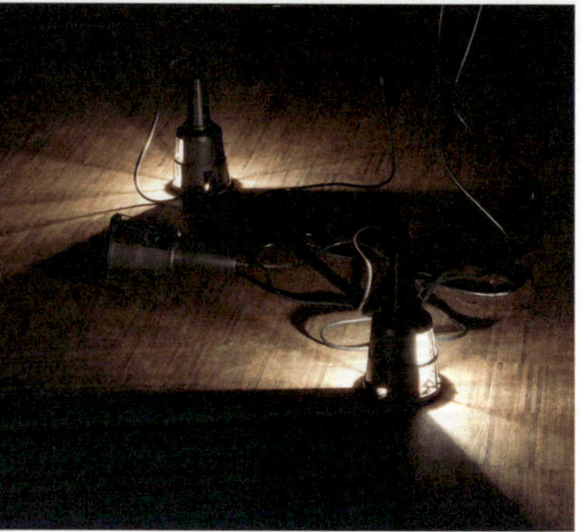

Crystal Castle

2010

mixed-media sound installation

**» on Hierarchies and Working
Conditions in the Field of Fine Arts**

Objects :
grey paint substrate,
power outlets, basement
lights, full-range
loudspeakers, cables,
playback equipment /
1000 x 500 x 400 cm
(set-up variable)

Sound :
8-channel composition /
hypnotic sound collage /
room resonance of
artist's personal studio
gained through
repeated re-playing and
re-recording of an audio
recording of the museum
Hamburger Bahnhof,
museum noises, fans, cut-ups
of art-related fragments
recorded from an answering
machine / diverse loops
(360:00) / CD 1 – track 8

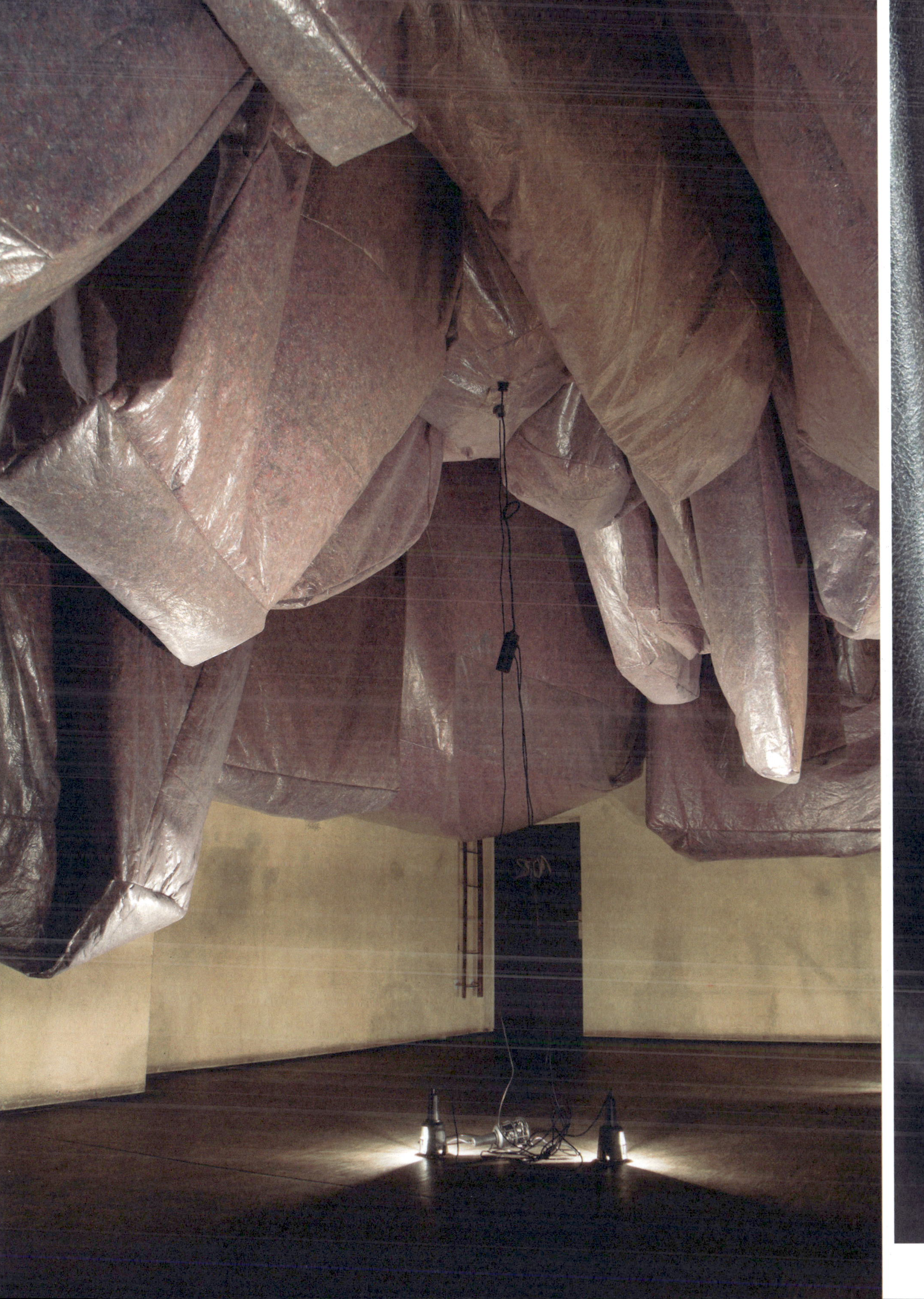

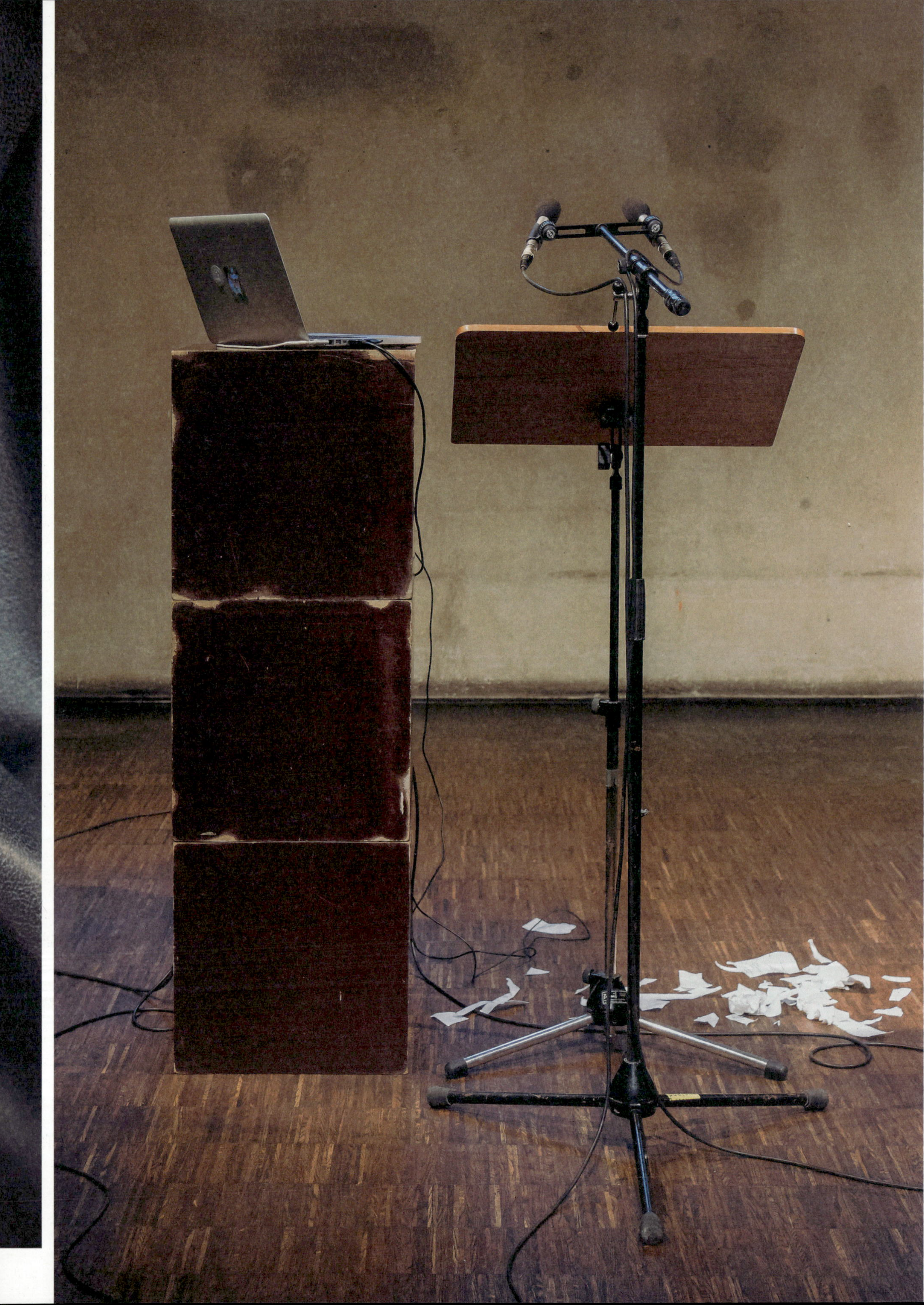

Sprachmusik

2012–17

Text : Stefan Roigk

A Concept, for Reading Aloud About Listening
» An Ode to Sound

Translation : Jim Campbell

**TEIL 1 DIE NACHT FRISST
ALLE IHRE KINDER**

Klang : leises Röcheln, Glucksen, leises Zischen
Stimme : Hauchen (langsam und mit vielen Pausen)

Stille …

Es ist nicht das Rauschen meines Nervensystems,
welches ich als leichtes Dröhnen aus der Gegend
des Fensters vernehme.

Es ist das weiche und einladende Geräusch des
Wassers, welches langsam die Heizungsrohre
emporkriecht, das poröse Kupfer des endlosen
Tunnelsystems reibt und die hölzerne Fußleiste
in Resonanz versetzt.

Stimme : wird klarer und deutlicher

Es verleiht dem einsamen Raum eine klangliche
Wärme, welche dieser eiskalten Winternacht auch
deutlich gut zu Gesicht steht …

Nur die Stille schafft dem Rauschen die nötige
Beachtung. Kein weiterer Laut erklimmt meine
Aufmerksamkeit!

(Kein Laut?)

…

**PART 1 THE NIGHT EATS
ALL HER CHILDREN**

Sound : quiet rattling, gurgling, soft hissing
Voice : breathy whispering (slow and often with pauses)

Silence …

It is not the noise of my nervous system, which
I hear as a light roar from the area of the window.

It is the soft and inviting sound of the water,
which slowly creeps up the steam pipes, rubs the
porous copper of the endless tunnel system and
resonates on the wooden skirting board.

Voice : becoming clearer and more distinct

It gives the lonely room a cold tonal warmth,
which is also writ large on the face of this icy
and cold winter night …

Only the silence provides necessary attention
for the rustling. No other sound climbs to my
recognition!

(No sound?)

…

Klang : Schaumgummi am Mikrofon
Stimme : bedroht, panisch

…

Im Moment des Zweifels
erkenne ich das leise Wispern:

Ein Zischen, filigran und zerbrechlich, in unregel-
mäßigen Stößen, sehr hochfrequent durchdringt
es den Raum in kaum hörbarer Lautstärke,
wechselt ab und an seine Frequenz, stoppt und
beginnt erneut mit einem kurzen Flirren.

Der Boden knackt vor Kälte. Die sich verziehen-
den Dielen schaffen ein mehrstimmiges Feld aus
hohlem Knirschen und bevölkern die statische
Leere mit räumlich differenzierten Klangpunkten.

Klang: langsam mit offenem Mund murmeln
Stimme: sehr undeutlich, langsam, müde: lethargisch
nach und nach deutlicher werdend

…

Ein tiefes Murmeln dringt aus der oberen Wohnung. Die Müdigkeit hat mich schon sehr benebelt, sodass ich mich durch das hypnotische
Dröhnen angesprochen fühle, ertappt in meinem
voyeuristischen Lauschen.

Doch wie jede Nacht ist es nur der alte Nachbar,
welcher vor dem Fernseher eingeschlafen war und
sich nun scheinbar seinen Weg zum Bett bahnt.

…

Sound : foam rubber on microphone
Voice : threatened, panicky

…

In a moment of doubt,
I realize the faint whispering:

A hiss, delicate and fragile, in irregular surges, of
a very high frequency, it permeates the space at
a barely audible volume, alternates its frequency,
stops and begins again with a brief whir.

The cold causes the floor to creak. The shifting
floorboards create a polyphonic field of hollow
grinding and inhabit the static void with spatially
differentiated sound points.

Sound : murmuring slowly with an open mouth
Voice : very slurred, slow, tired: lethargic
then, little by little, becoming more distinct

…

A deep murmur penetrates from the upper
apartment. The fatigue has addled me extremely,
so that I feel addressed by the hypnotic drones,
caught in my voyeuristic eavesdropping.

However, like every night it's just the old neighbor,
who had fallen asleep in front of the TV and is now
apparently making his way to bed.

…

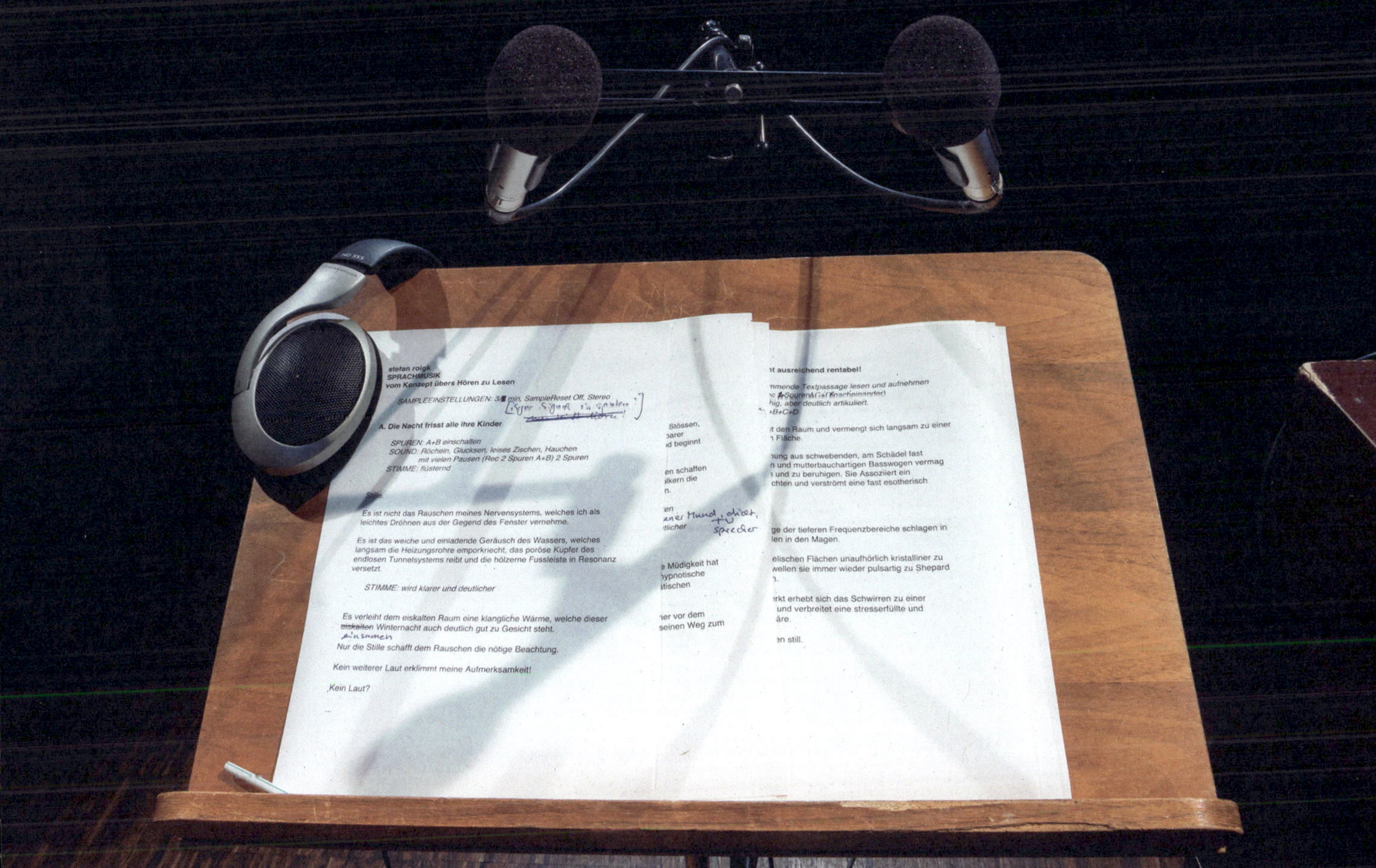

Klang : stehende Flächen, Seufzer,
Kehlkopfgesang, perkussive Klänge
Stimme : klar und deutlich, zackig

Das Grummeln verstummt ...

Dann das Schlurfen und Schaben der abgenutzten Pantoffeln auf rohem Holz. So als gäbe es ein Fenster zum Hof. Es breitet sich langsam aus, durchzieht dann die komplette Deckenfläche und verstummt mit einem dumpfen Knall am linken Rand meines Zimmers.

Extrem gedämpft und nach kurzer Pause ...

setzt es im Flur seinen holperigen Rhythmus fort.

...

Sound : sustained „pad" sounds, sighs,
throat singing, percussive sounds
Voice : clear and distinct, snappy

The rumbling stops ...

Then the shuffling and scraping of worn-out slippers on bare wood. As if there is a window onto the courtyard. It spreads slowly first, then runs through the entire ceiling area and falls silent with a thud on the left side of my room.

After a short break and extremely muted ...

it continues its bumpy rhythm in the hall.

...

Klang : langsam knirschend und schlürfend, röchelnd, dumpf, Pusten in Flasche
Stimme : ruhiger, langsamer, flüsternd

Mein Atem gewinnt durch die Nähe zum Kopfkissen an Lautstärke und erfüllt dröhnend meinen gesamten Kopf.

Mein Magen knurrt. Ich drehe mich um und werde von Stille erfüllt ...

Leise Krümel fallen vom Fensterrahmen. Prasseln wie in Zeitlupe aufgelöstes Brausepulver auf den Fußboden. Wie Sternenstaub.

Eine tiefe Woge öffnet das knirschende Fenster. Ein heulendes Wummern durchdringt horngleich die Starre und umspielt die zärtlichen Geräusche der fallenden Partikel.

Ein Papierstück bewegt sich. Es säuselt einen langgezogenen Ton, tanzt filigrane Frequenzen und vermischt sich mit dem quietschenden Scharren der Jalousien an der porösen Außenwand.

Auf und ab, wiegen Sie mich in den Schlaf.

Der Nacht entgegen.

Sound : slow crunching and slurping, heavy breathing, blowing into bottle
Voice : calmer, slower, whispering

Close to the pillow, my breath gains volume and occupies, droning, my entire head.

My stomach is growling. I roll over and am filled with silence ...

Quiet crumbs are falling from the window frame. They patter like effervescent powder dispersed in slow-motion onto the floor. Like stardust.

A deep swell opens the creaky window. A howling rumbling penetrates the rigidity like a horn and swirls around the gentle sounds of falling particles.

A piece of paper moves. It whispers a long tone, dances filigree frequencies and mixes with the squeaky scraping of blinds on the porous outer wall.

Up and down, they rock me to sleep.

Towards the night.

TEIL 2 EIN GLAS, RANDVOLL
MIT HUPENDEN AUTOS

Klang : die ersten sechs Zeilen lesen und wiederholen
Stimme : dröhnend, rhythmisch, mantraartiger Singsang
(lethargisch, monoton, langsam, steigernd)

Dröhnen, Dröhnen, Dröhnen.
Dröhnend, dröhnend, dröhnend.

…

Stimme : benebelt, zum Ende hin immer werden die
helleren Passagen deutlicher und spitzer gelesen, singen

Dröhnen, schwaches Verb!
Und trotzdem nimmt es einen ein.
Hallt immerzu, schwatzt dumpf daher.
Und dröhnt doch immer weiter.

Es dröhnt.
Dröhnt schwer und warm. Ganz zugedröhnt.
Umschlingt den Raum, und dann den Kopf,
Ein Läuten tiefer Glocken.

Mit hellem Schmerz. Dröhnt es fortan;
und immerdar.
Blendet wie Licht; bleibt doch ganz dumpf.
Schlägt ein im Bauch und dröhnt ganz warm.

Dröhnen.
Und spitz konkret.
Dröhnen.
Schält sich heraus.
Dröhnen.
Ein zwiebelgleiches Schwirren.

PART 2 A GLASS, BRIMMED
WITH HONKING CARS

Sound : read and repeat the first six lines
Voice : droning hum, rhythmic, mantra-like singsong
(lethargic, monotone, slow, building)

Drone, drone, drone.
Droning, droning, droning.

…

Voice : muddled/fuzzy, the lighter passages are read
more distinctly and sharply towards the end, singing

To drone. A weak verb!
And yet it occupies one's mind.
Echoes constantly, chatters dully.
But still remains droning.

It drones.
Drones heavy and warm. Renders stoned.
Embraces the room, and then my head.
A ringing of deep bells.

With piercing pain. It roars from now on;
and forever.
Blinds like light; but still remains dull.
Strikes the midriff and drones even warmer.

Droning.
And peaking concretely.
Droning.
Peels out.
Droning.
An onion-like buzzing.

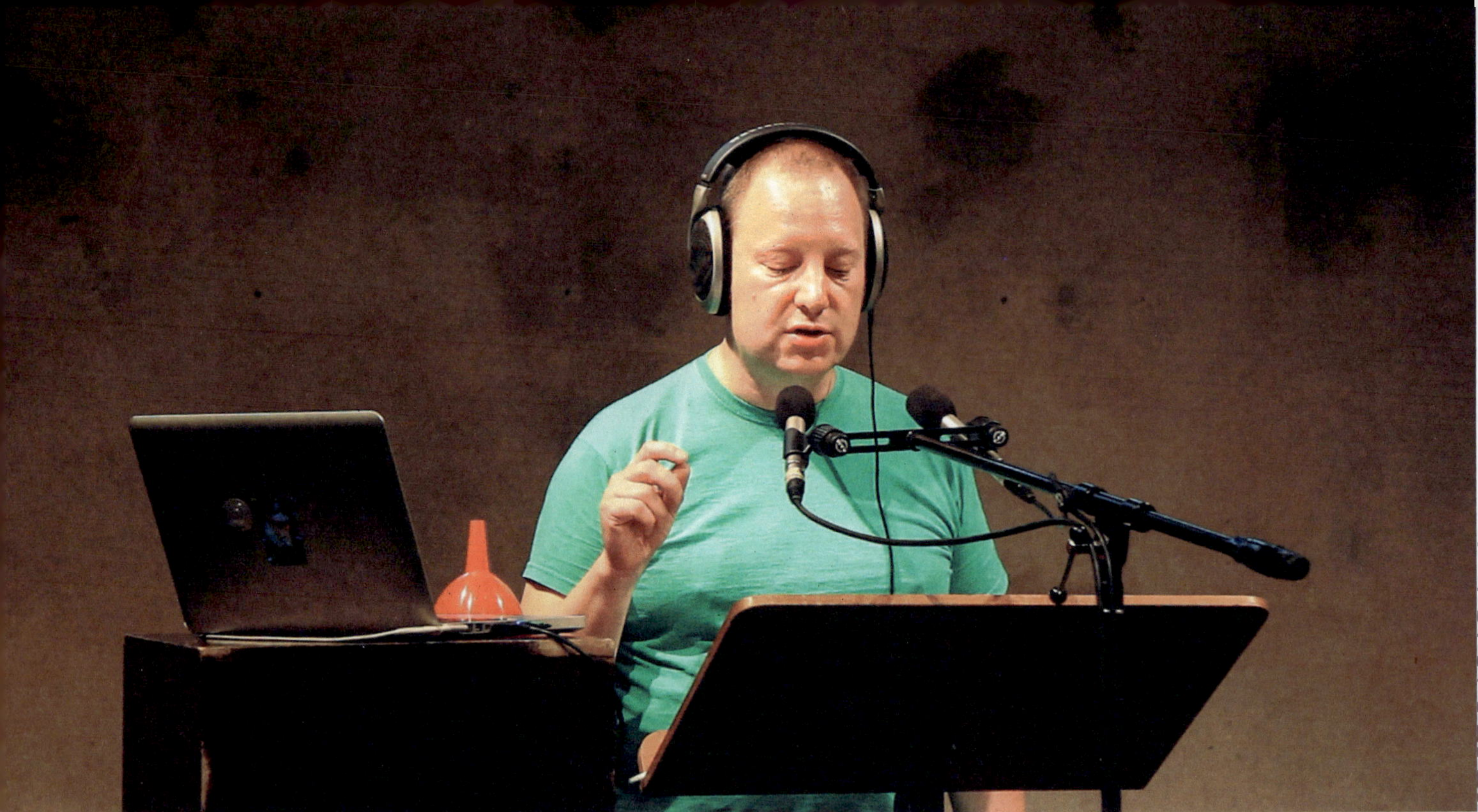

<table>
<tr><td>

TEIL 3 EVOLUTION IST NICHT AUSREICHEND RENTABEL!

Klang : Zischen, Surren, Krächzen,
kurze Flächen, in Flasche pusten, Strohhalm
Stimme : aufgewühlt, aber deutlich

Subtil breiten sich im Hintergrund die um
Oktaven gepitchten Gesänge einer Nachtigall im
sommerlichen S-Bahn-Damm aus und verhelfen
der eben noch synthetisch erscheinenden Klang-
welt zu einem fast natürlichen Charakter.

In mantraartigen Schleifen wiederholt sich der
komplexe Lockruf und begräbt die dröhnenden
Schwingungen unter einem stark rhythmischen
Geflecht unerwidert verhallender Geborgenheit.

</td><td>

PART 3 EVOLUTION IS NOT ADEQUATELY ECONOMICAL!

Sound : hissing, humming, croaking, brief interrupted
„pad" sounds, blowing into bottle, drinking straw
Voice : agitated but clear

The pitch-shifted chants of a nightingale in the
background spread out subtly in the estival city
rail-line embankment. It lends the soundscape,
a moment ago still synthetic, an almost natural
character.

The complex mating call recurs in mantra-like
loops and buries the roaring vibrations under a
strong rhythmic network of fading security.

</td></tr>
</table>

TEIL 4 DAS LEBEN STEHT UND FÄLLT MIT DEM RAUSCHEN

Klang : leise wispern und winseln, singen und pfeifen
Stimme : betulich singend, Gedicht lesend

...

Oh Du mein Klang,
wie Du ziselierst und knisterst,
leise verstreichst,
und im Rauschen des Mondes,
langsam schwindest.

Oh Du mein Klang,
wie Du Dich langsam erhebst,
herumtänzelst und braust,
wogenartig aufplusterst und -bäumst,
in der Stille des leeren Raumes.

Oh Du schmerzliches Geräusch,
wie Du lauerst auf meinem Thron,
den Kopf verstopfst,
und mein Ohr,
für Form und Klang verschließt.

Oh Du zartes Sausen,
wie Du verhalten,
stets drüber schwebst,
und Gewissheit mir gibst,
selbst den tobendsten Lärm
durch Flirren zu spalten.

...

PART 4 LIFE STANDS AND FALLS WITH A RUSHING SOUND

Sound : soft whispering and whimpering, singing and whistling
Voice : singing fussily, reciting a poem

...

My dear sound,
how you garnish and crackle,
softly pass,
and in the noise of the moon,
slowly fade away.

My dear sound,
how you slowly rise,
tripping and rushing,
puffing and rearing up waving,
in the silent and empty space.

Oh my painful noise,
how you lurk on my throne,
block my head,
and seal my ears,
for form and sound.

Oh my gentle breeze,
how you cautiously,
hover above, always,
and give me certainty,
to split even the most raging noise
by shimmering.

...

TEIL 5 DER EPHEMERE MOMENT

Klang : Papier reißen und knüllen, leise Vokale
singen, röcheln, Flächen hauchen, Modulationsgeräusche
Stimme : ganz ruhig lesen, lieblich
(wie eine Kindergeschichte)

Das Vibrieren eines leicht gefüllten Weinglases
auf einer hölzernen Küchenarbeitsplatte. Aus-
gelöst durch die verständnislosen Hilfsarbeiter,
welche die obige Mauer mithilfe eines Stemm-
hammers und Brechstangen dem Erdboden
gleichmachen.

Das Glas, verhalten, subtil;
wie eine weit entfernte Fahrradklingel.

... Bleibt stehen.

In der anschließenden Pause rieseln Aberhunderte
minimal kleinster Klangpartikel im verbliebenen
Schacht gen Erdmittelpunkt und reiben, poltern
und brechen in mikrobenartiger Weise im Inneren
der Wand.

Sie wirken extrem räumlich, dicht, intim, fast so,
als wären sie im eigenen Kopf, als würde sich die
Schädeldecke lösen und langsam, aber beständig
zu Staub zerfallen.

...

PART 5 THE EPHEMERAL MOMENT

Sound : tearing and crumpling paper, soft singing of
vowels, labored breathing, aspirating sustained sounds,
modulation sounds
Voice : reading with complete calm, mellow
(as if reciting a story for children)

The vibration of a nearly empty wine glass on a
wooden kitchen counter. Triggered by the un-
comprehending laborers, as they demolish the
upper wall with a caulking hammer and crowbars.

The glass, mild; subtle;
like a far-off bicycle bell.

... It stops.

In the subsequent break, hundreds of tiny
sound-particles trickle in the remaining shaft
towards the center of the Earth. Scratching,
rubbing, rumbling and cracking like microbes
inside of the wall.

They appear to be extremely spatial, dense, in-
timate, almost as if they were in one's own head,
as if the skullcap were being removed and slowly
but steadily turned to dust.

...

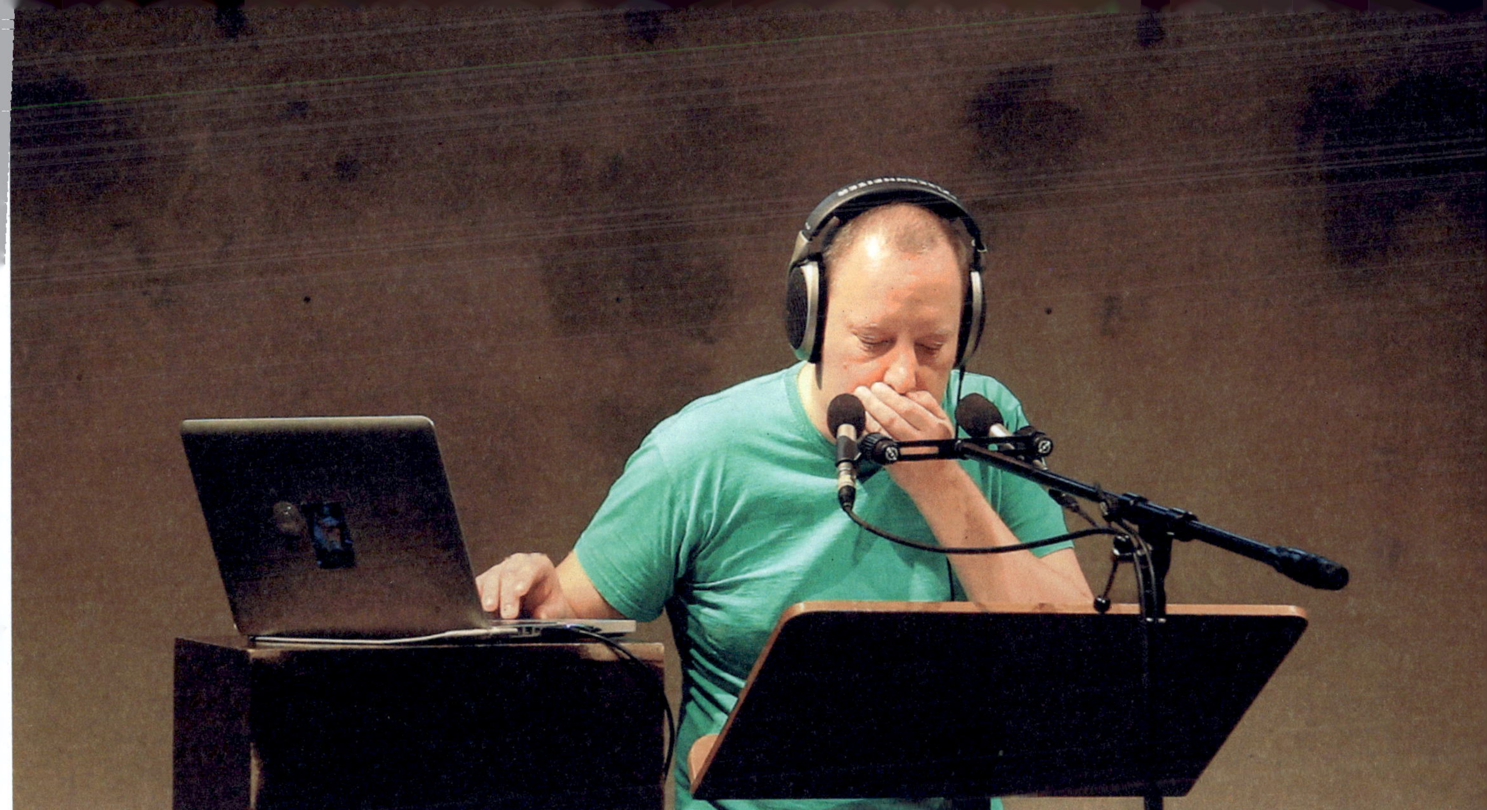

| TEIL 6 **VON HINTEN NACH VORN UND WIEDER ZURÜCK** | PART 6 **FROM BACK TO FRONT AND BACK AGAIN** |

Klang : guttural, röcheln, keuchen, leise Drones aufbauen (leise mit Kehlkopf und Gaumen, je mehr Drones, desto harmonischer und ruhiger)
Stimme : flüstern, ruhig und leise sprechend

Sound : guttural, rasping, panting, soft drones begin to build (softly with larynx and gums – the more the drones emerge, the more harmonious and calm it becomes)
Voice : whispering, speaking calmly and quietly

Die synthetische Tonarchitektur wird zu einem Dschungel aus Räumen und Echos.

The synthetic sound-architecture becomes a jungle of spaces and echoes.

... Löst sich auf.

... Decomposed.

Ziseliert in feinste Frequenzen und prescht plötzlich druckvoll nach vorn.

Decorates in the finest frequencies and suddenly punches forward.

... Breitet sich aus.

... Spreads out.

Pflanzt sich wie eine Hydra in mehrstimmigen Crescendi fort.

Like a hydra it propagates in polyphonic crescendos.

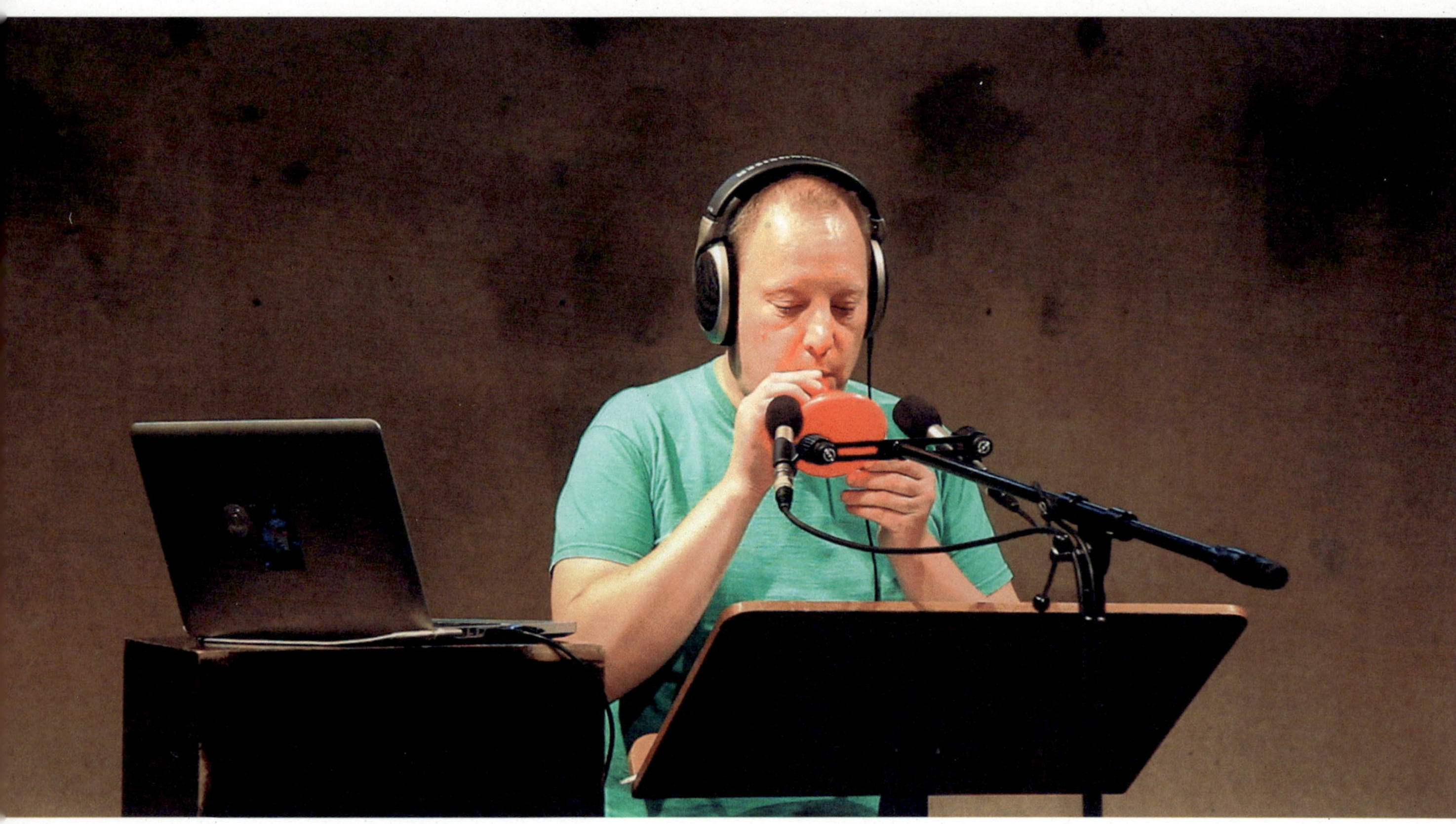

Klang : ruhiges zischen, rauschen, pfeifen, strohhalm
Stimme : leise lesend, flüstern, aufzählen

Sound : calm hissing, whooshing, whistling, drinking straw
Voice : reading softly, whispering, reciting

...

...

Sobald das stürmende Gewitter unerwartet verstummt, wuchert es pilzartig an gleich mehreren Stellen wieder hervor.

Where the tempestuous storm ceases unexpectedly, it proliferates anew, fungal and deafening, at several places simultaneously.

Girlandenförmig schält sich der prasselnde Regen seinen Weg durch den Klang.

Like a garland, the crackling rain peels its way through the noise.

Beruhigt die aggressive Stimmung.

Soothes the aggressive mood.

Beruhigend.

Soothing.

Beruhigen die aufgeregte Stimmung.

Soothes the agitated mood.

multi-channel system, stereo microphones, max/MSP patch, computer / aleatoric sound processing of the recorded vocal improvisations / 25 – 45 minutes / a studio recording of "Sprachmusik" was published on CD in 2017 by Tochnit Aleph / 32:07 / CD 1 – track 9 + CD 2 – track 4

Klang : tiefes atmen, Stille, Feedbacks
Stimme : immer ruhiger werden

Sound : deep breathing, silence, feedback
Voice : gradually becoming calmer and calmer

Verschlingt sich in komplexen Perkussionsformen.

Intertwines in complex percussive forms.

Wurzelförmig greifen die Klänge ineinander, werden länger, verschmelzen. Haften, kleben an einander. Tentakelartig.

Like roots, the sounds fit into one another, become longer, fused. Adhere, stick together. Like tentacles.

Das Ruckeln der vorbeifahrenden Straßenbahn.

The bucking of the passing tram.

Das dichte Gewebe
der surrenden Nachttischlampe.

The dense tissue
of my whirring bedside lamp.

Tiefes Brummen des Kühlschrankes.

The low humming of the fridge.

Das Atmen meines schlafenden Sohnes.

The breathing of my sleeping son.

Löst sich voneinander.

Peels off.

Lichtblitze.

Flashes of light.

Tiefes Atmen.

And deep breathing.

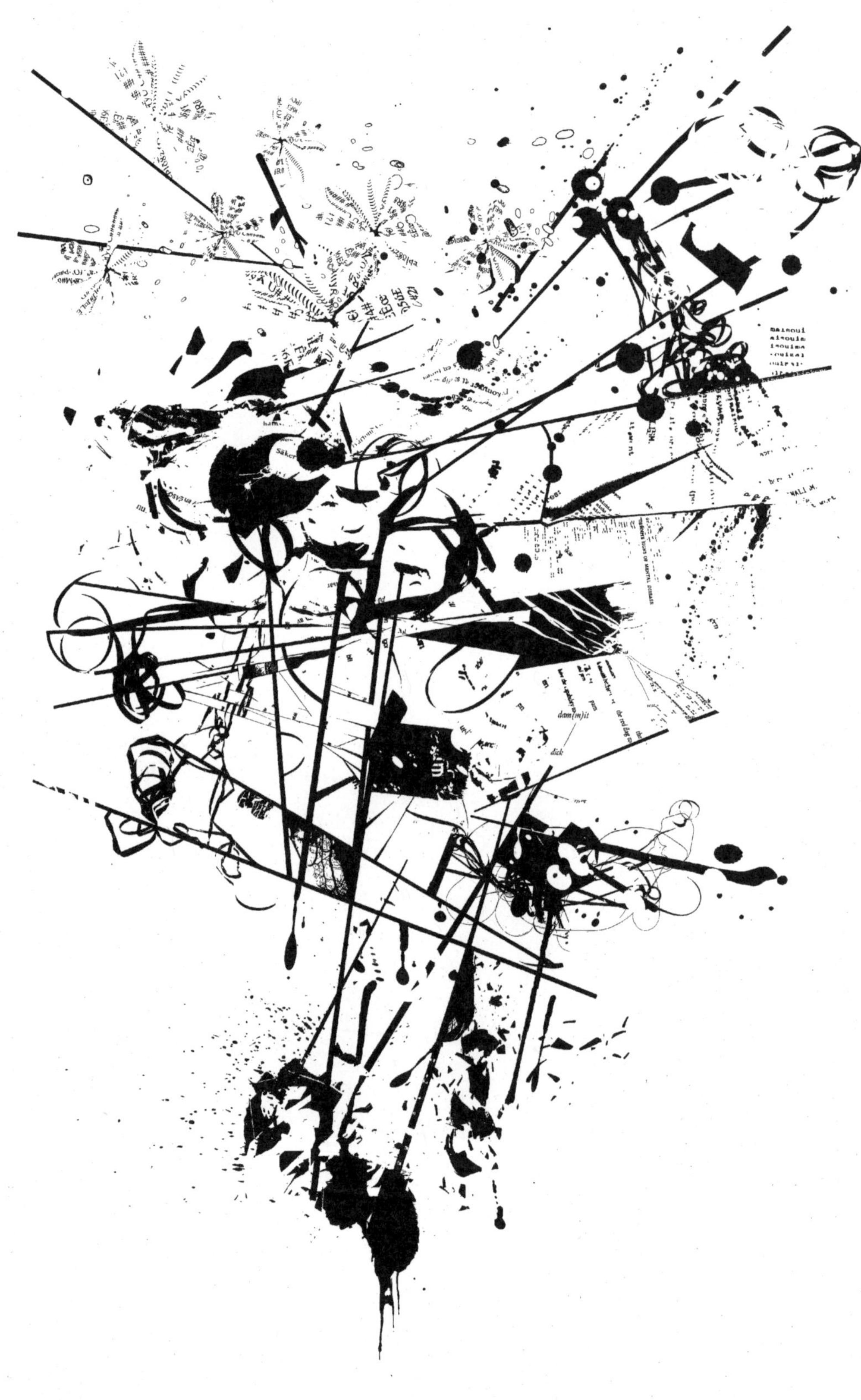

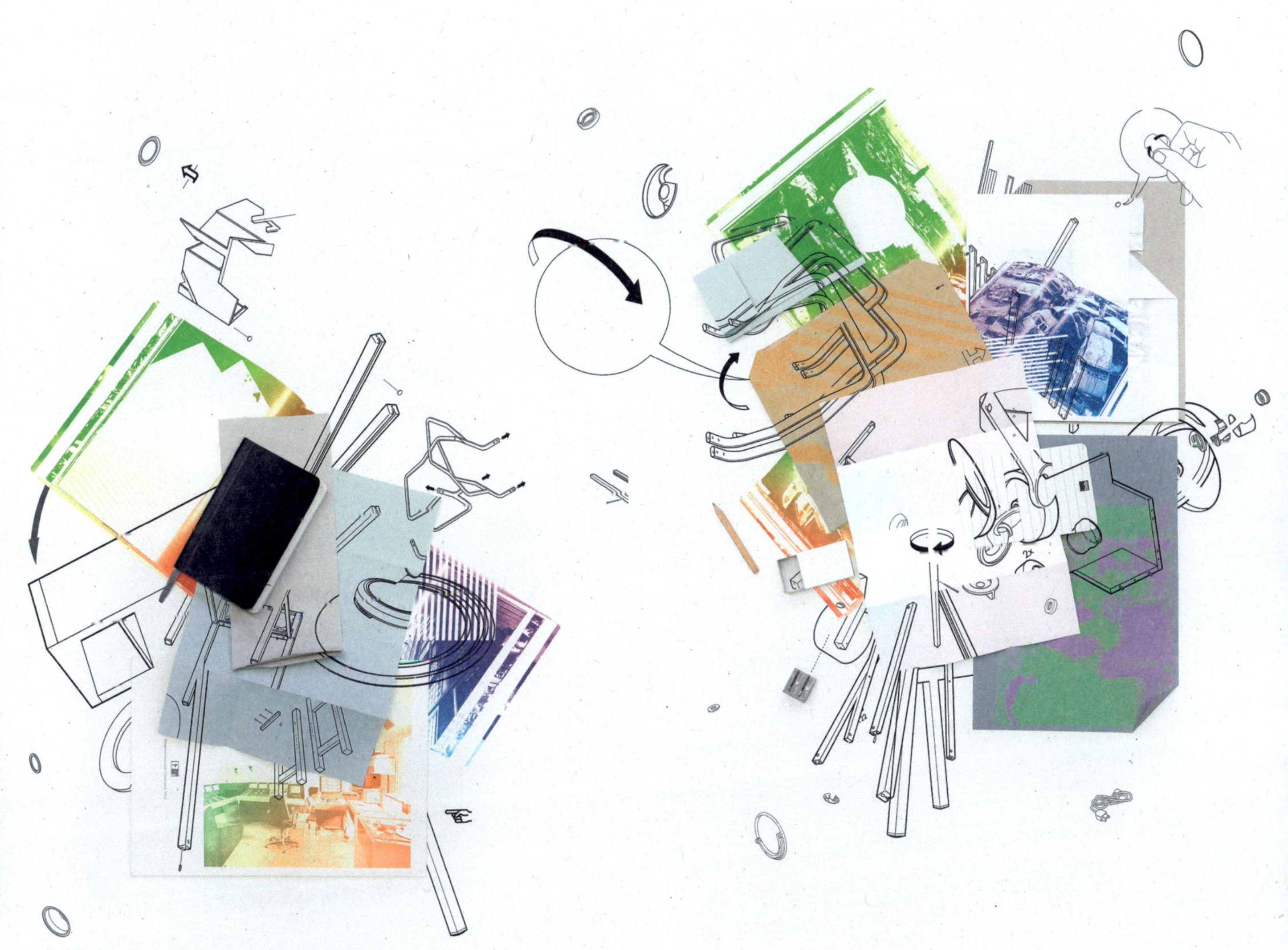

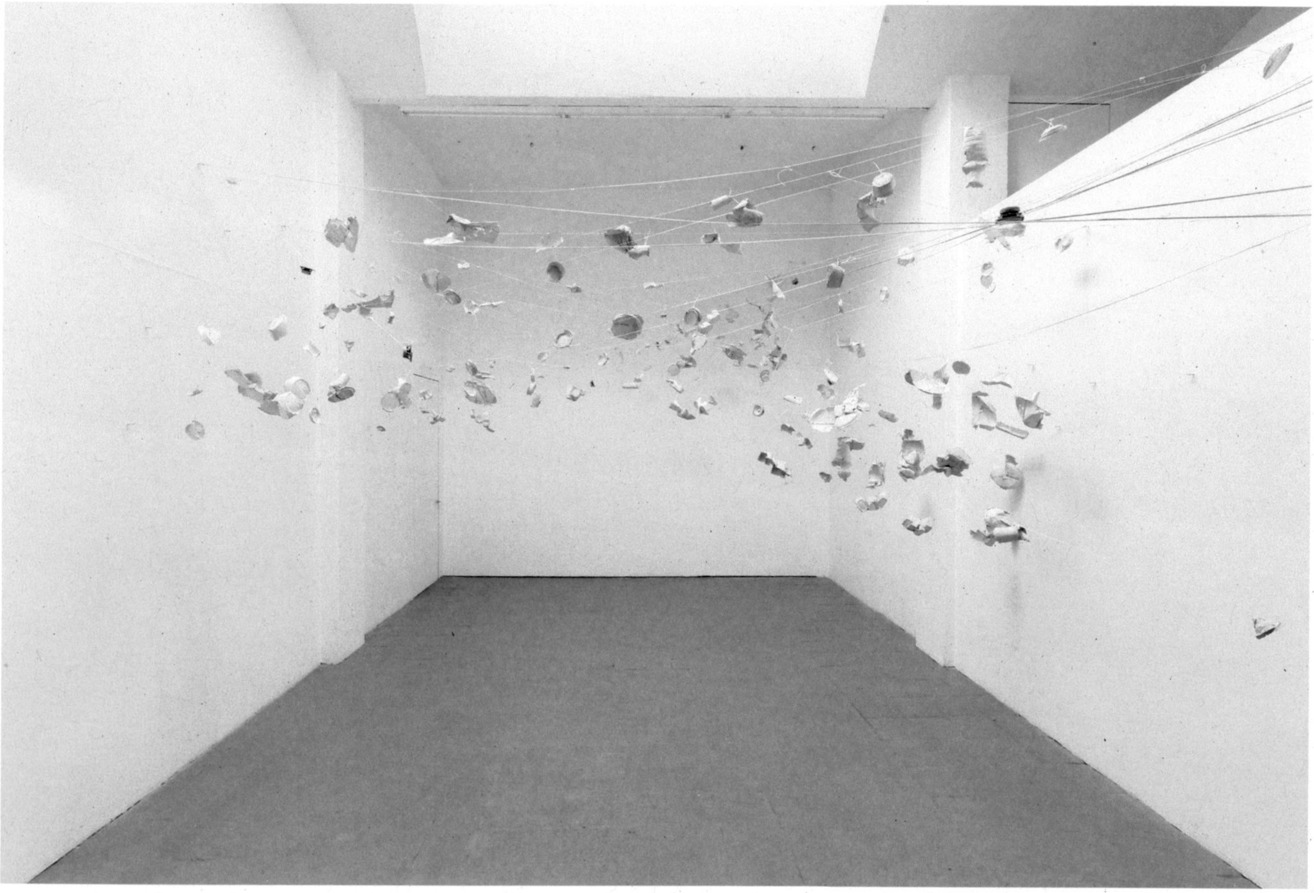

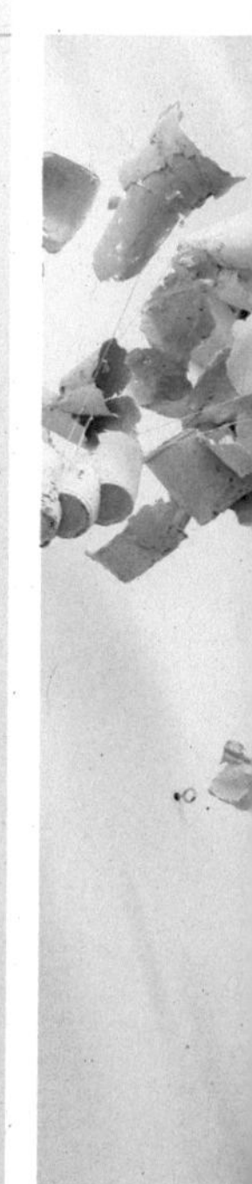

Objects : paper mâché castings from deformed plastic packaging and disposable dishes, nylon string, cable ties, full-range loudspeakers, cables and playback equipment / 800 x 500 x 600 cm (size variable)

Sound : 8-channel composition / dense sound field composed of squeaking, shattering, crunching, rattling, rubbing, pushing, blowing and falling noises produced with foam rubber, disposable dishes made of cardboard and plastic, foil and polystyrene / loop (60:00) / CD1 – track 3

Bursting Confidence

2013

mixed-media sound installation

» Transfer of the Editing Techniques and Aesthetics of Musique Concrete Into the Third Dimension

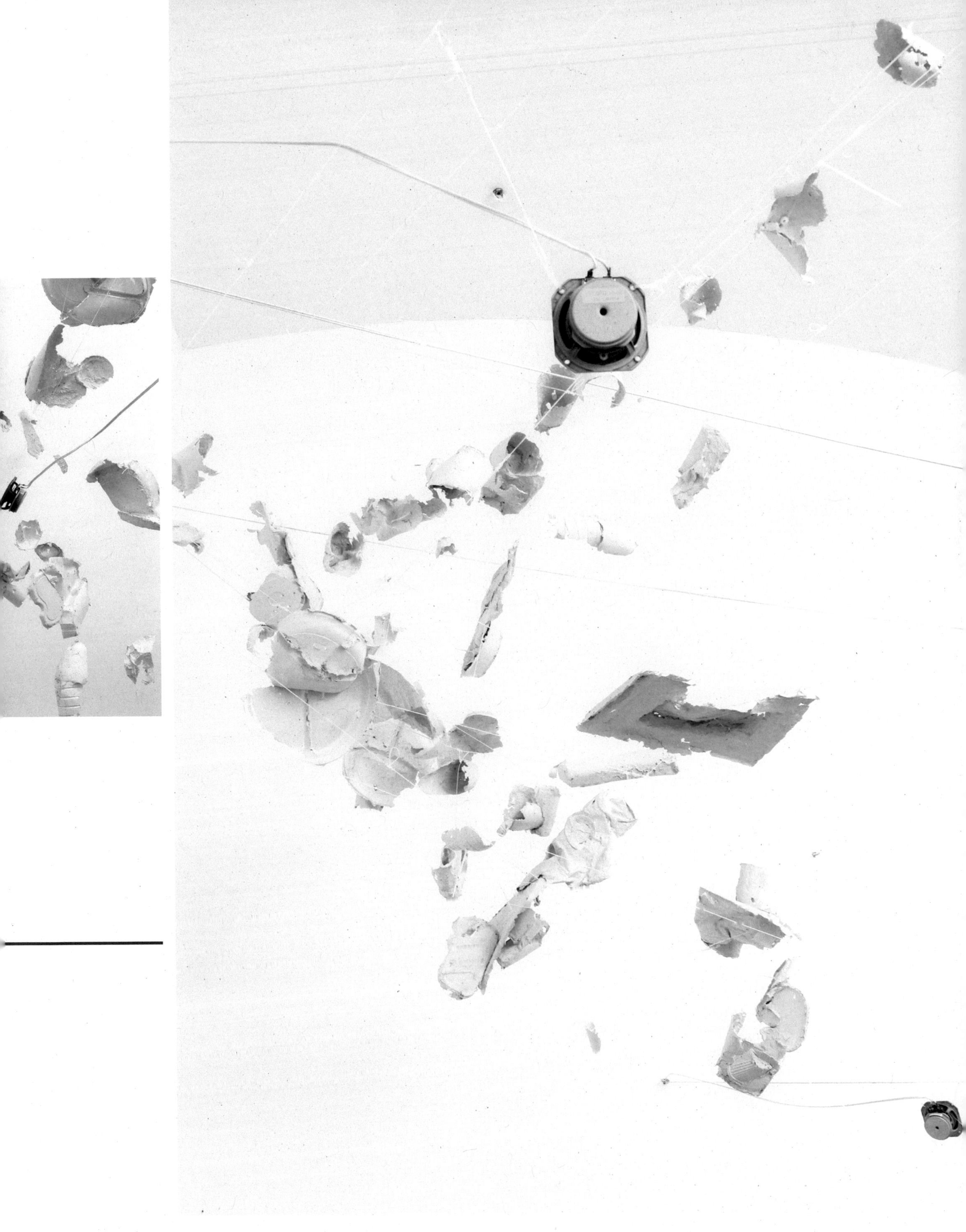

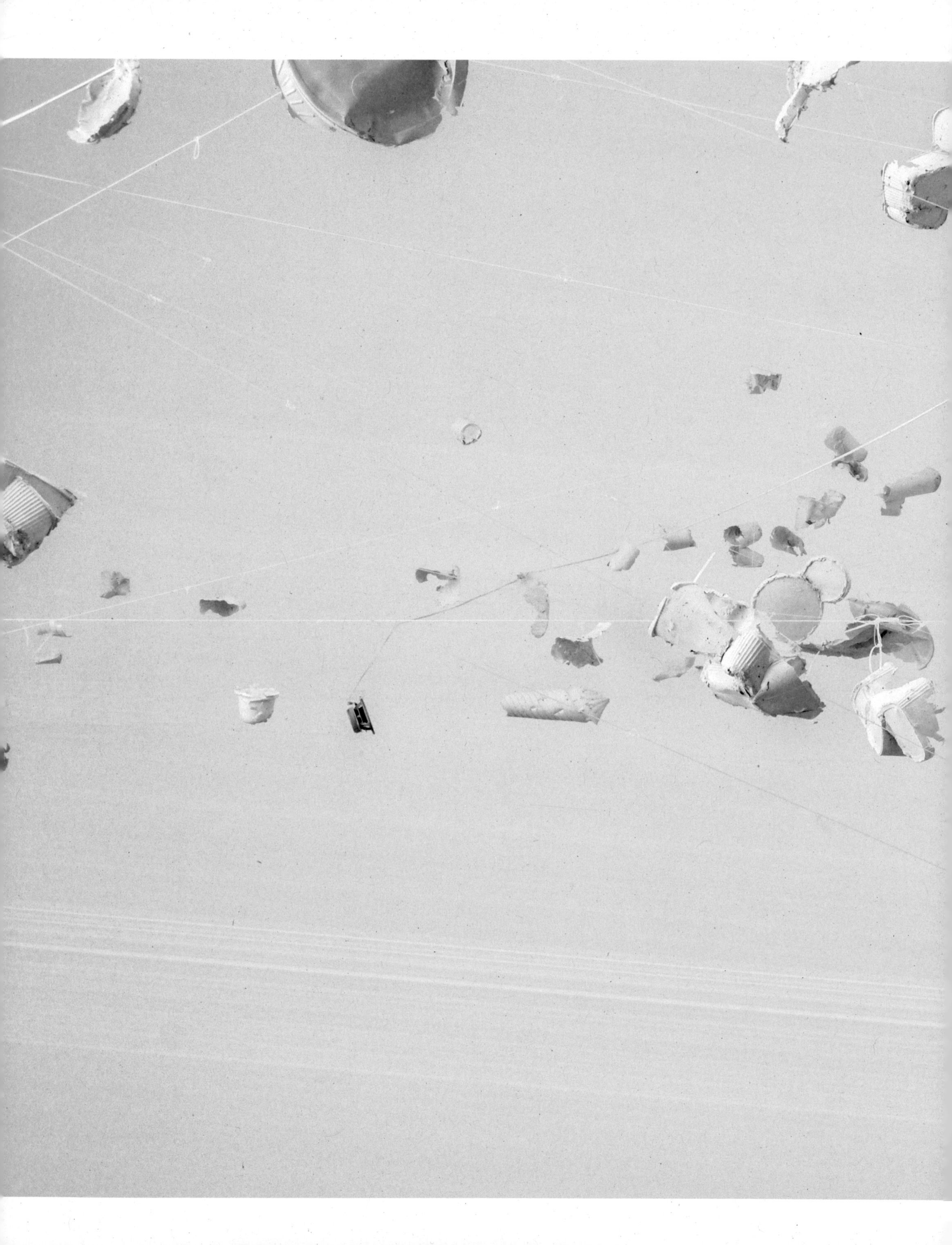

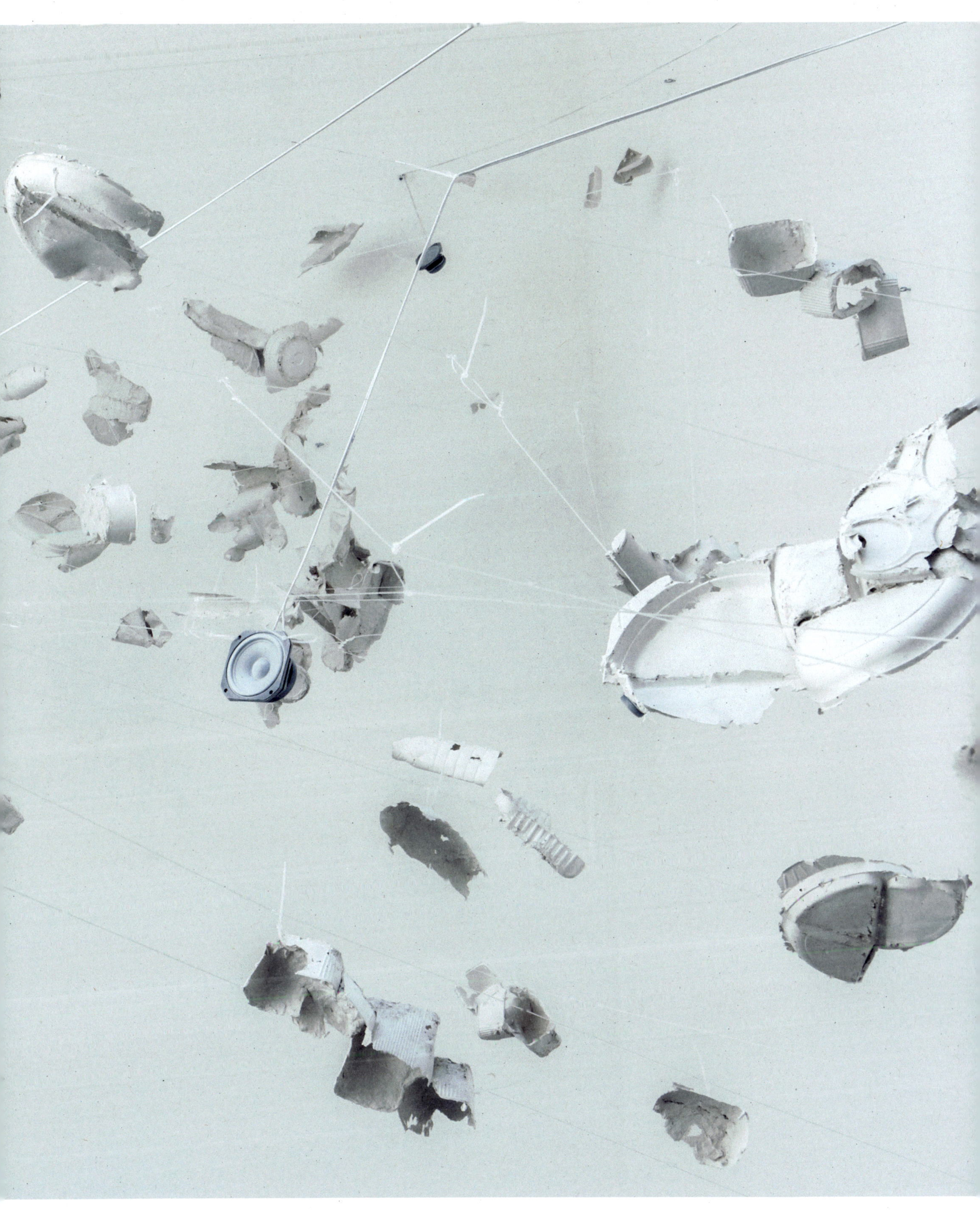

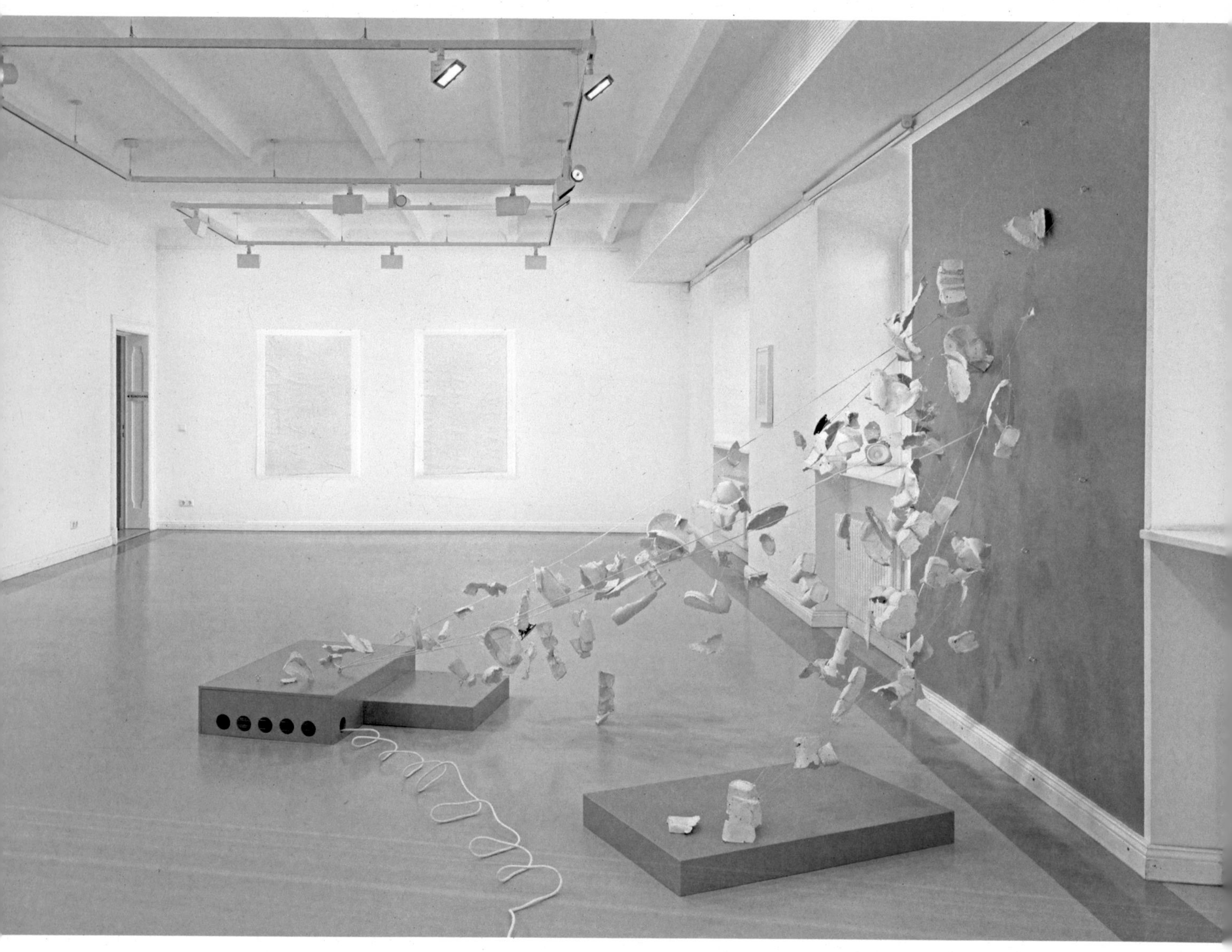

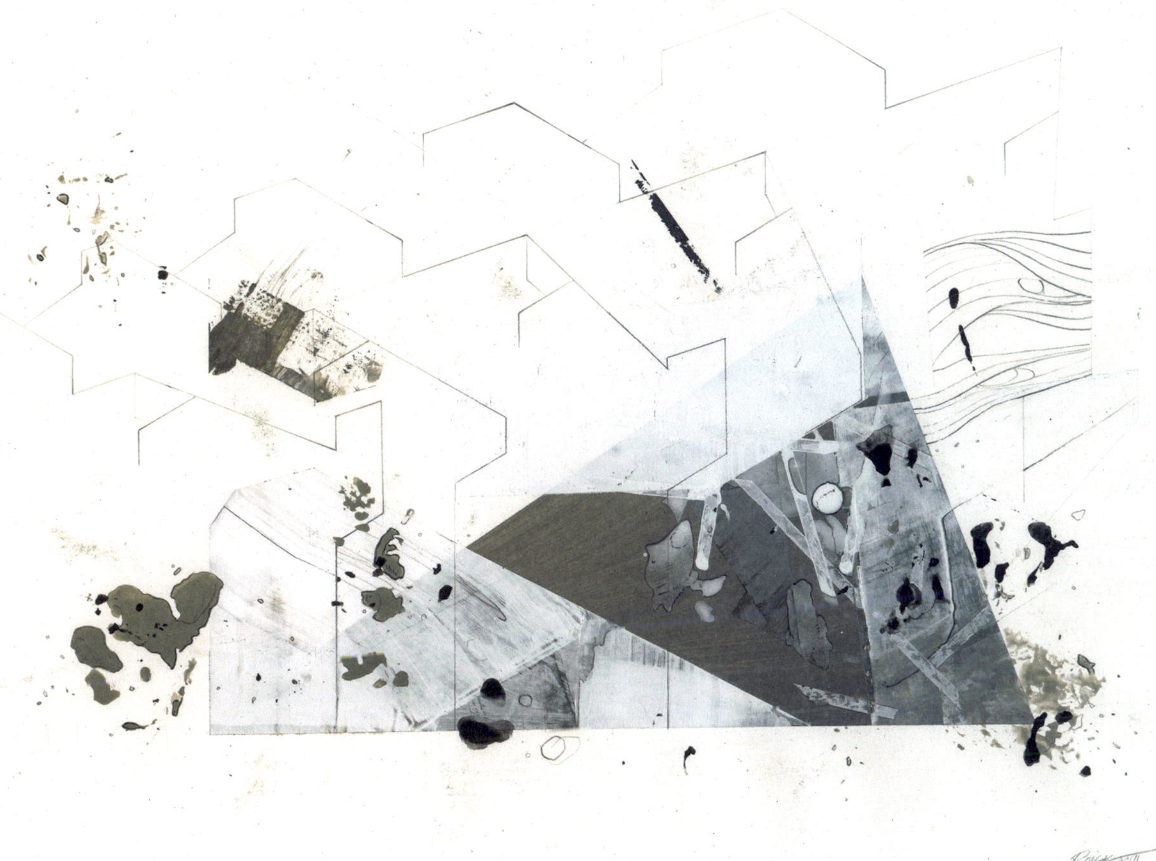

Musikalische Grafiken

2015–17 ————————————————————

8-part series of drawings

» Drawings in the Tradition of Visual
Music: Instead of Being Brought to Life
in a Sonic Interpretation by Musicians,
They Resound as Acoustic Associations
in the Eye of the Beholder

Material :
pencil, fineliner, acrylic
paint, Letraset letters and
audiotape on paper

Format :
41 x 29 cm

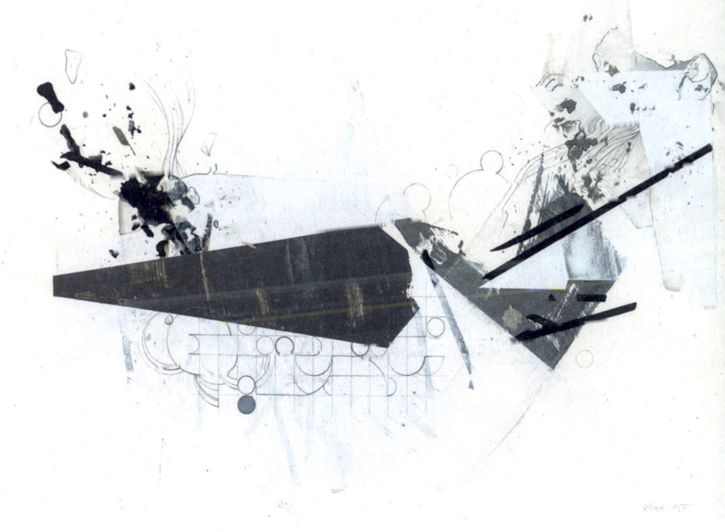

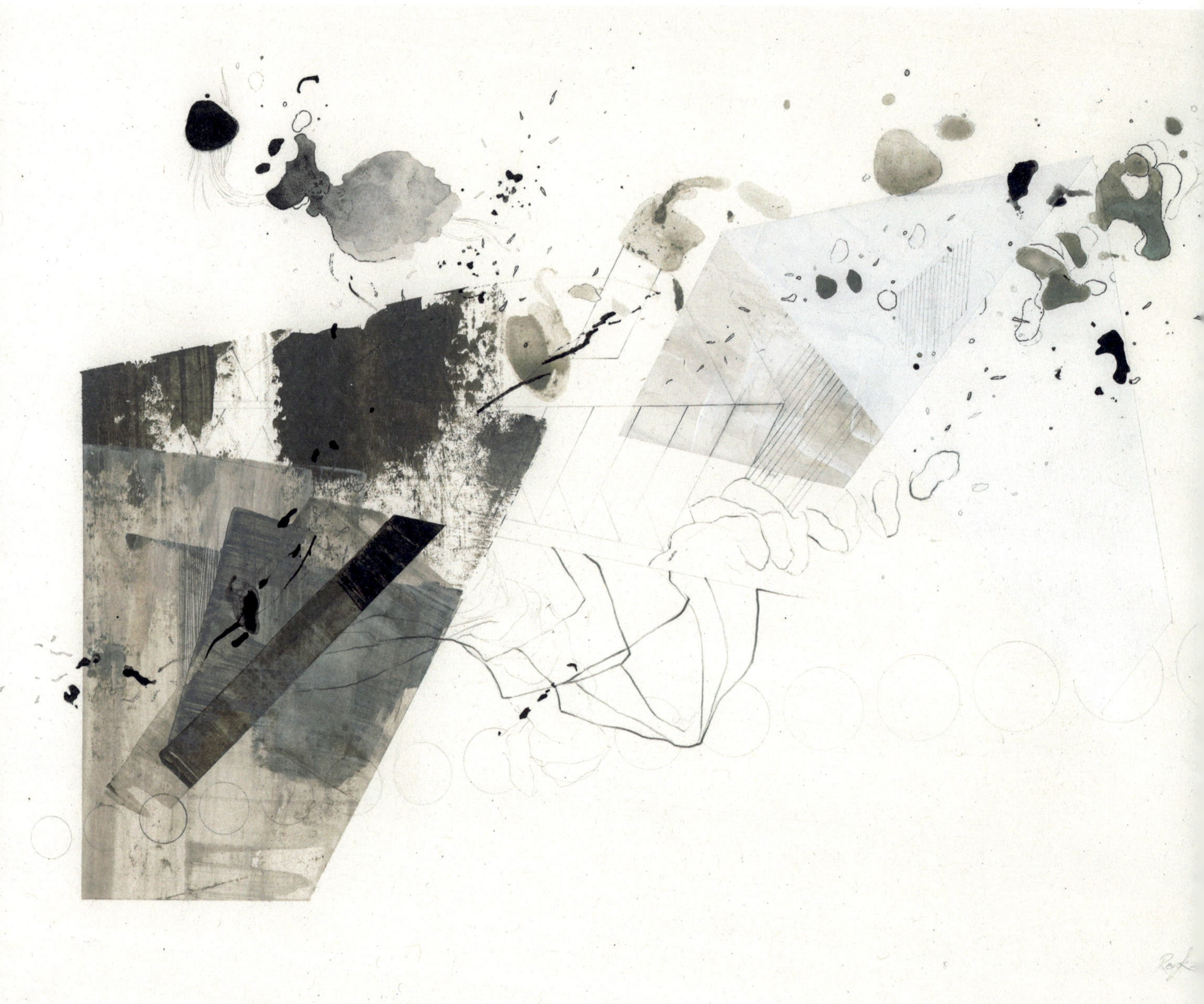

Imaginary Soundscape No. 6

2012–13 ————————————

6-piece object ensemble

» Sound Imaginations Coagulated Into Silicone – Tangible in the Flesh, Without Audible Sound

Objects :
black silicon, wire,
microphone stands,
polystyrene and
wooden picks **/**
300 x 450 x 120 cm

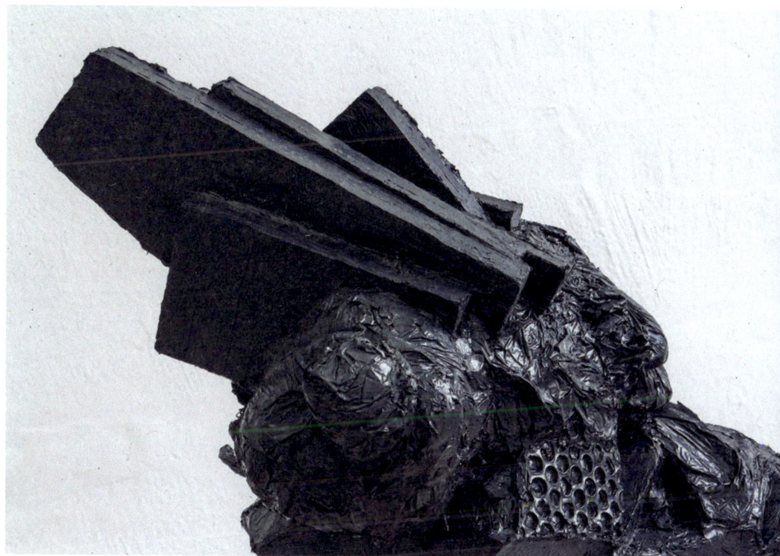

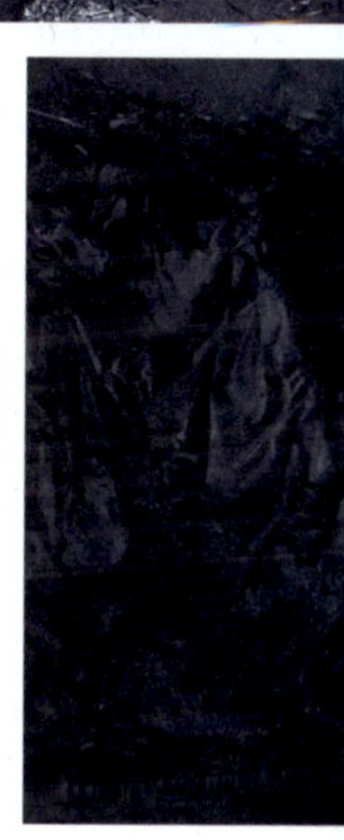

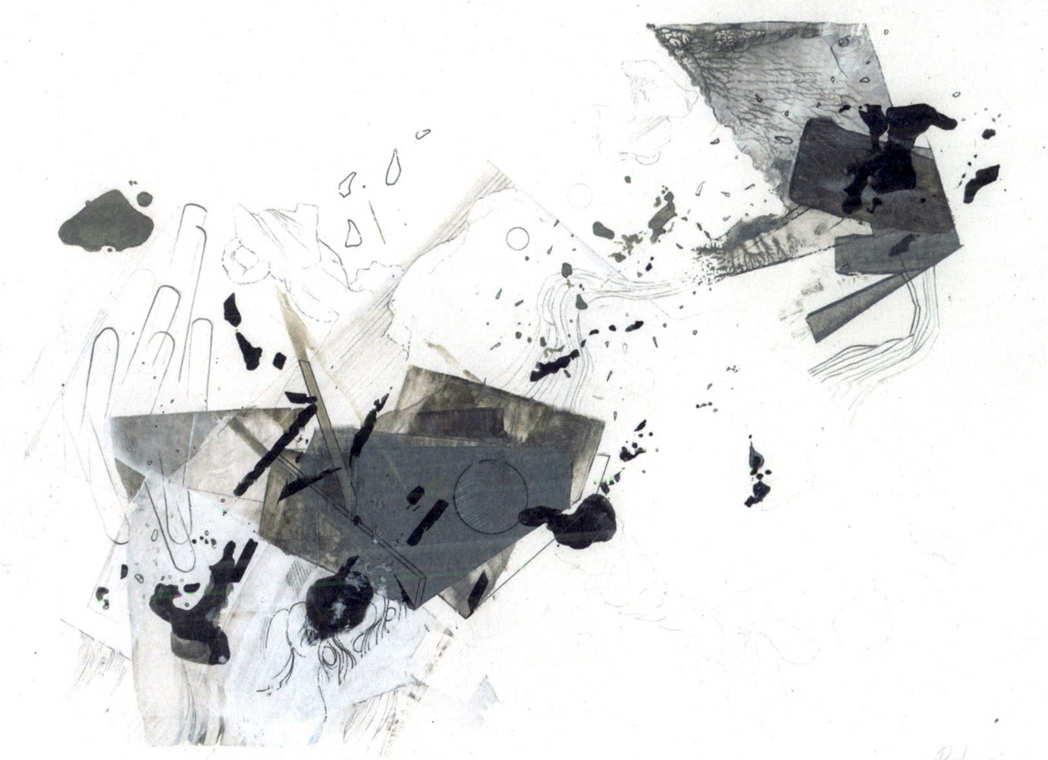

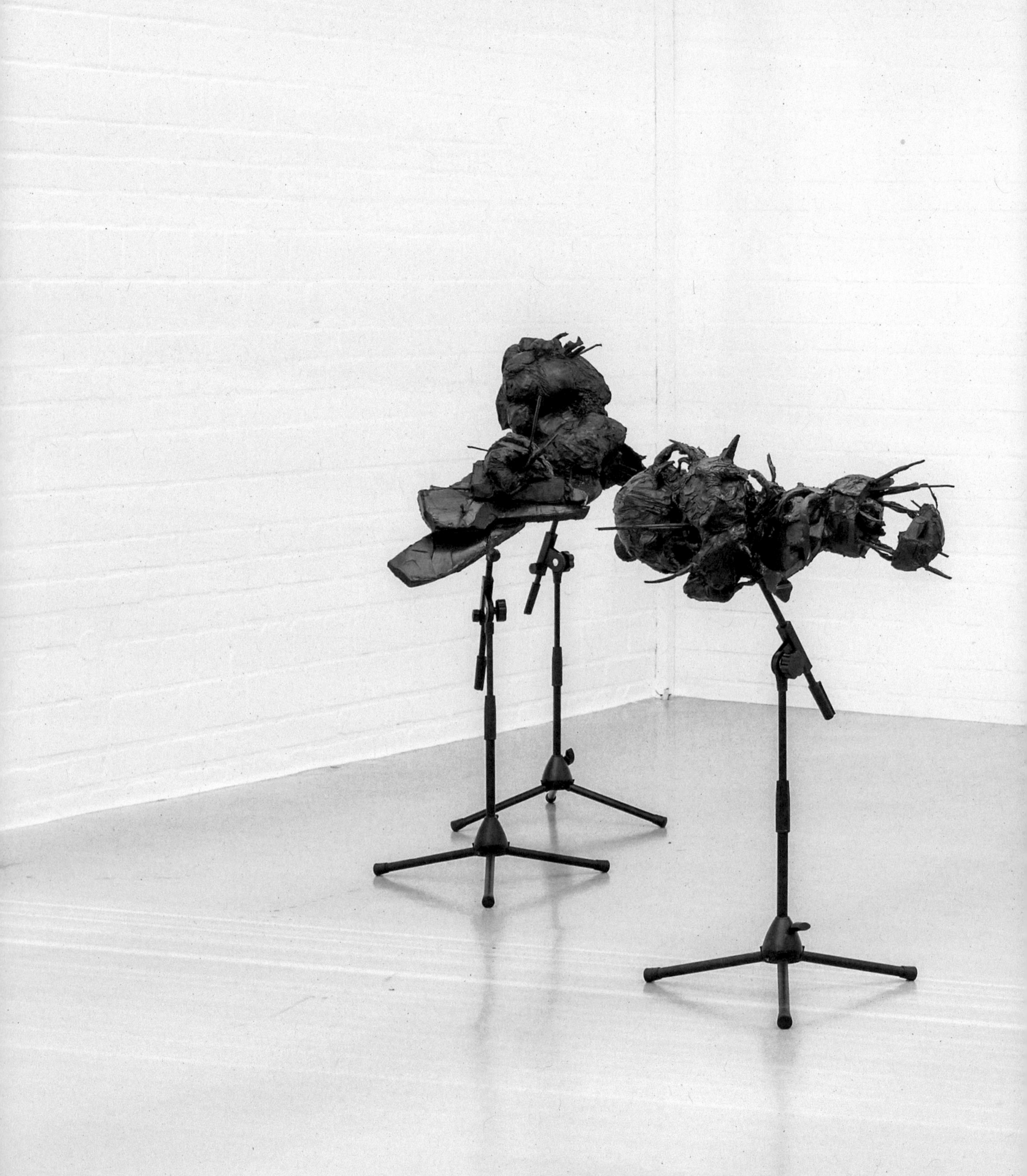

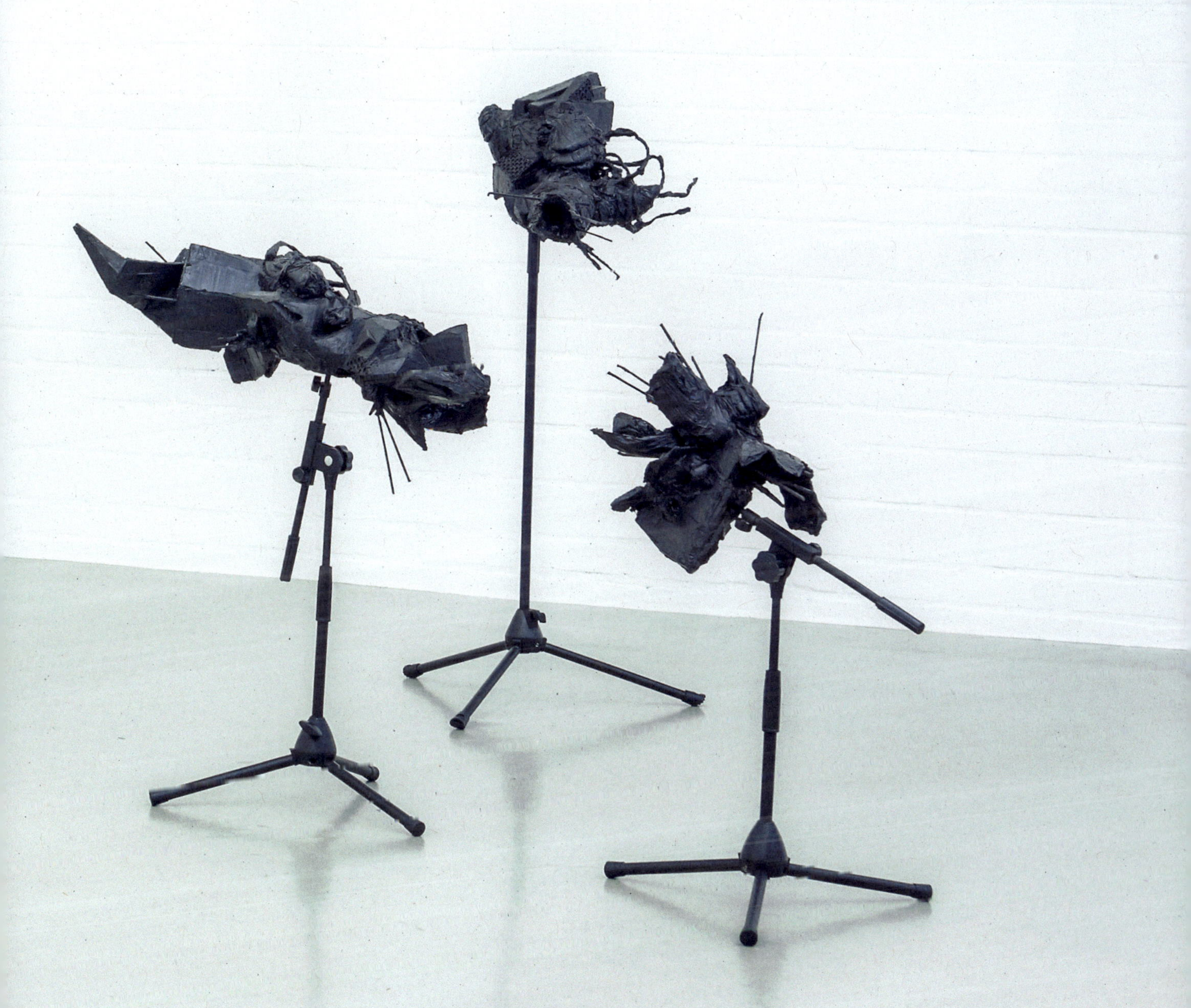

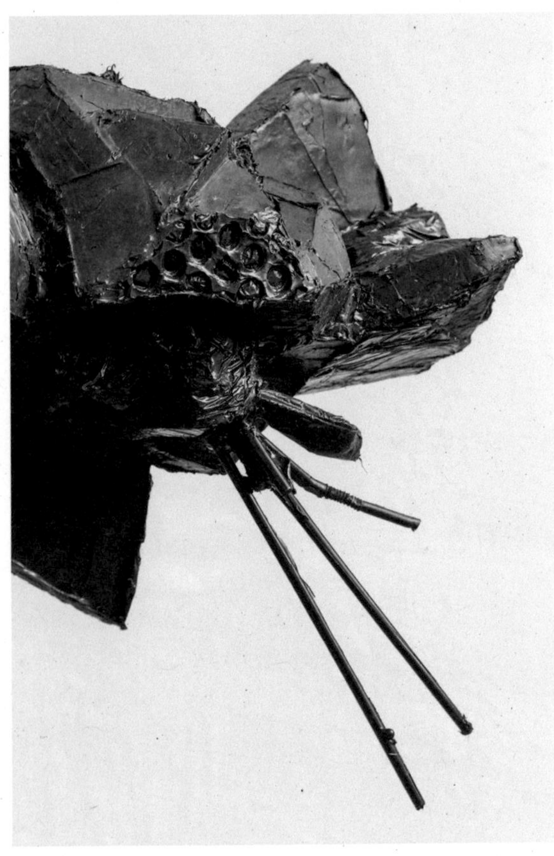

Objects :
paper mâché and
silicone castings from
deformed plastic
packaging, doormats,
fabric tape, full-range
loudspeakers, cables and
playback equipment /
700 x 500 x 50 cm

Sound :
6-channel composition /
dense sound field composed
of rubbing, crackling,
squeaking and scratching
with bubble wrap,
disposable dishes, paper and
polystyrene / loop (60:00) /
CD 2 – track 3

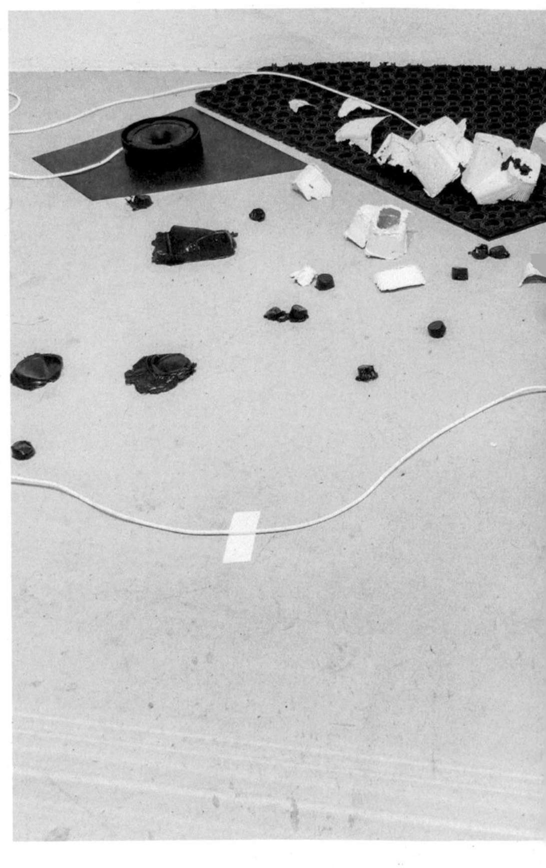

Expanded

2013

mixed-media sound installation

**» Transformation of the Concept
of Musical Graphics Into an Intermedial
Amalgamation of Sculpture and Sound**

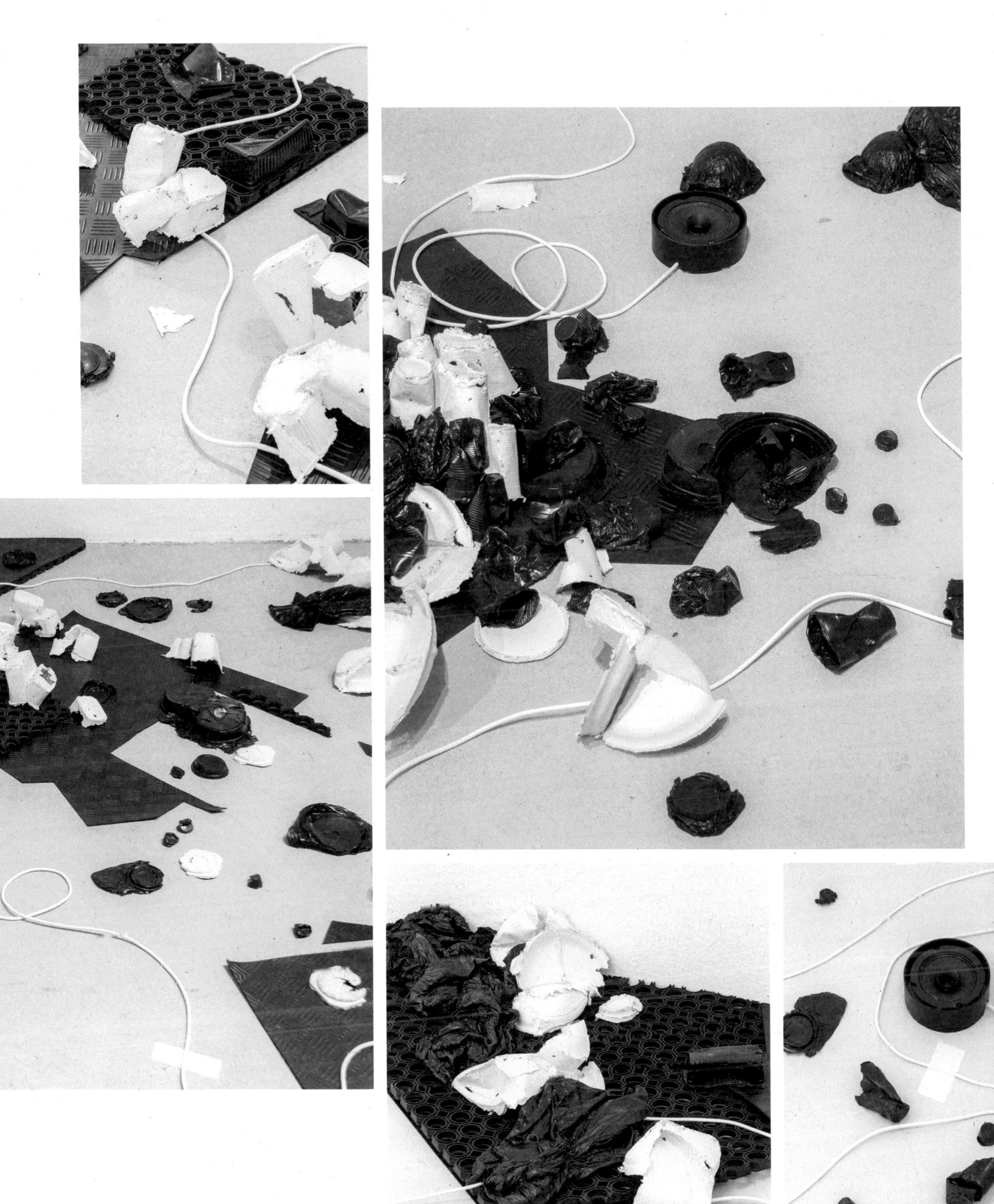

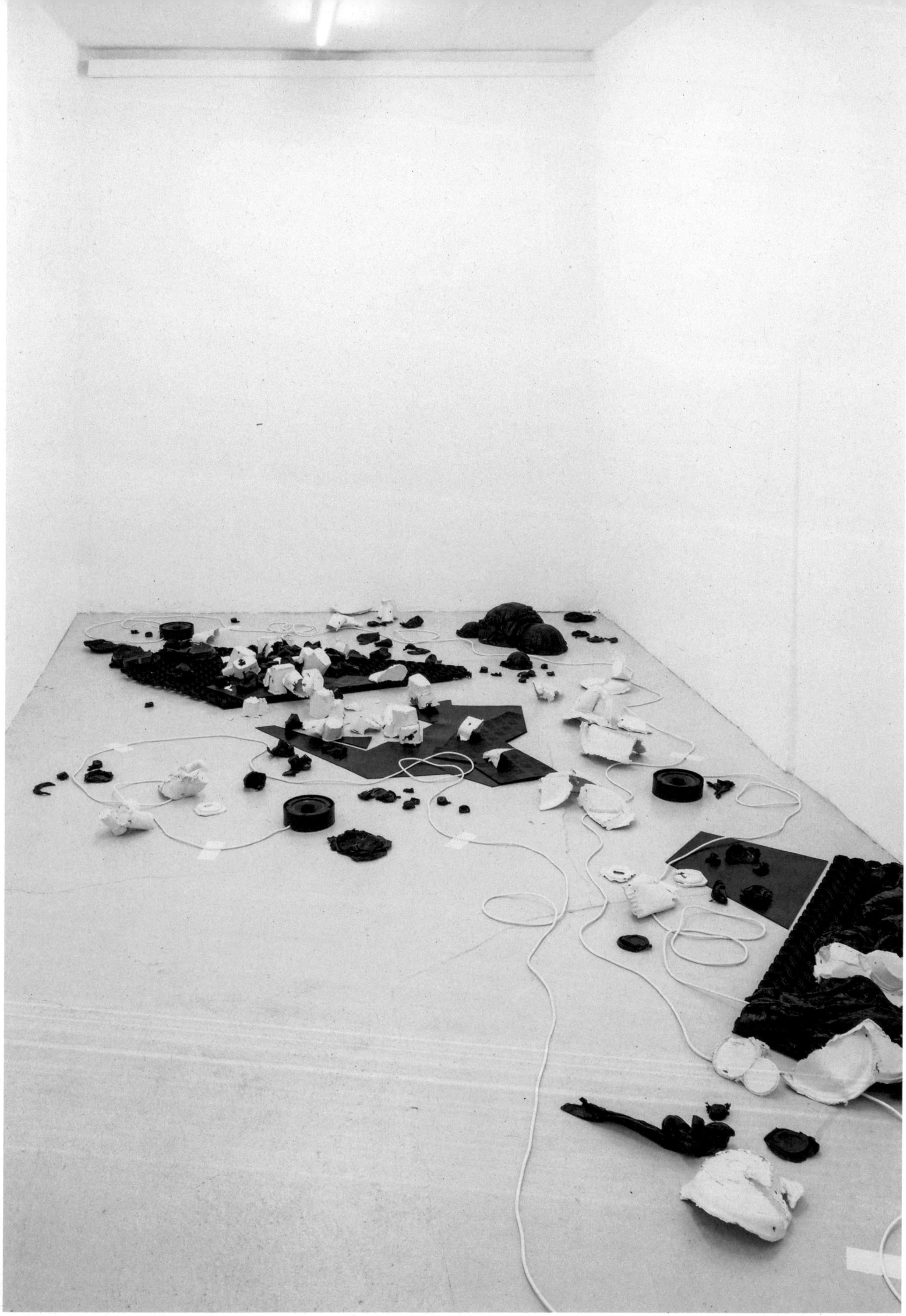

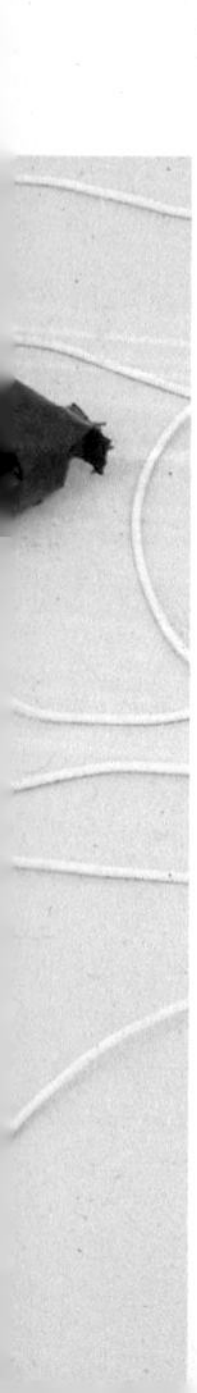

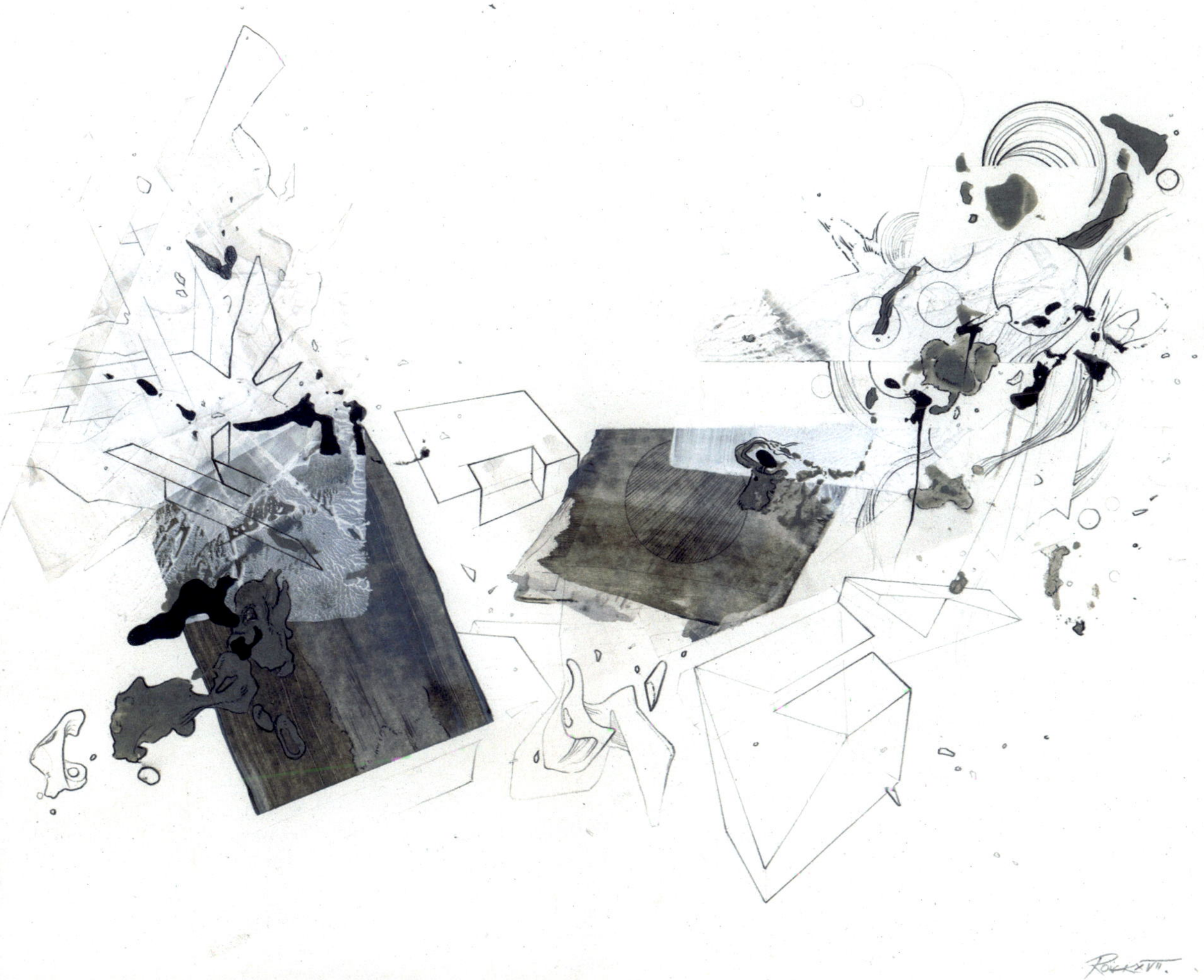

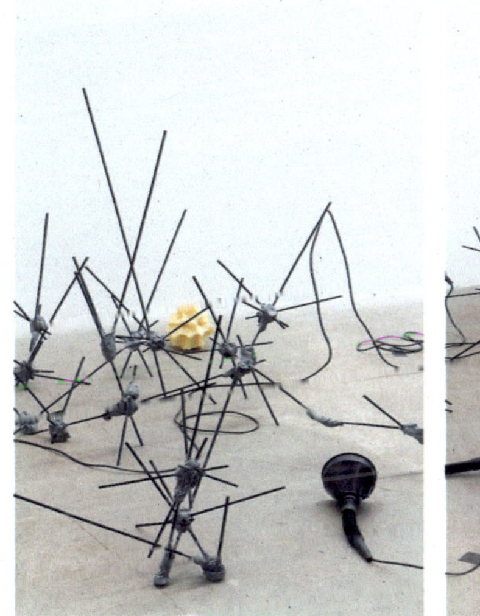
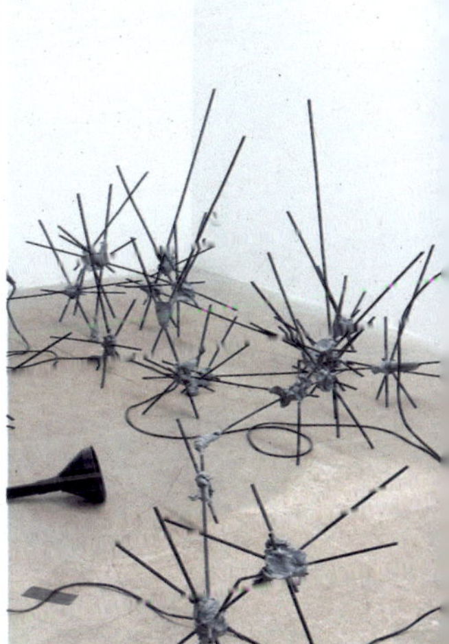

ZOO

2022 —————————————

mixed-media sound installation
in co-operation with Daniela Fromberg
» an Acoustic Enclosure

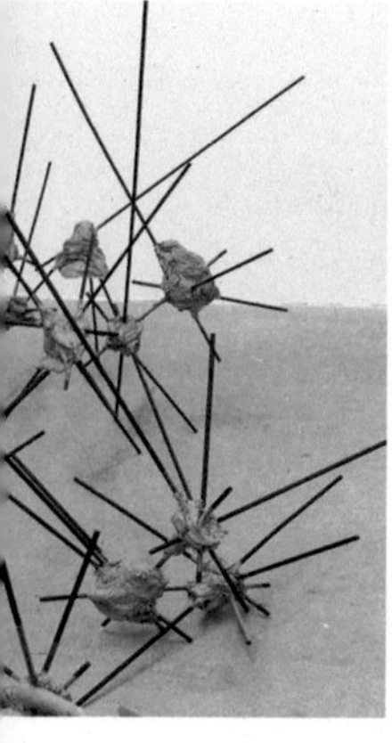

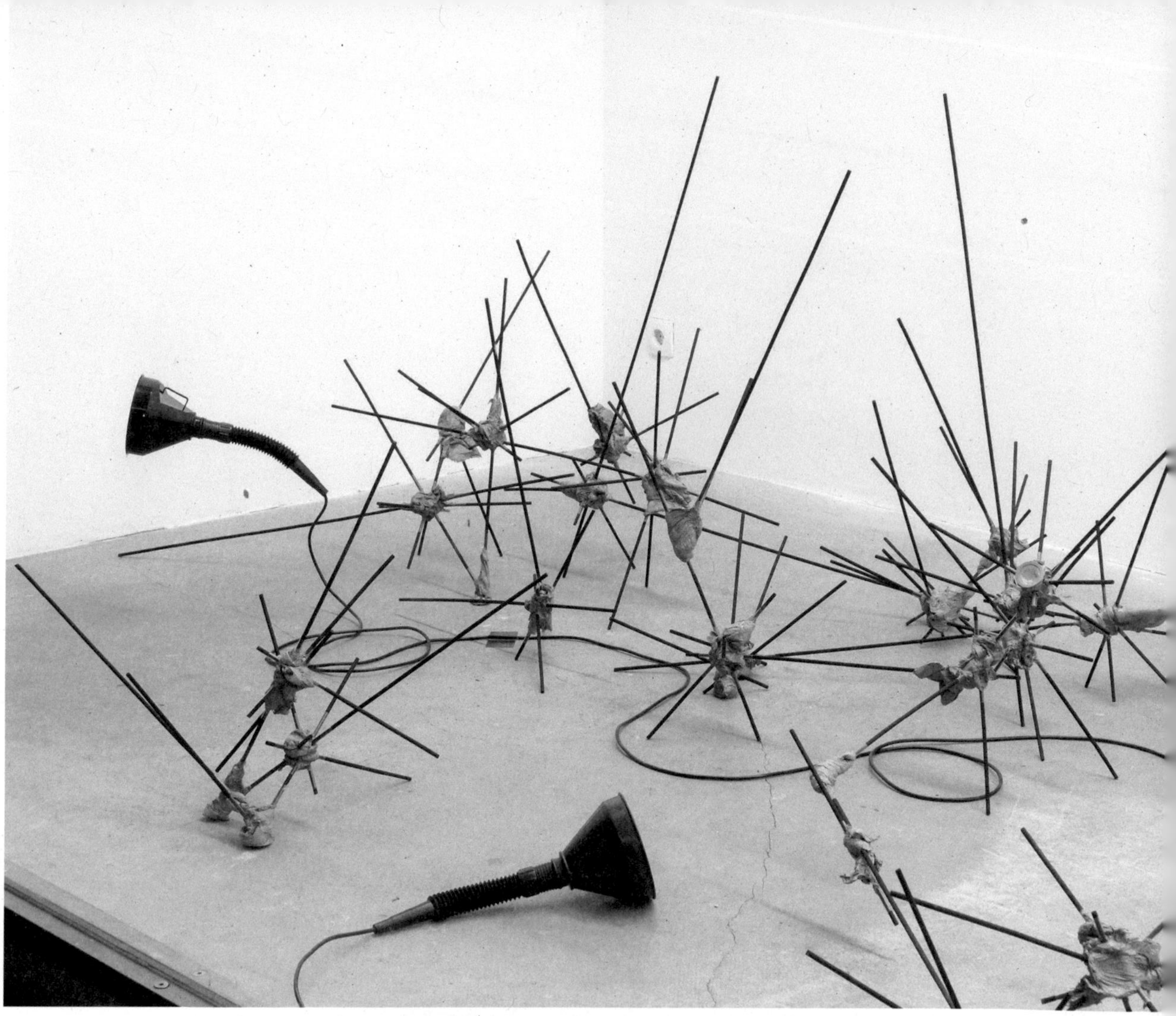

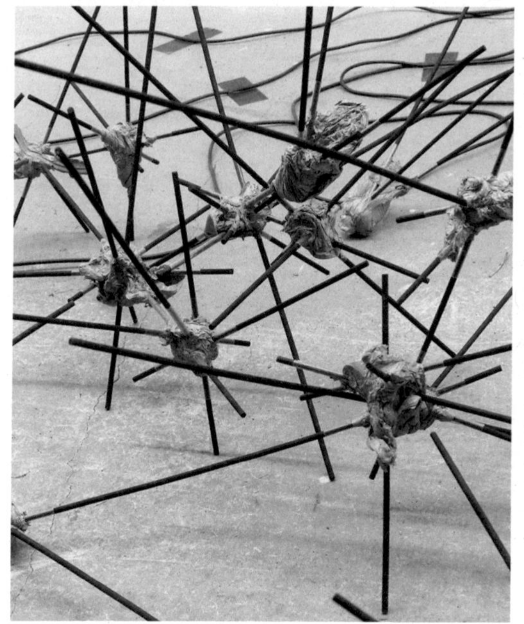

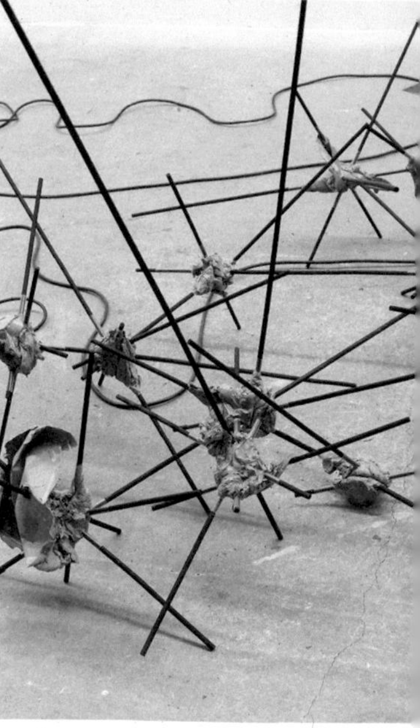

Objects :
interlocking structures
made of wire, straws and grey
silicone, round beechwood
bars painted black, full-range
loudspeakers inside black
polyethylene oil funnels,
cables and playback equipment
/ 200 x 800 x 150 cm
(size variable)

Sound :
4-channel acousmatic
composition **/** very dense and
hypnotic sound field composed
of buzzing-squeaking
pinecones on internal plaster
with hollow parts, tips of
branches scratching on concrete
flooring, room recording of an
atelier house, whistling thermos
bottle and a telephone dial tone
/ loop (8:58) **/ CD 2 – track 5**

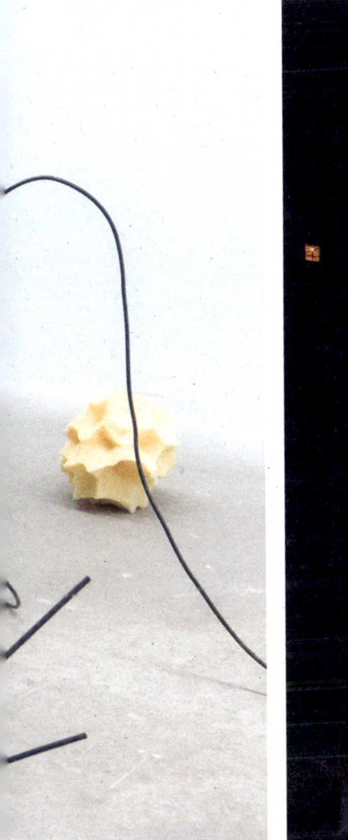
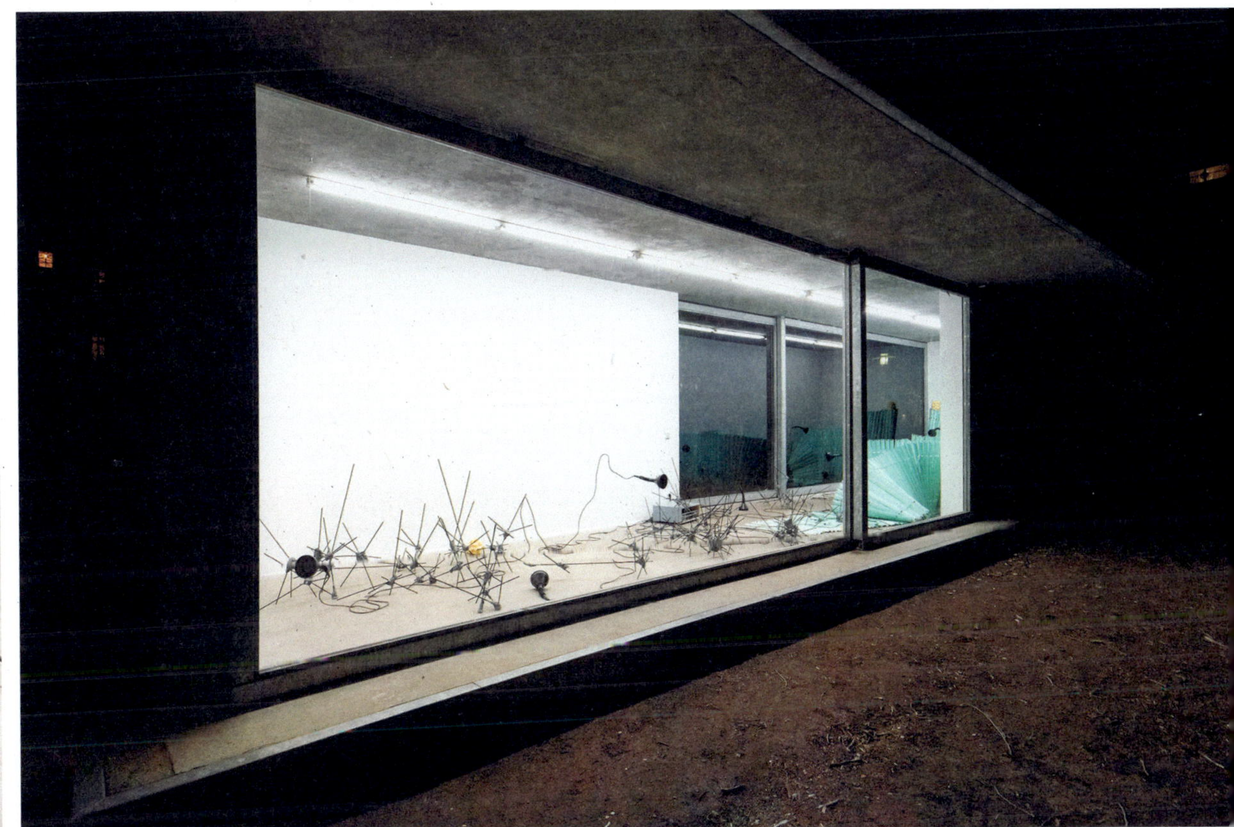
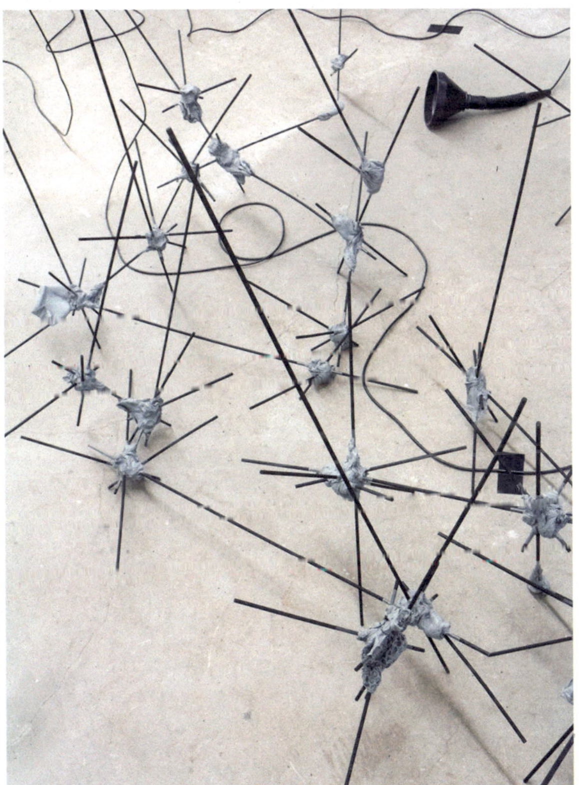
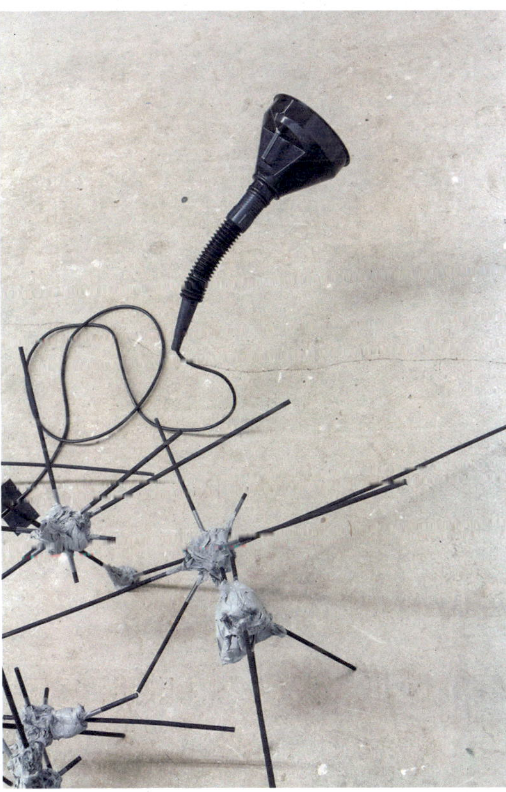

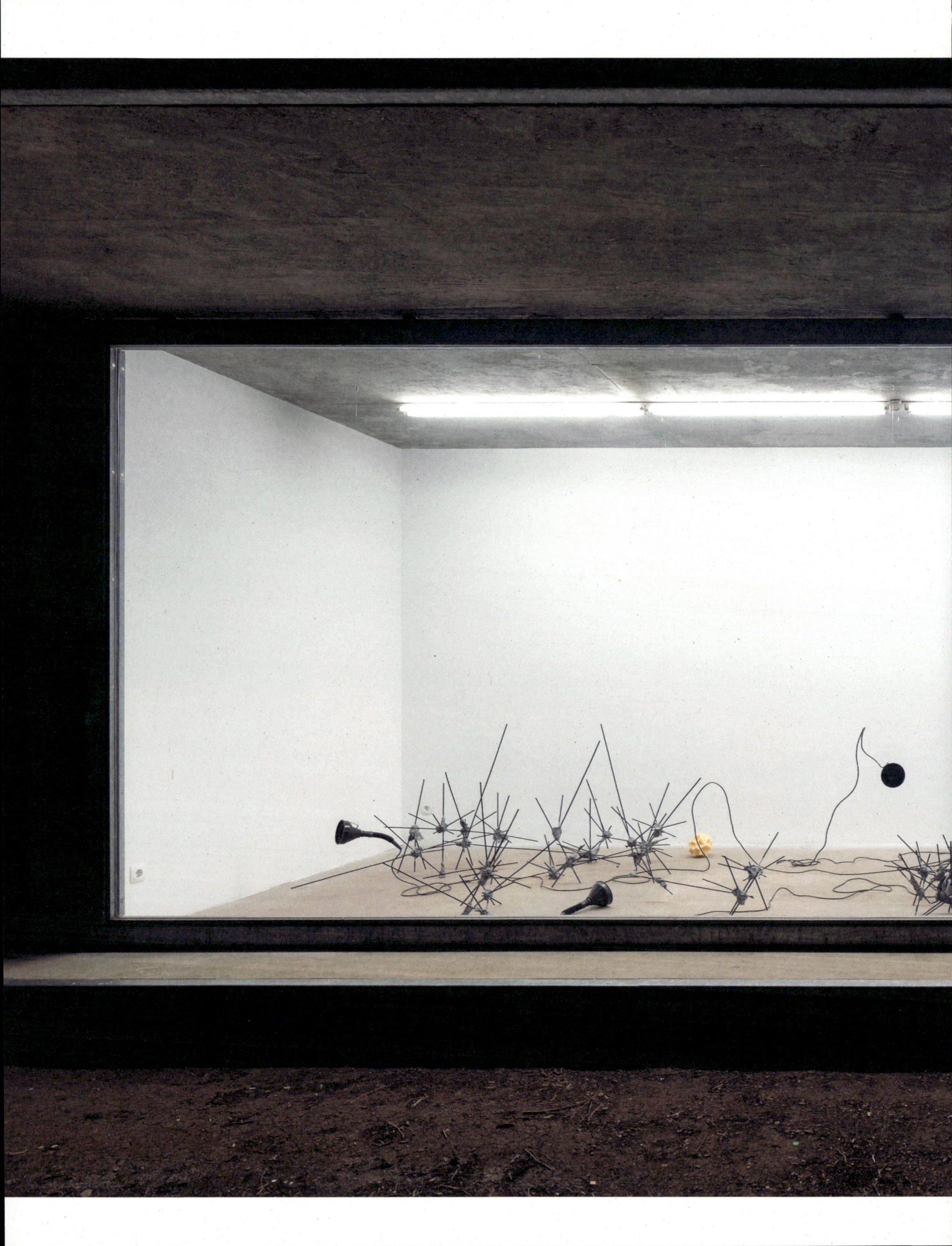

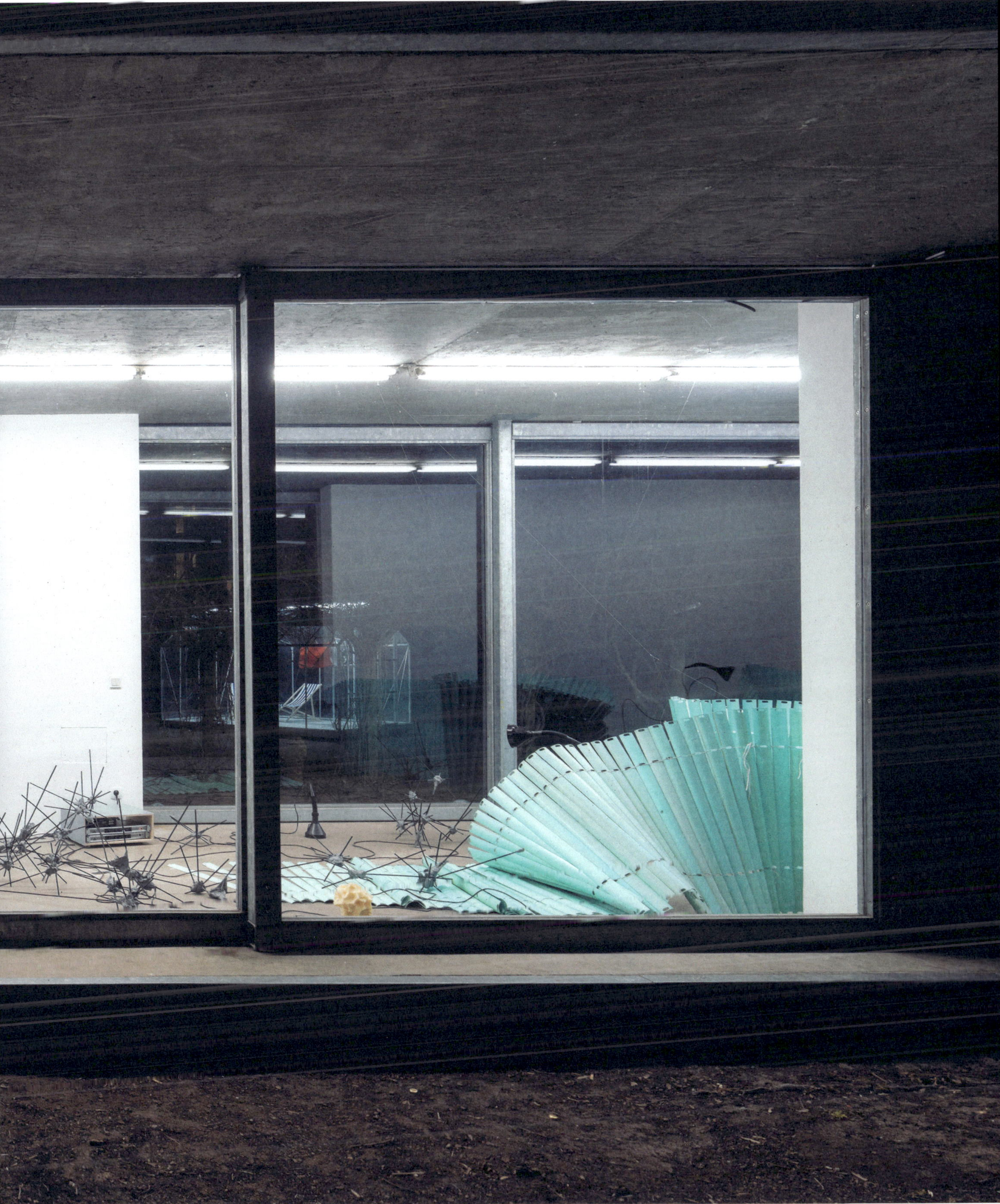

Entfaltung

2015–16

mixed-media sound installation
**» the Path of the Flaneur Becomes the Timeline
of an Everyday Acoustic Experience**

Objects :
castings from water bottles
in paper mâché, acrylic paint,
polystyrene, plastic coverings,
orange and black funnels,
tile adhesive, full-range
loudspeakers, cables and
playback equipment **/**
700 x 500 x 300 cm
(size variable)

Sound :
8-channel acousmatic
composition **/** hypnotically
flowing sound field **/** signal
from an overnight train,
falling wooden picks, blowing
through straws, plastic water
bottles hitting one another,
creaking wooden floorboards,
paper and plastic bags **/**
loop (54:48) **/** CD 1 – track 13

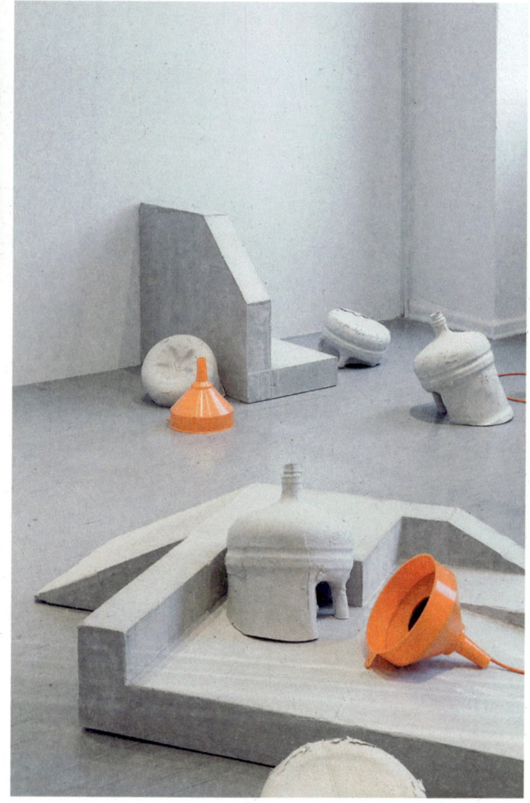

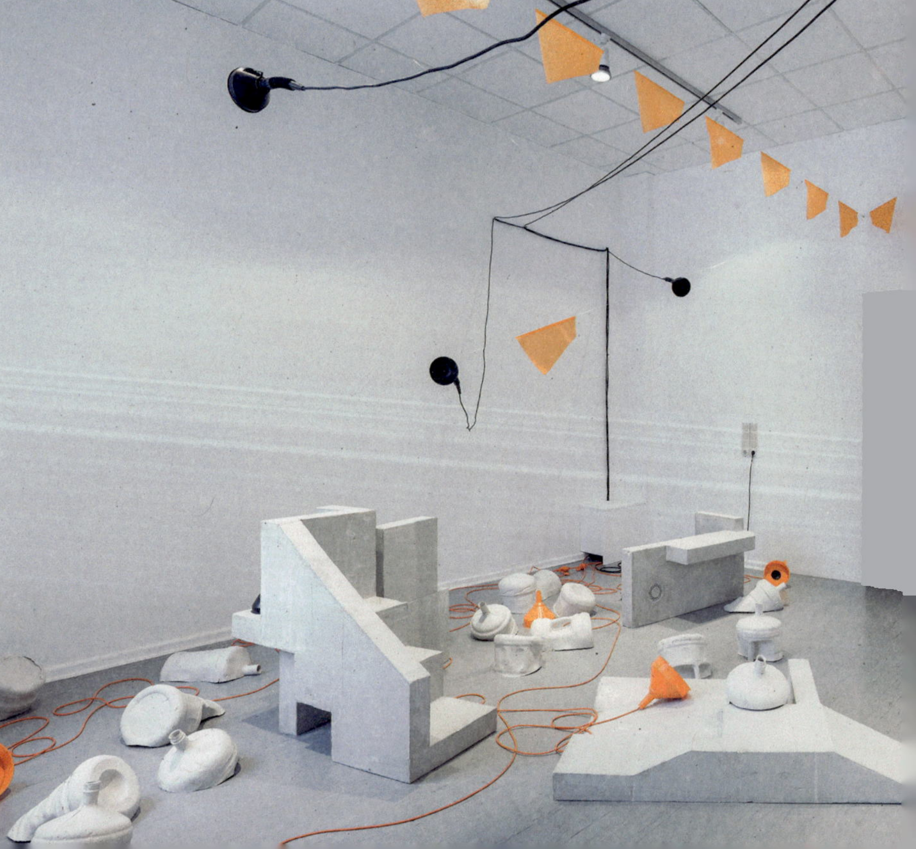

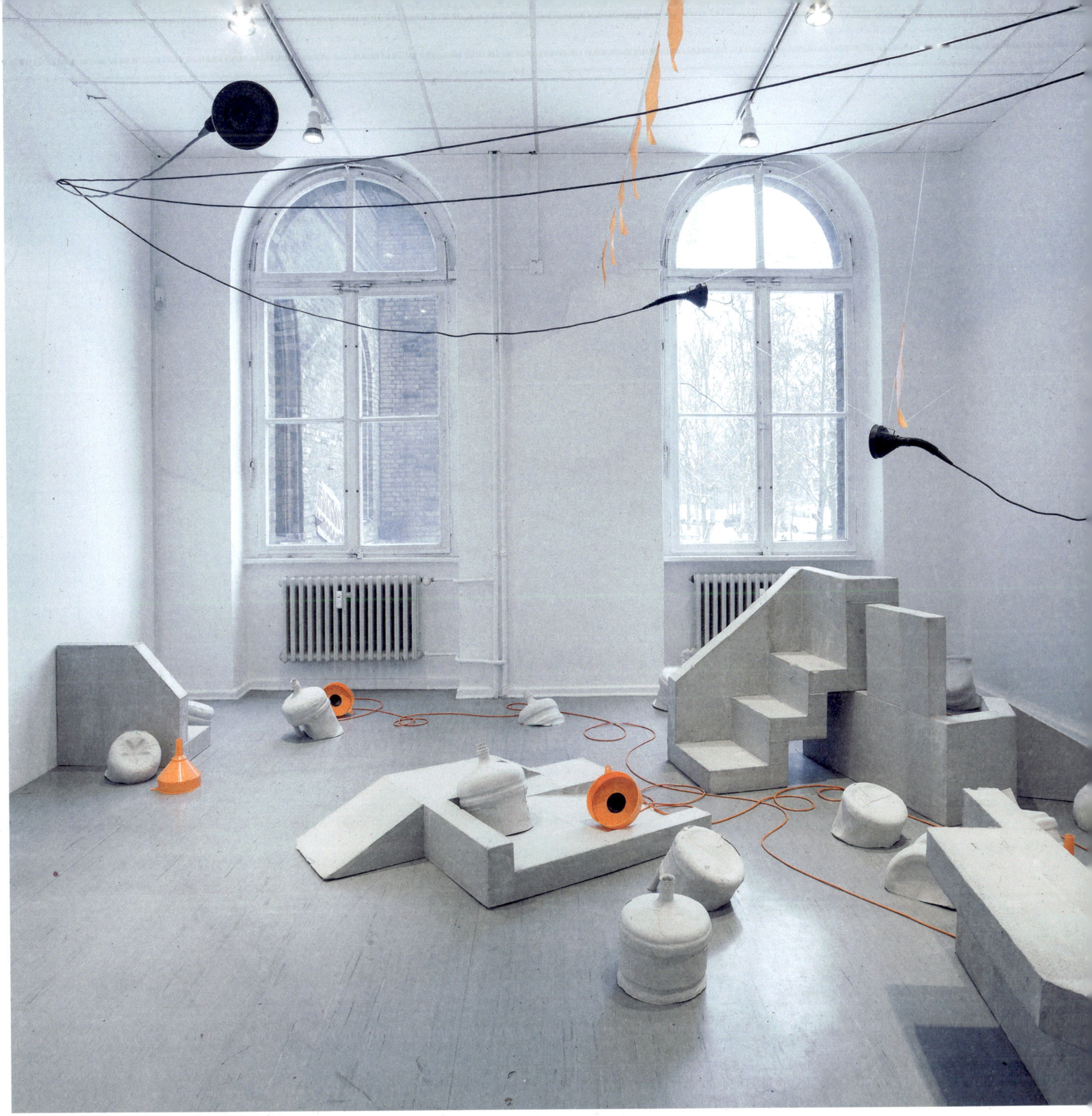

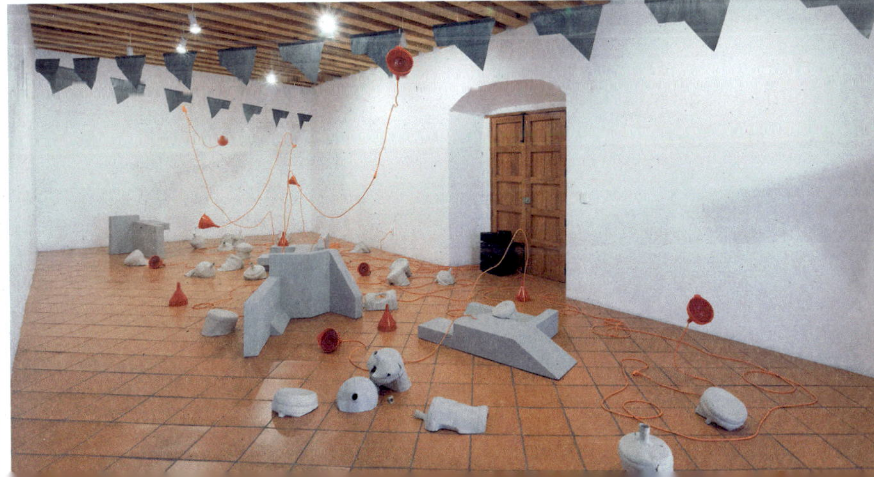

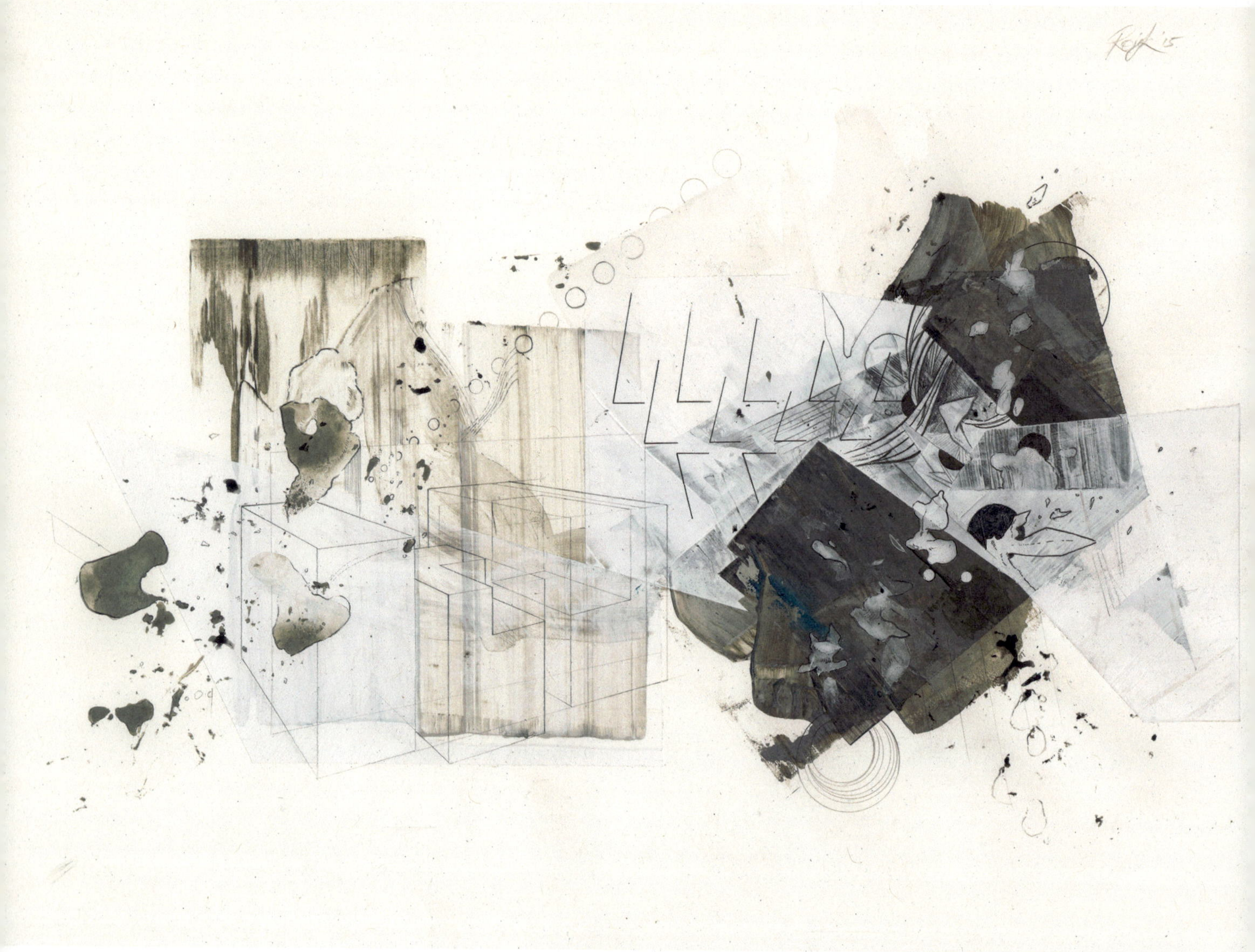

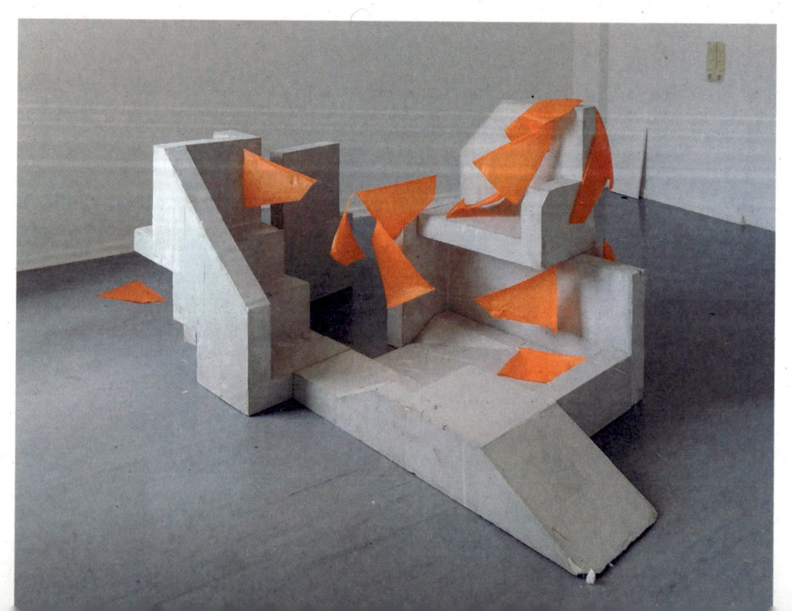

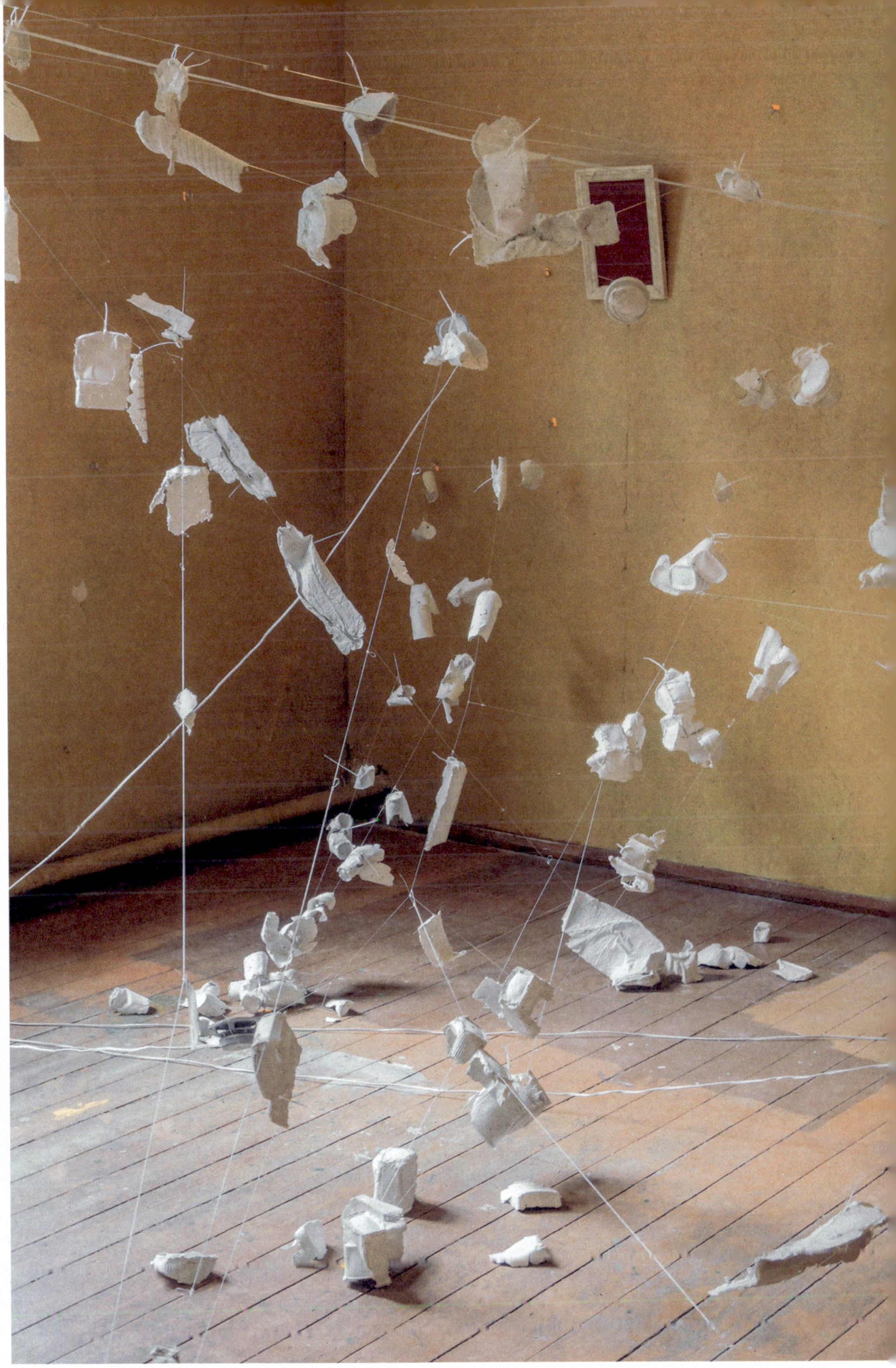

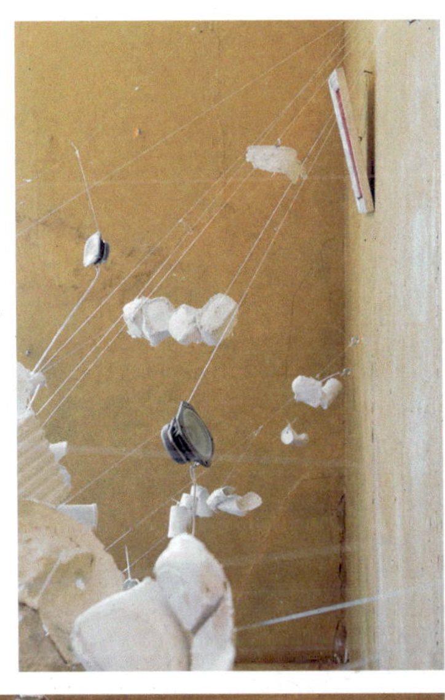
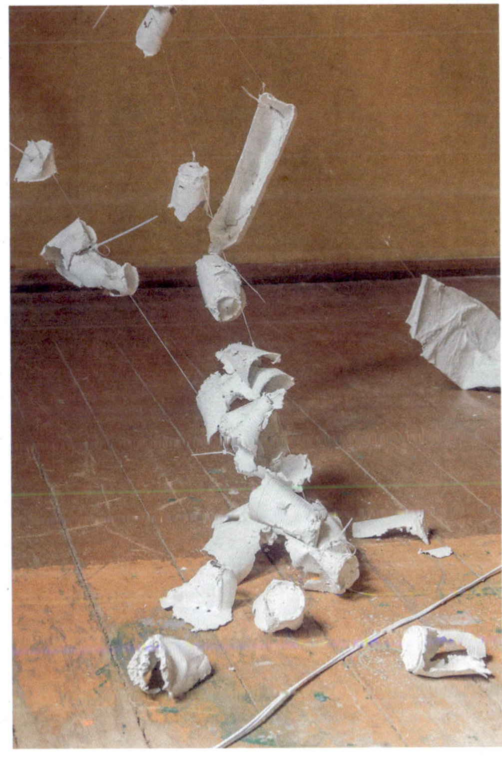

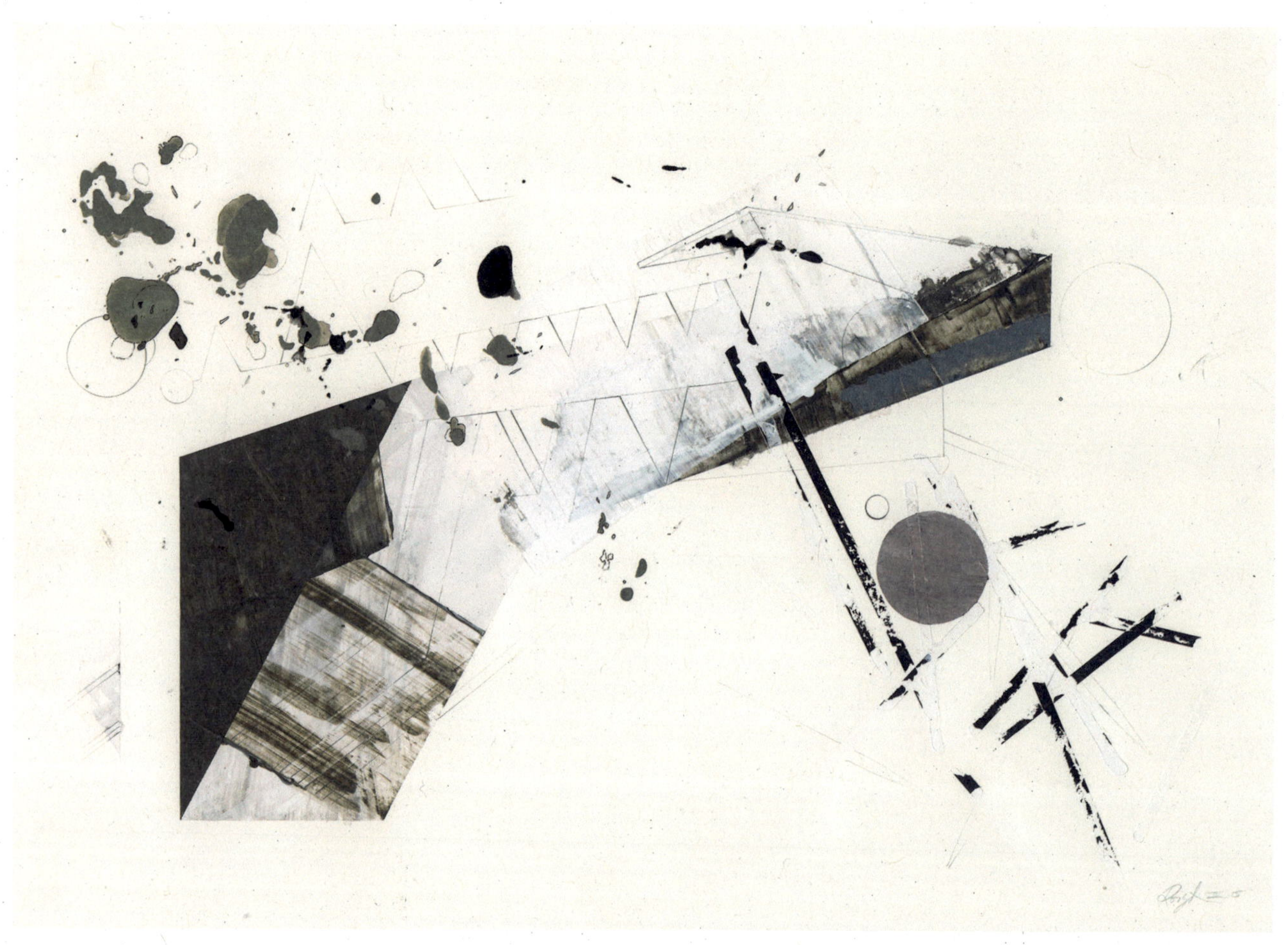

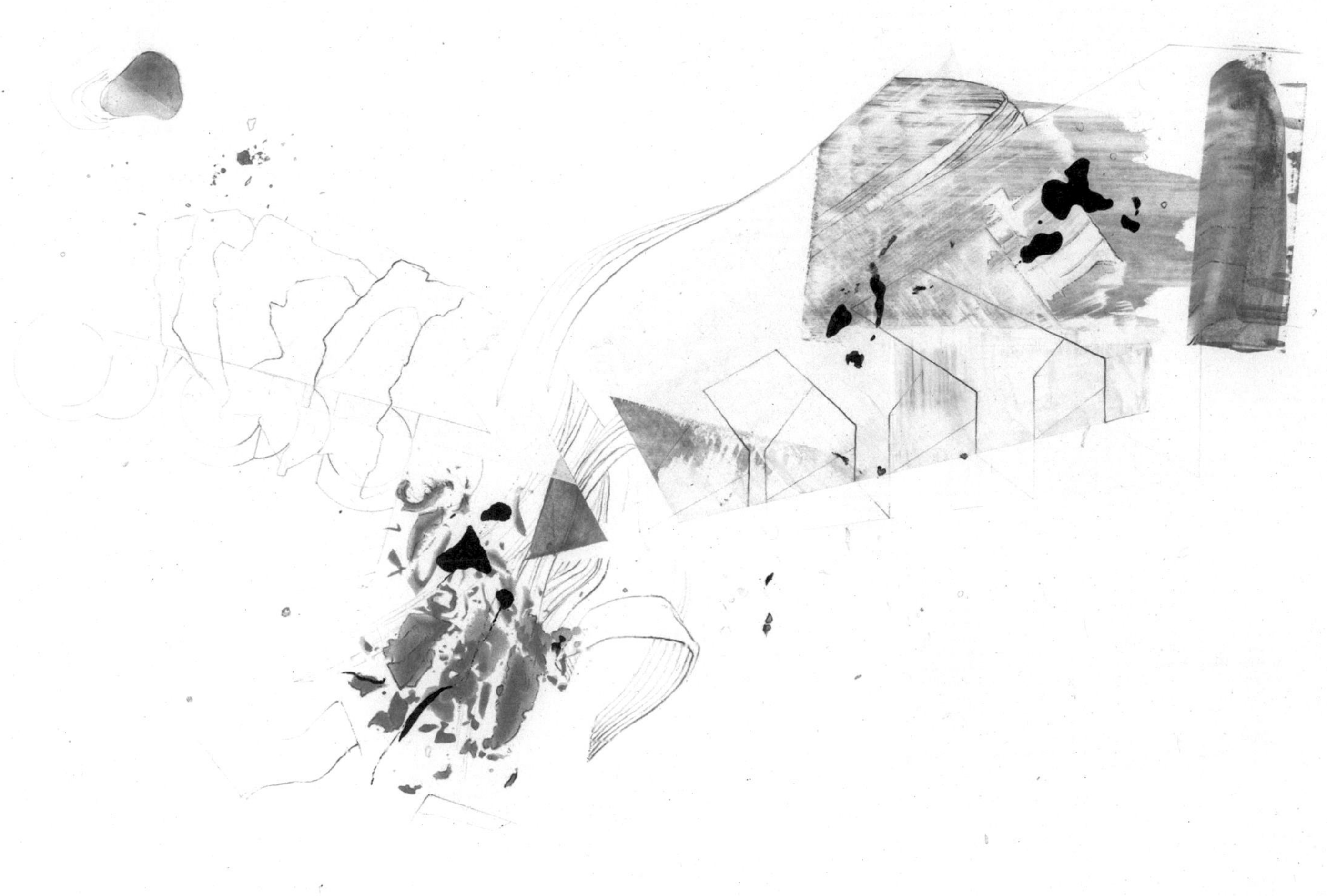

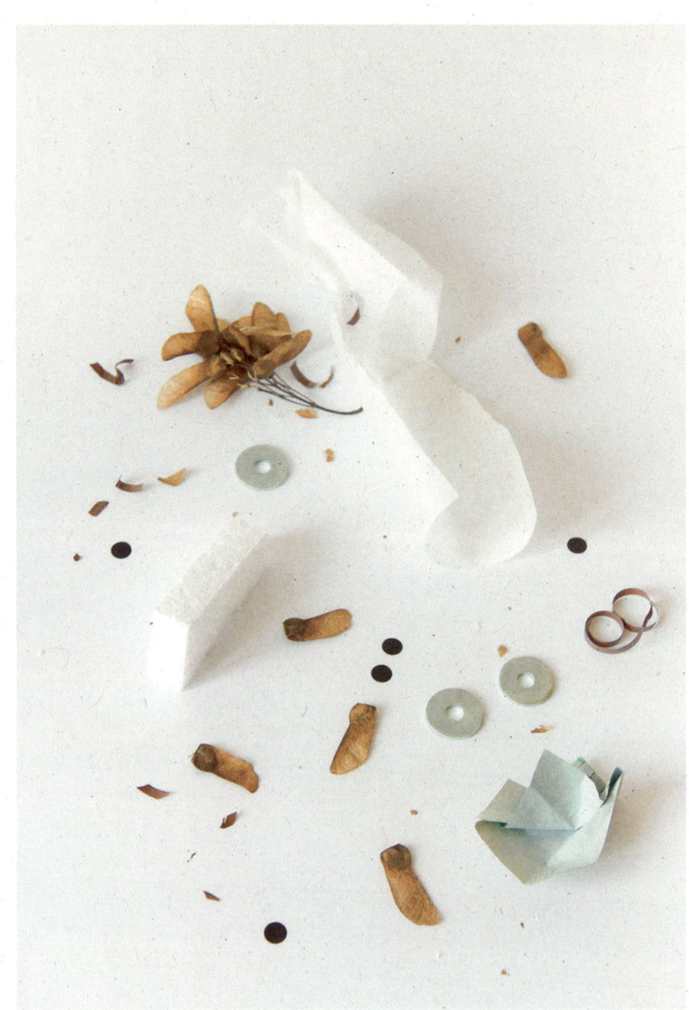

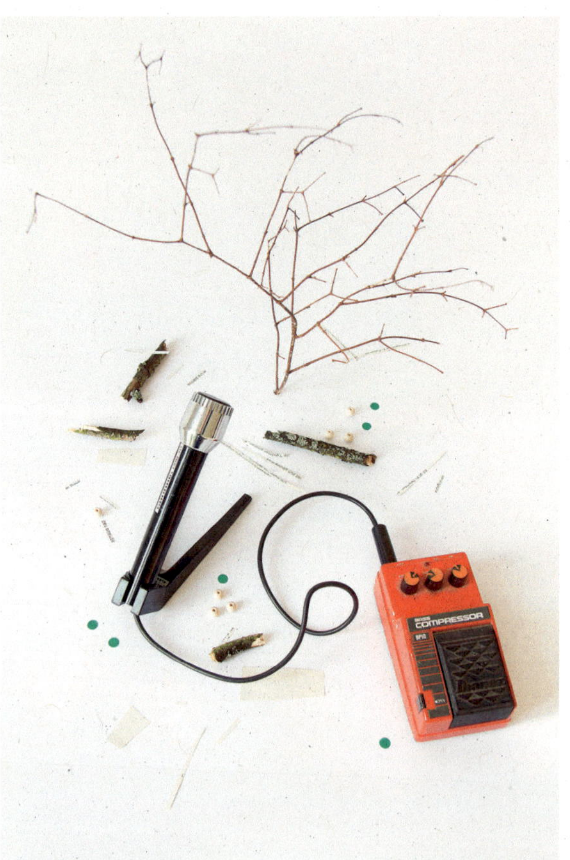

illustrations for the concert series
"Biegungen im Ausland" **/** 2014

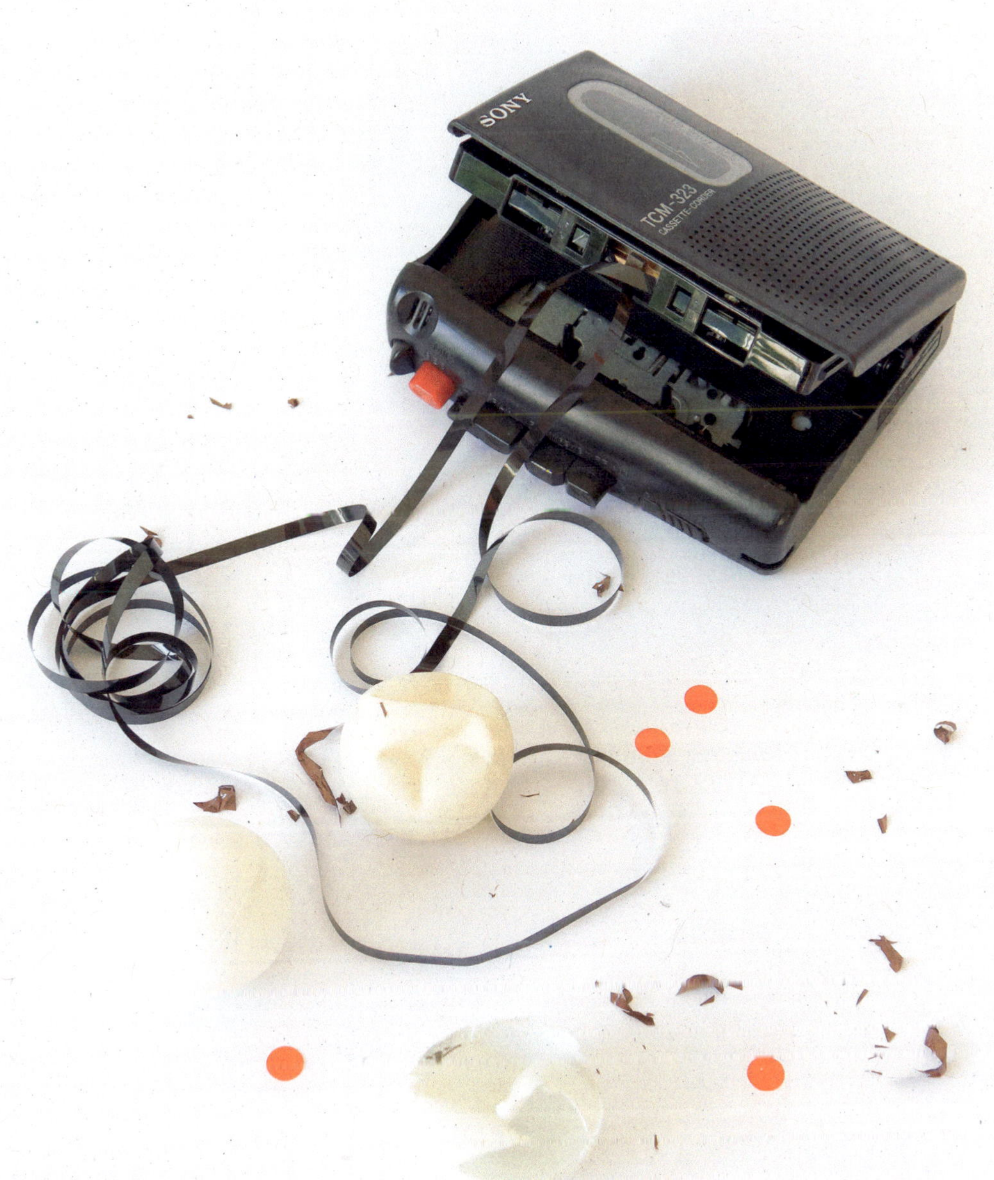
SONY
TCM-323
CASSETTE-CORDER

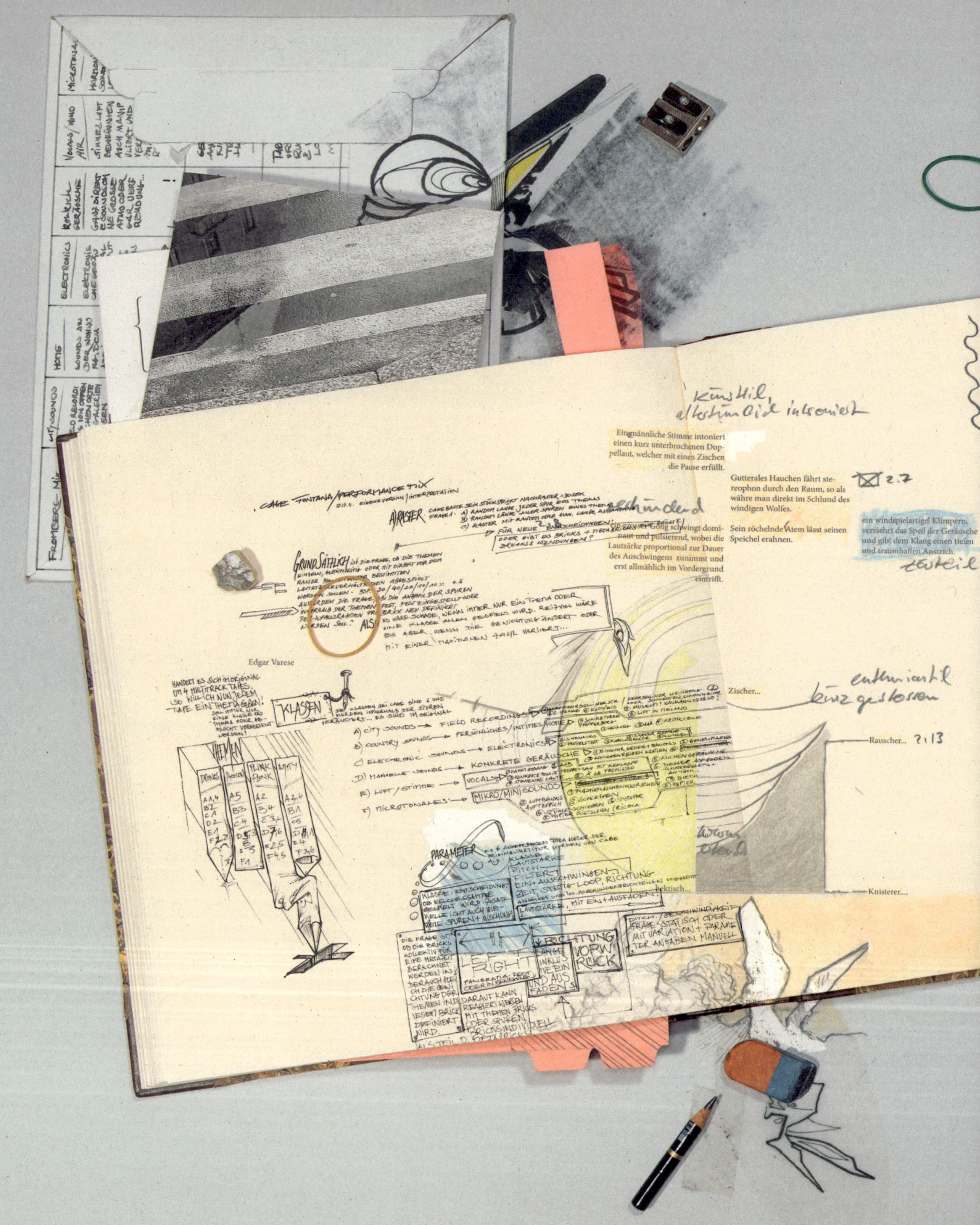
Eingmännliche Stimme intoniert einen kurz unterbrochenen Doppellaut, welcher mit einen Zischen die Pause erfüllt.

Gutterales Hauchen fährt stereophon durch den Raum, so als währe man direkt im Schlund des windigen Wolfes.

Sein röchelnde Atem lässt seinen Speichel erahnen.

ein windspielartigel Klimpern, verziehrt das Speil der Geräusche und gibt dem Klang einen tiefen und traumhaften Anstrich

Ein grosser Gong schwingt dominant und pulsierend, wobei die Lautsärke proportional zur Dauer des Auschwingens zunimmt und erst allmählich im Vordergrund eintrifft.

Edgar Varese

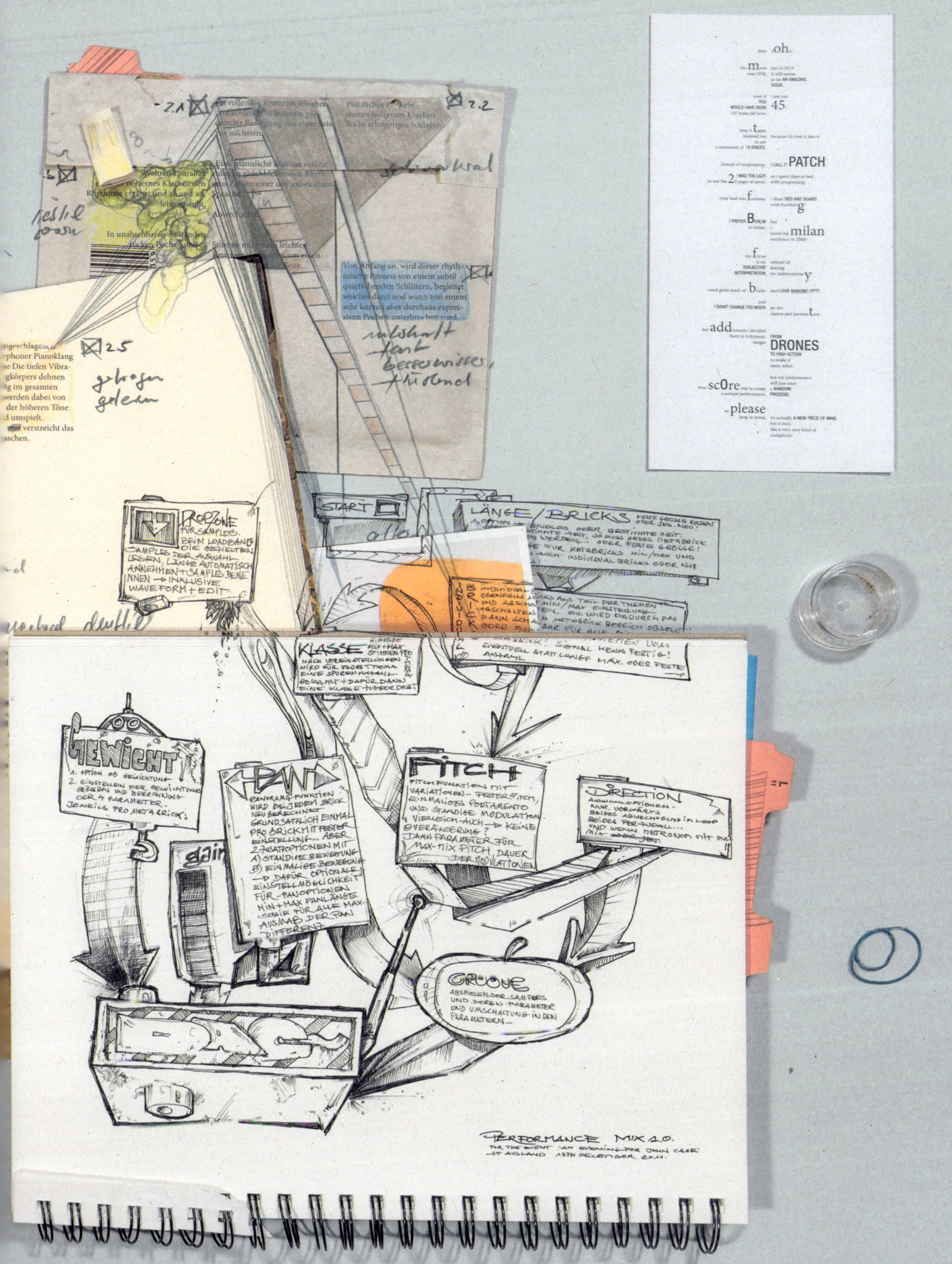
dear .oh.
the m... was 1994, but in 2019 it still seems to be AN AMAZING ISSUE.
even if YOU WOULD HAVE BEEN 107 years old now, I am just 45.
your t ...tapes inspired me to use a maximum of 16 VOICES, because it's root is also 4.
instead of composition, I CALL IT PATCH
2 I WAS TOO LAZY to use the 20 pages of score, as i spent days in bed with programming.
your host was f ontana, i share BED AND BOARD with fromberg g
I PREFER B ERLIN to milan, but i loved my milan residency in 2008.
my f ocus is on SUBJECTIVE INTERPRETATION, instead of aiming for indeterminac y
i used grids made of b ricks and LOUD BANGING DITTY
and I DIDNT CHANGE TOO MUCH on the classes and parame t ers.
but add itionaly i devided them in 4 dynamic ranges FROM DRONES TO HIGH ACTION to make it more mine.
your sc0re was to create a unique performance. but my performance will just start a RANDOM PROCESS.
so please keep in mind, it's actually A NEW PIECE OF MINE. but it feels like a very nice kind of complicity!
PERFORMANCE MIX 1.0.
FOR THE EVENT "AN EVENING FOR JOHN CAGE" AT AUSLAND 17TH DECEMBER 2011.
GEWICHT
GAIN
PAN
PITCH
DIRECTION
BASS
GROOVE
KLASSE
START
LÄNGE / BRICKS
PROP.ONE

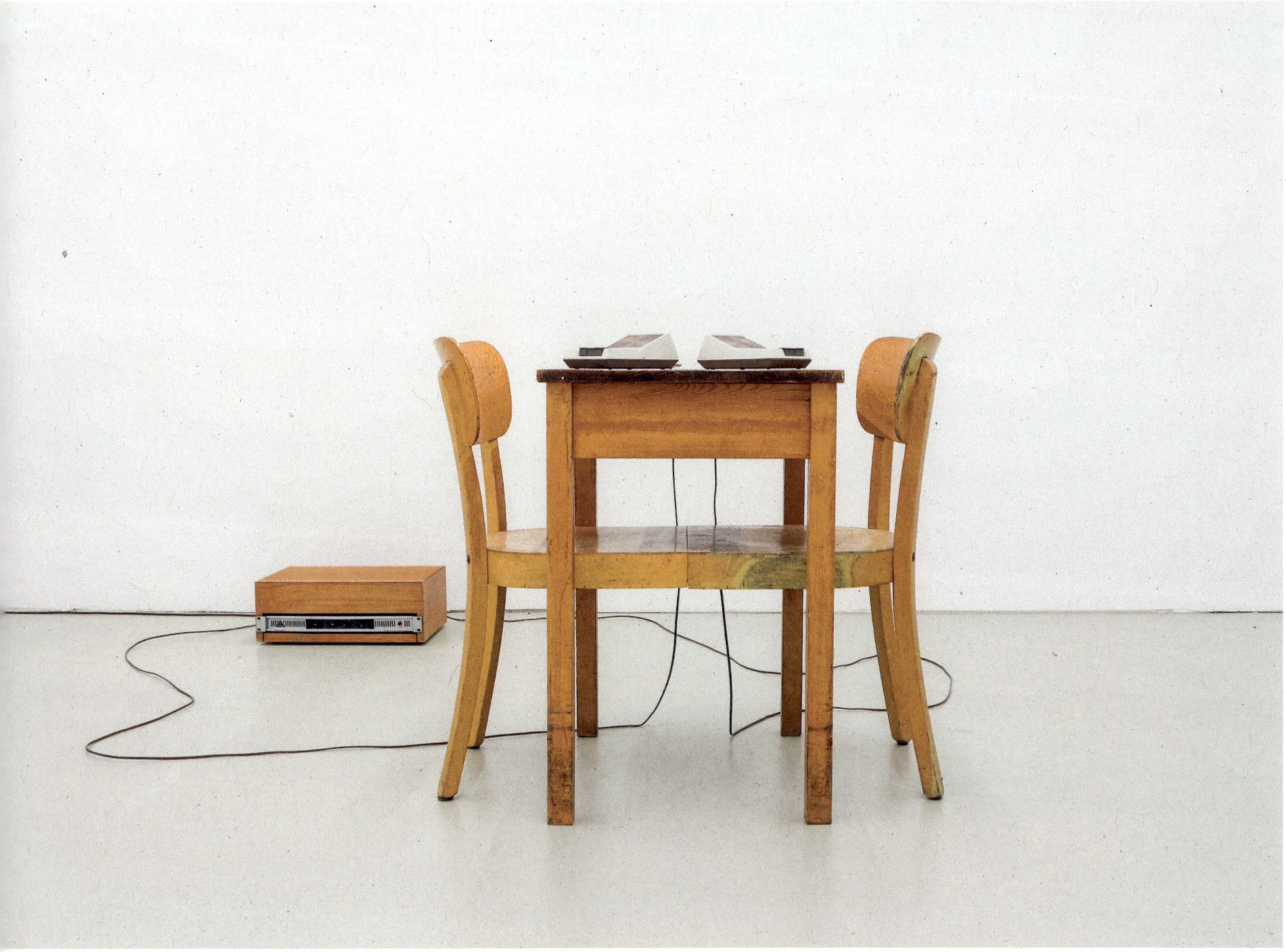

Schweigen ist Gold

2015 ——————

mixed-media sound installation
**» Two Voices Struggle to Be the Authority
of an Acoustic Interpretation**

Objects :
vintage wooden table,
modified vintage wooden
chairs, modified hi-fi
loudspeaker, intercoms, cables
and playback equipment
/ 200 x 250 x 150 cm

Sound :
2-channel composition
/ voice, ventilators, feedback,
breathing noises **/** monologues
and dialogues **/** poetic
descriptions of sounds
/ loop (8:03) **/** CD 1 – track 4

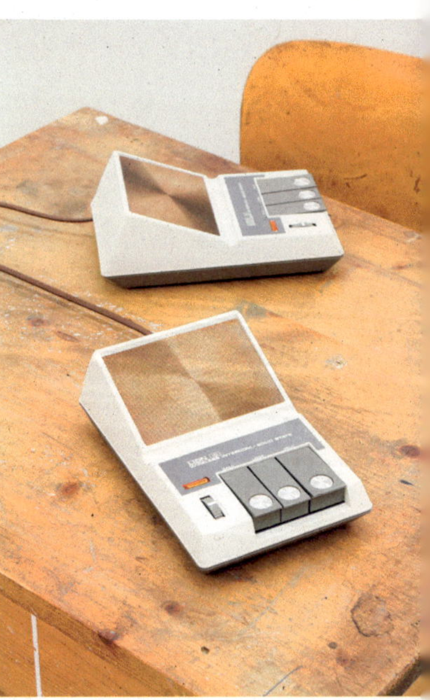

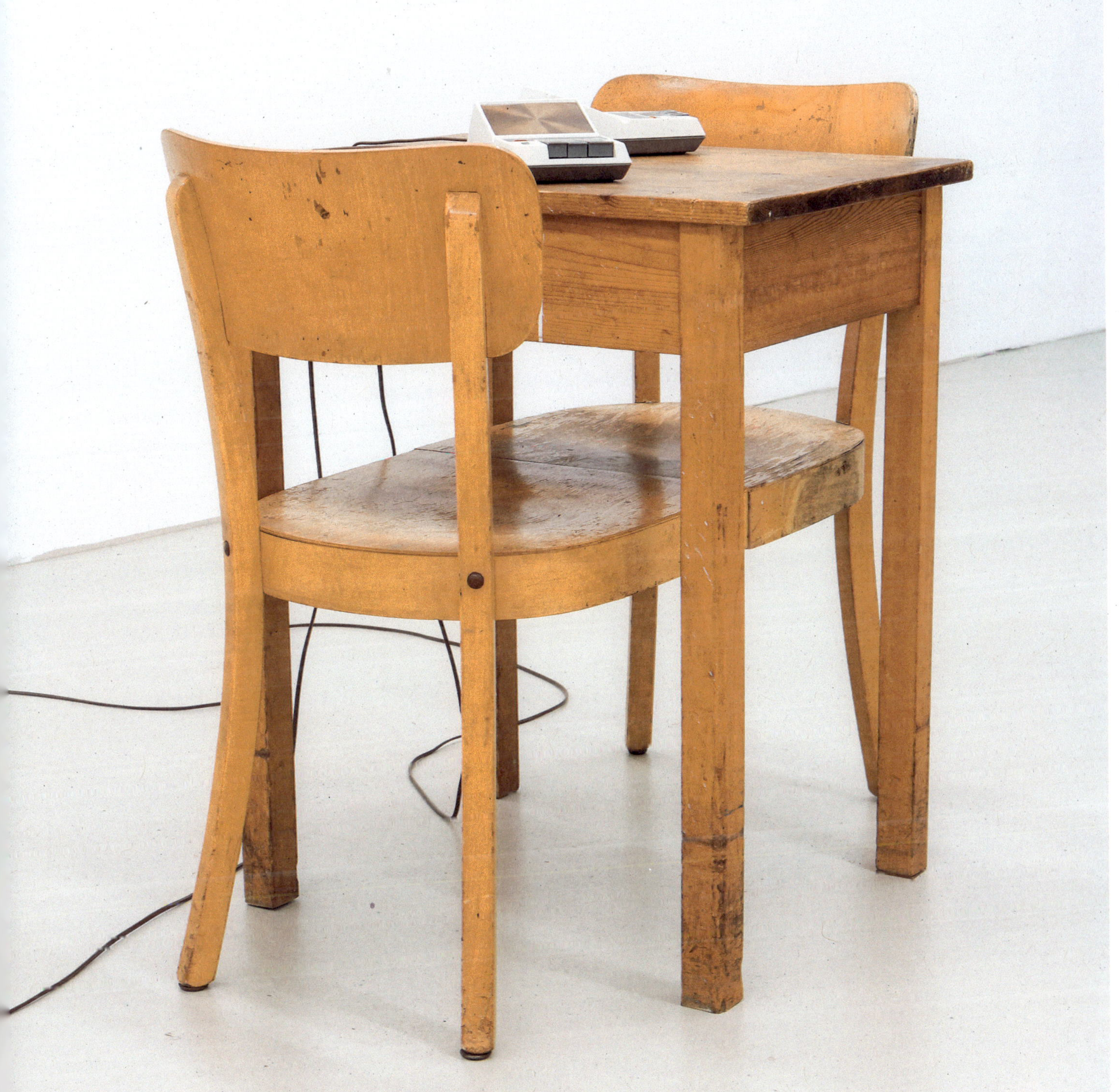

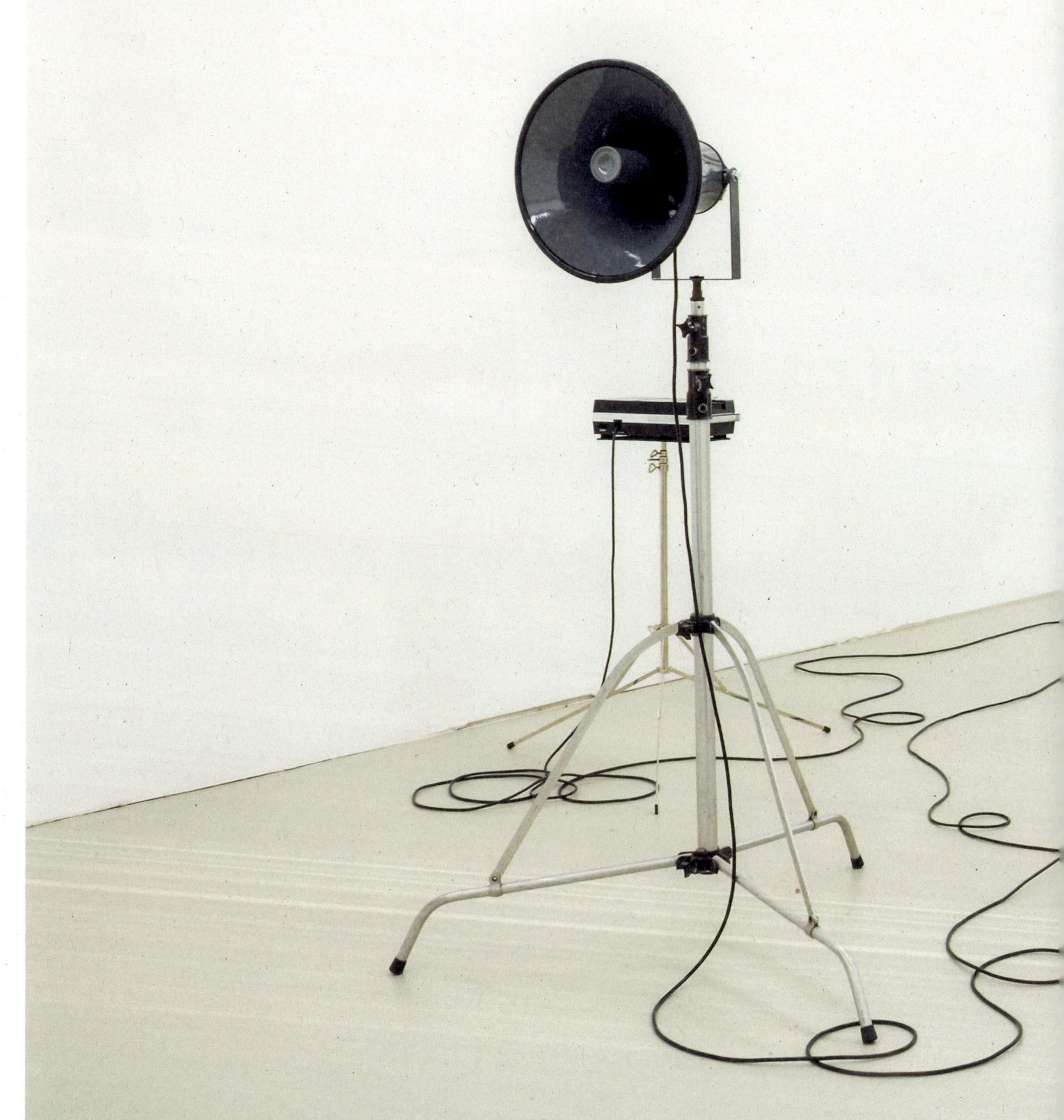

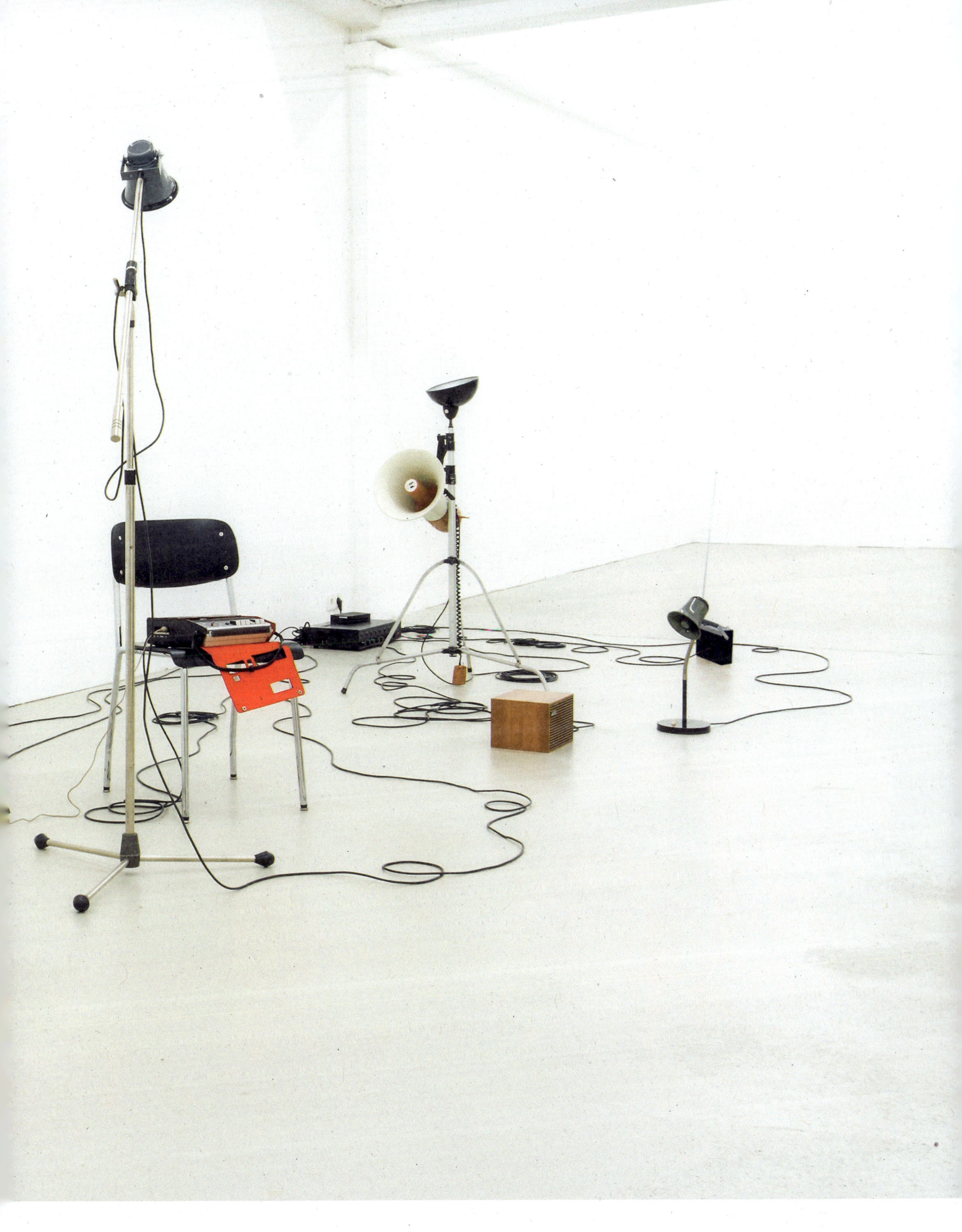

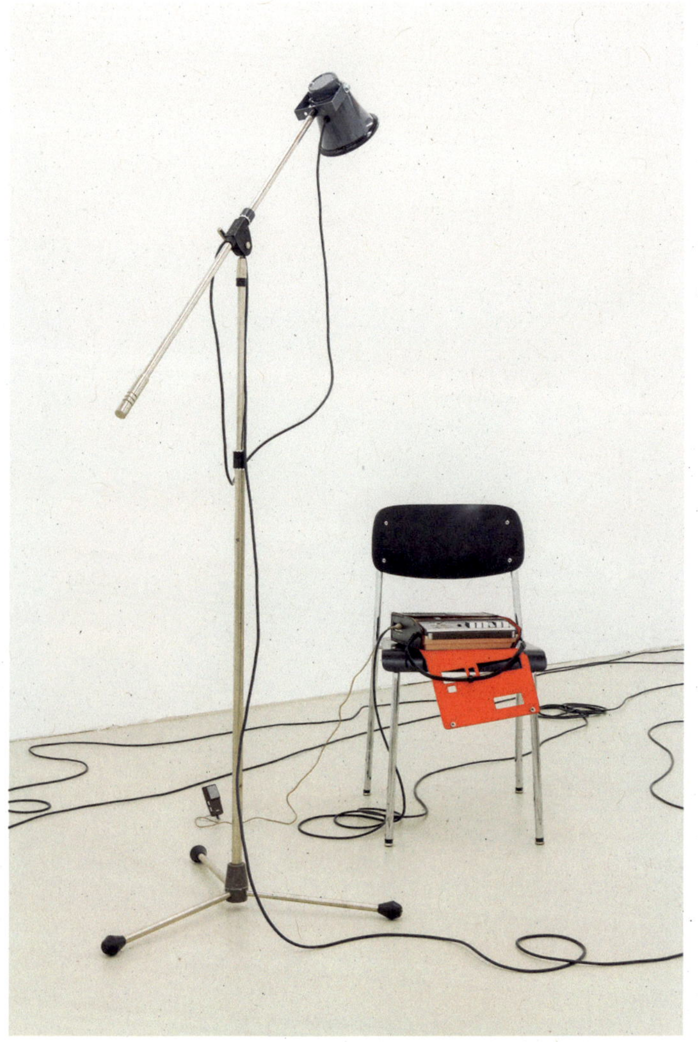

Worte wie Schall und Raum

2016 ———

mixed-media sound installation

» the History of Noise in Music as an Installation Theatre Piece: Poetic Descriptions of the Sonic Aspects Of Selected Key Works From the Artist's Record Collection

Objects :
chair, lamp stands, various loudspeakers, megaphone, vintage portable radio, vintage cassette recorder, cables and playback equipment / 600 x 200 x 250 cm

Sound :
8-channel composition / voice / an arrangement of whispered, cried, shouted and spoken sound descriptions arranged as a chaotic Babylonian chorus of voices with intensely theatrical density and dynamics / loop (33:30) / CD 1 – track 1 + 11 + CD 2 – track 1, 6 + 14

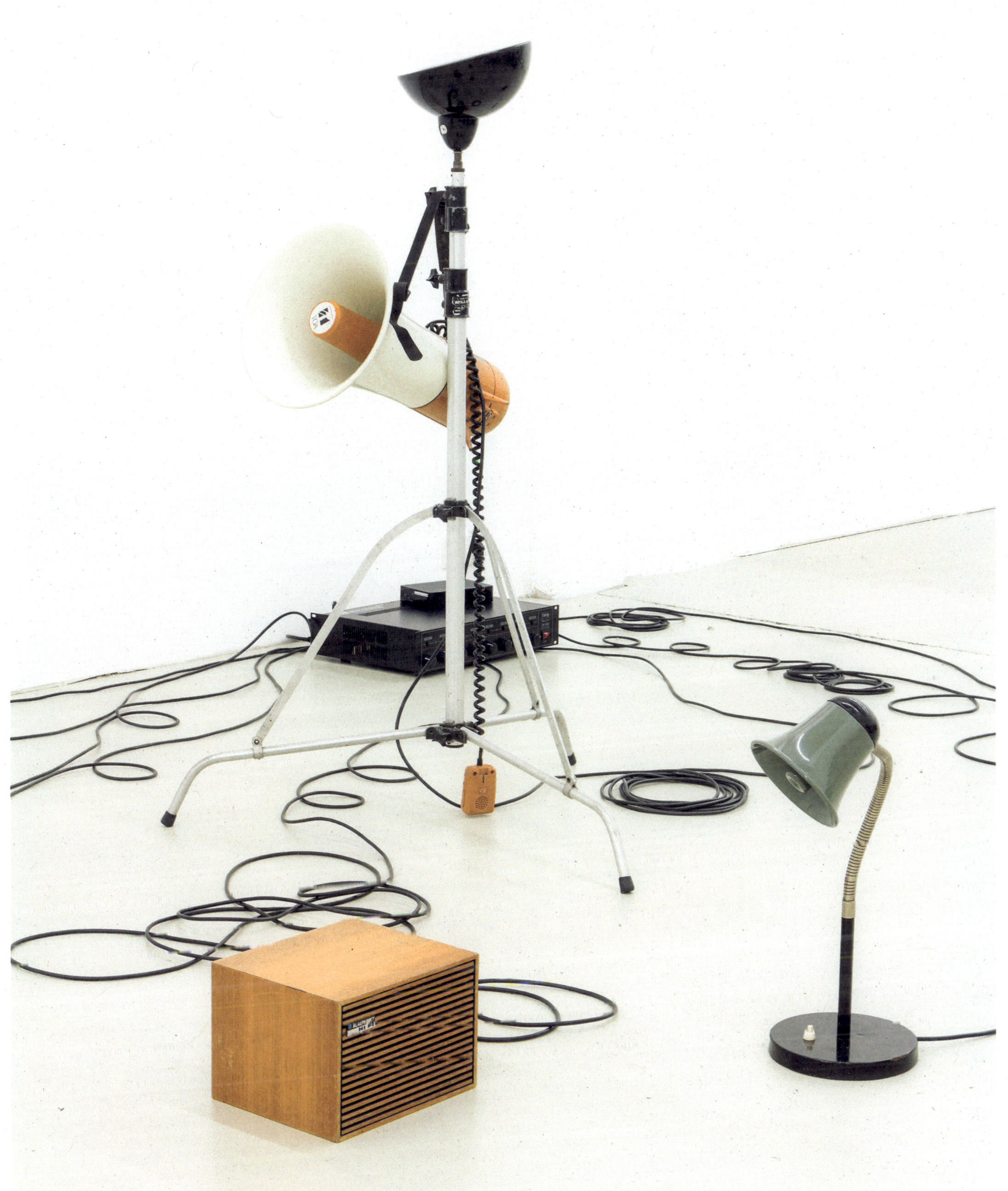

Objects :
polystyrene, plaster, acrylic
paint, books coated in
black varnish, desk lamps,
intercoms, fan heaters, drain
filters, doormats, full-range
loudspeakers, cables and
playback equipment **/**
400 x 200 x 50 cm

Sound :
7-channel acousmatic
composition **/** breathing,
whispered to-do lists,
hissing, falling chestnut
cases, refrigerator hum, room
recordings of the studio,
static, crackling fallen leaves,
bells, electronic interference
noises and feedback **/**
loop (8:30) **/ CD 2 – track 11**

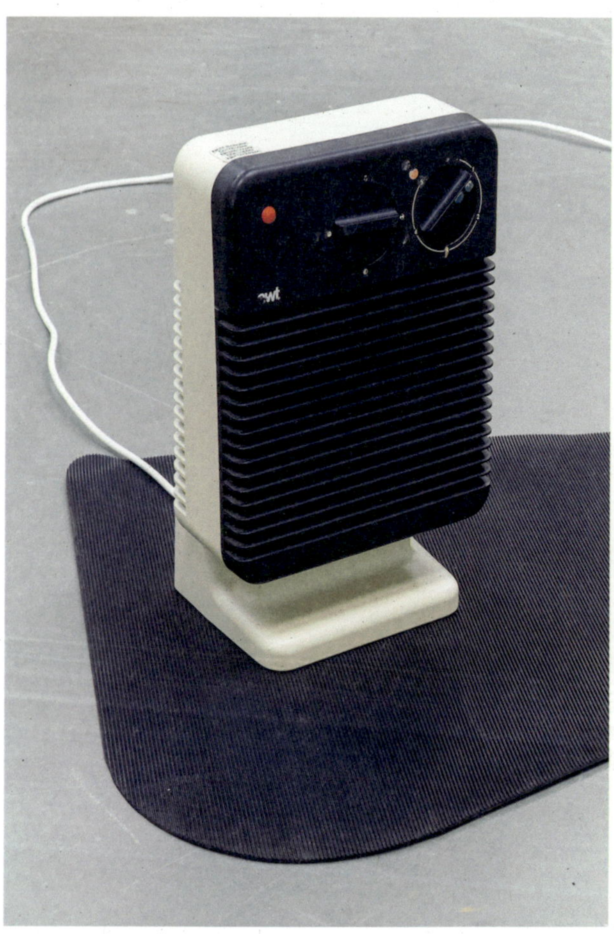

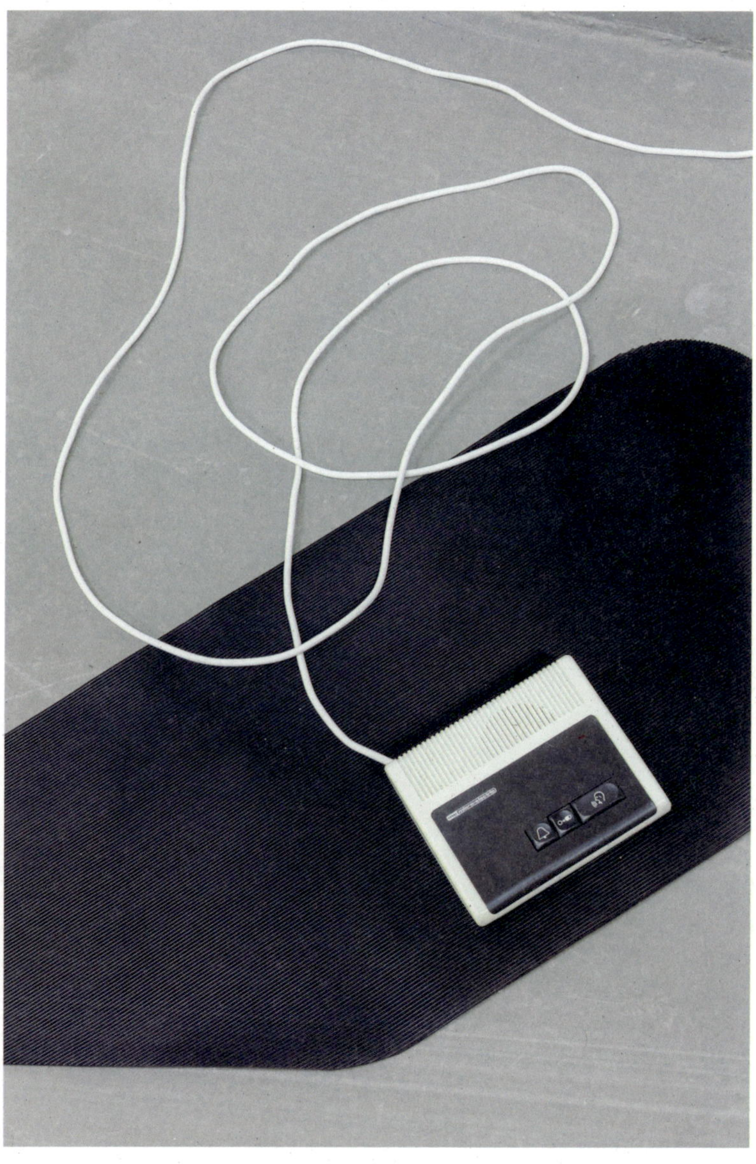

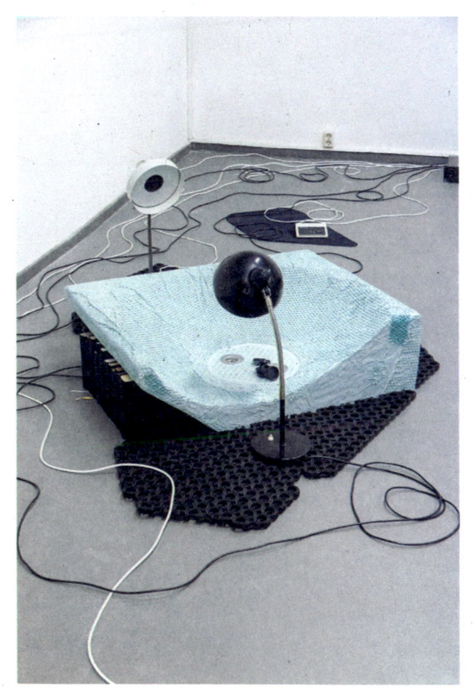

A Path Is Formed by Laying One Stone at a Time

2018

mixed-media sound installation
» To-Do Lists — or How the Sense of Duty Hinders the Creative Process

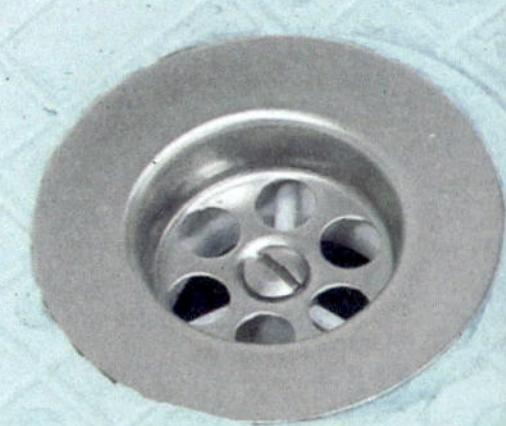

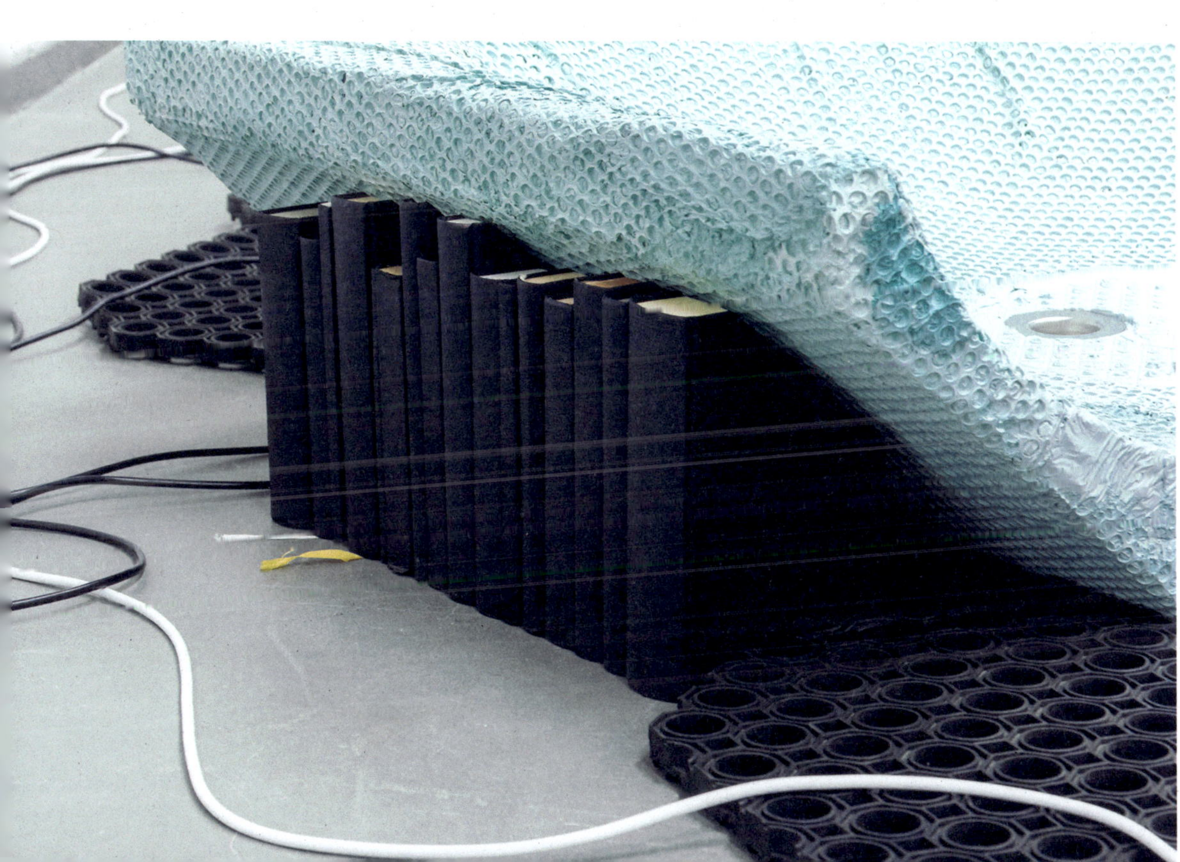

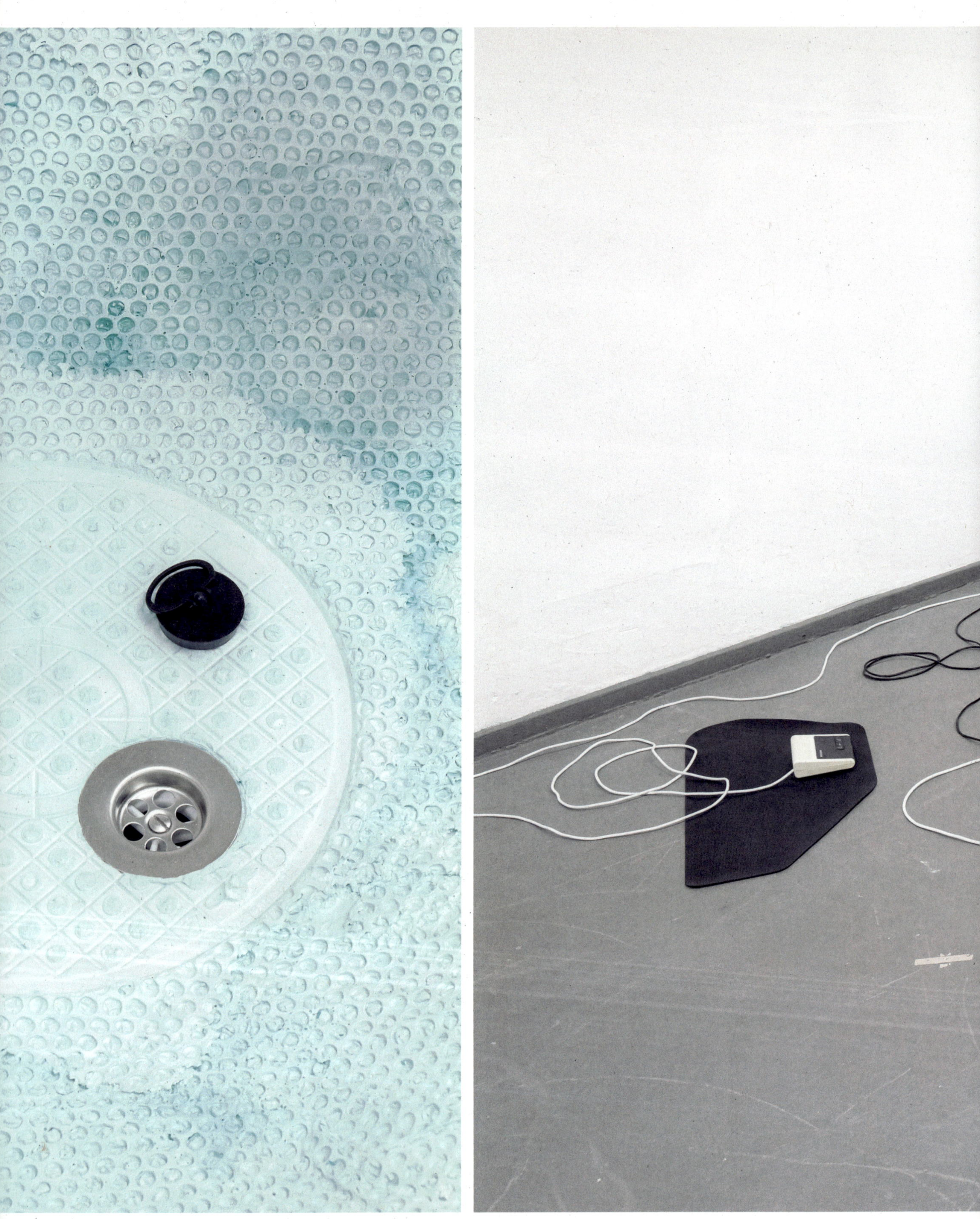

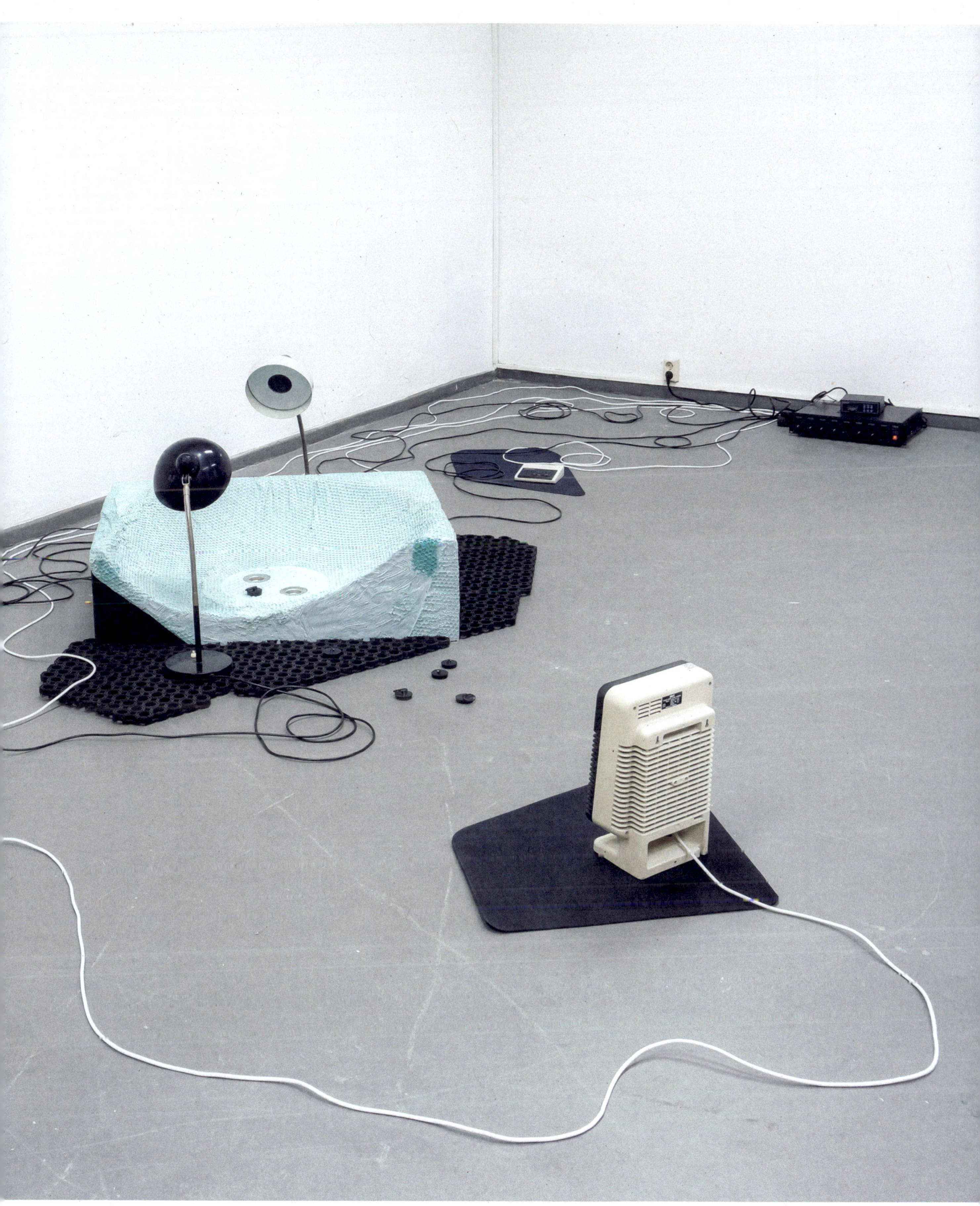

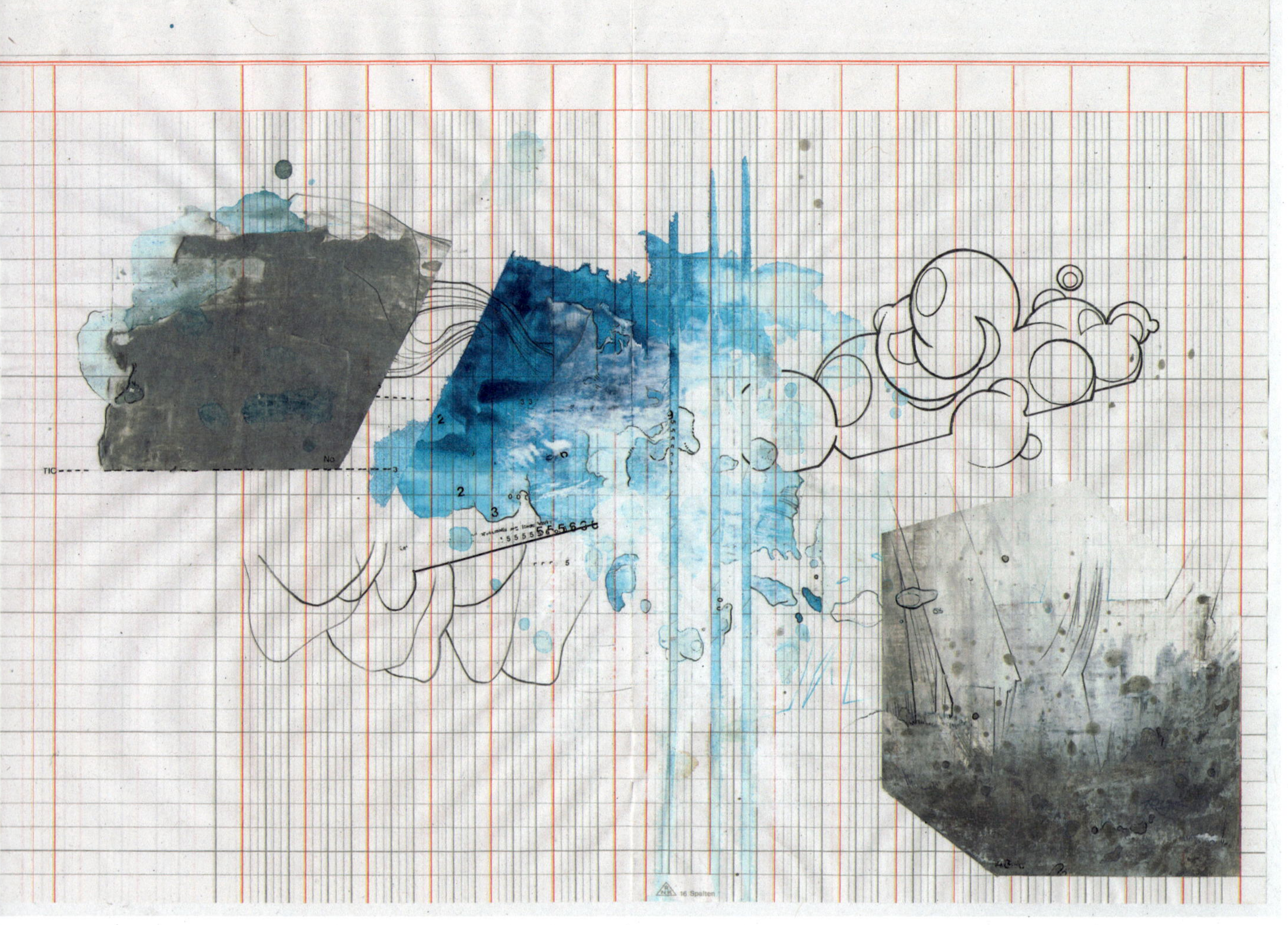

Musikalische Grafiken / Schrattenberg

2018—19 ——————————

7-part series of drawings

» Drawings in the Tradition of Visual Music: Instead of Being Brought to Life in a Sonic Interpretation by Musicians, They Resound as Acoustic Associations in the Eye of the Beholder

Material :
acrylic paint,
pencil, fineliner,
Letraset letters
on pre-printed
accounting forms

Format :
41 x 29 cm

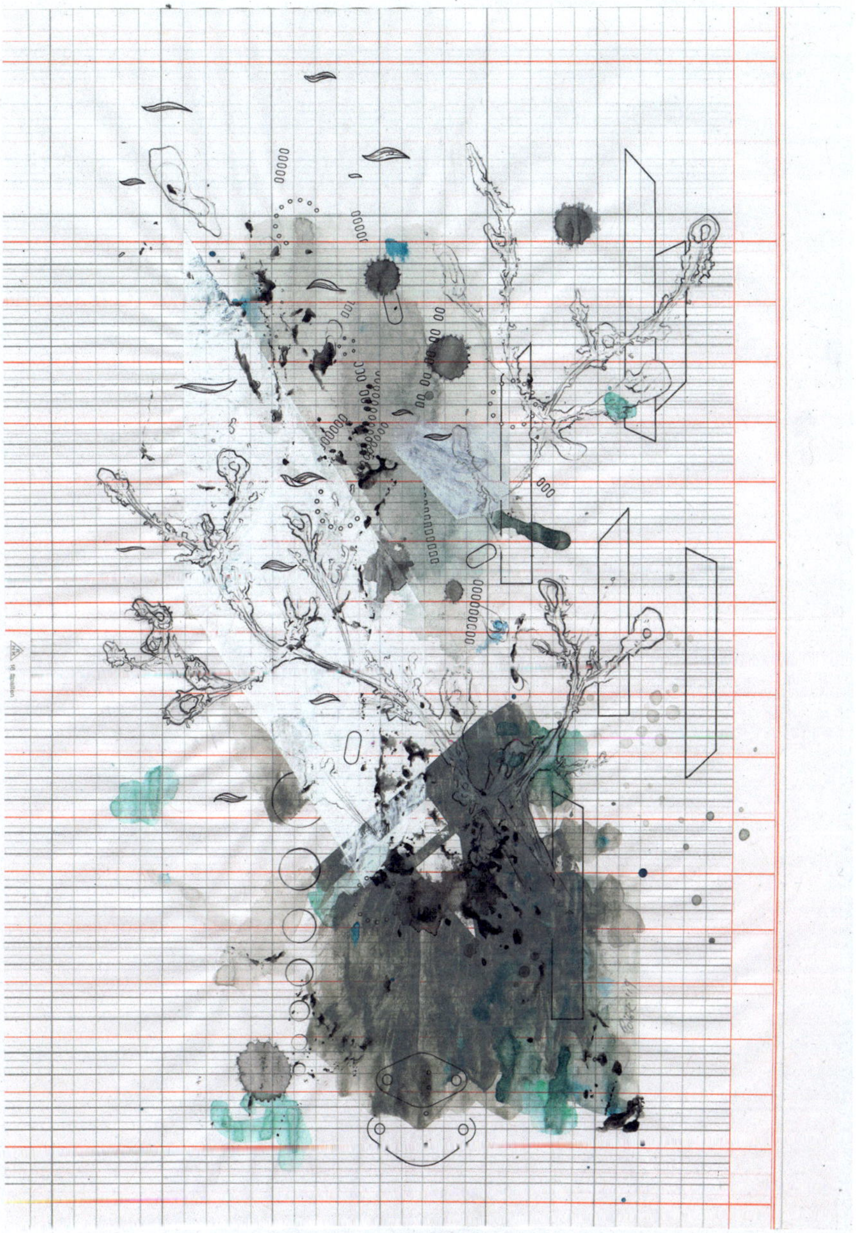

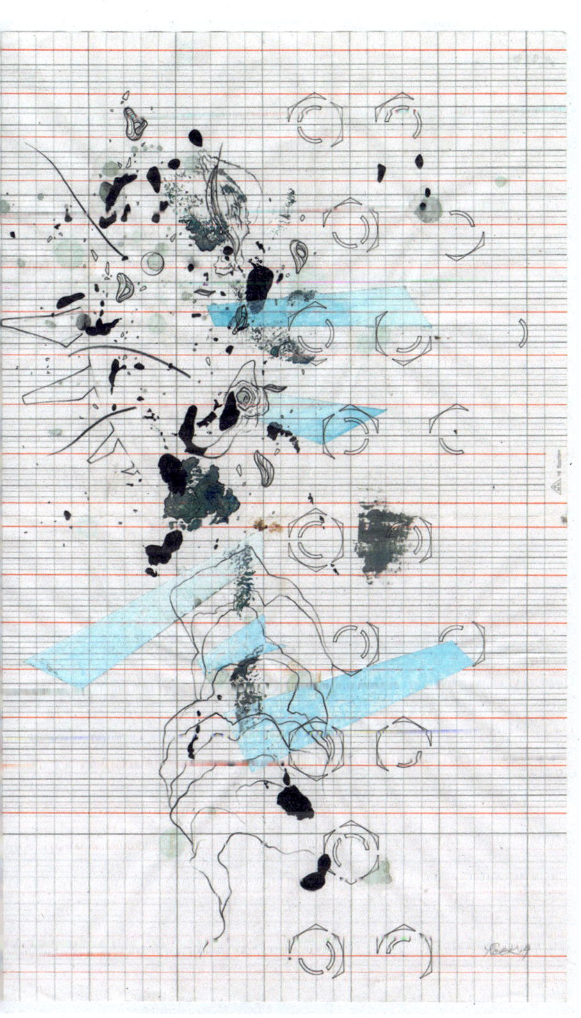

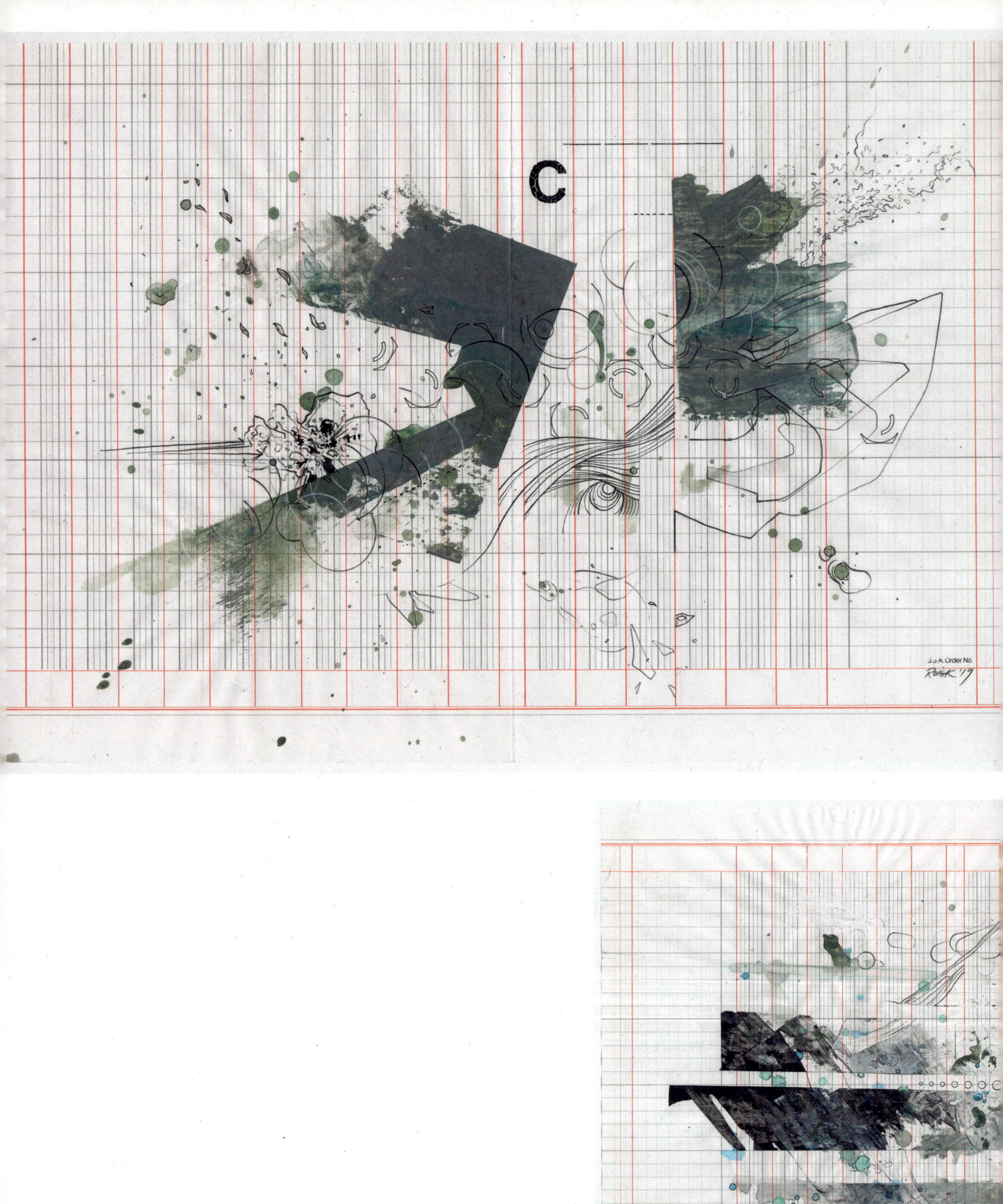

C
J.S.A. Order No
Rofok '19

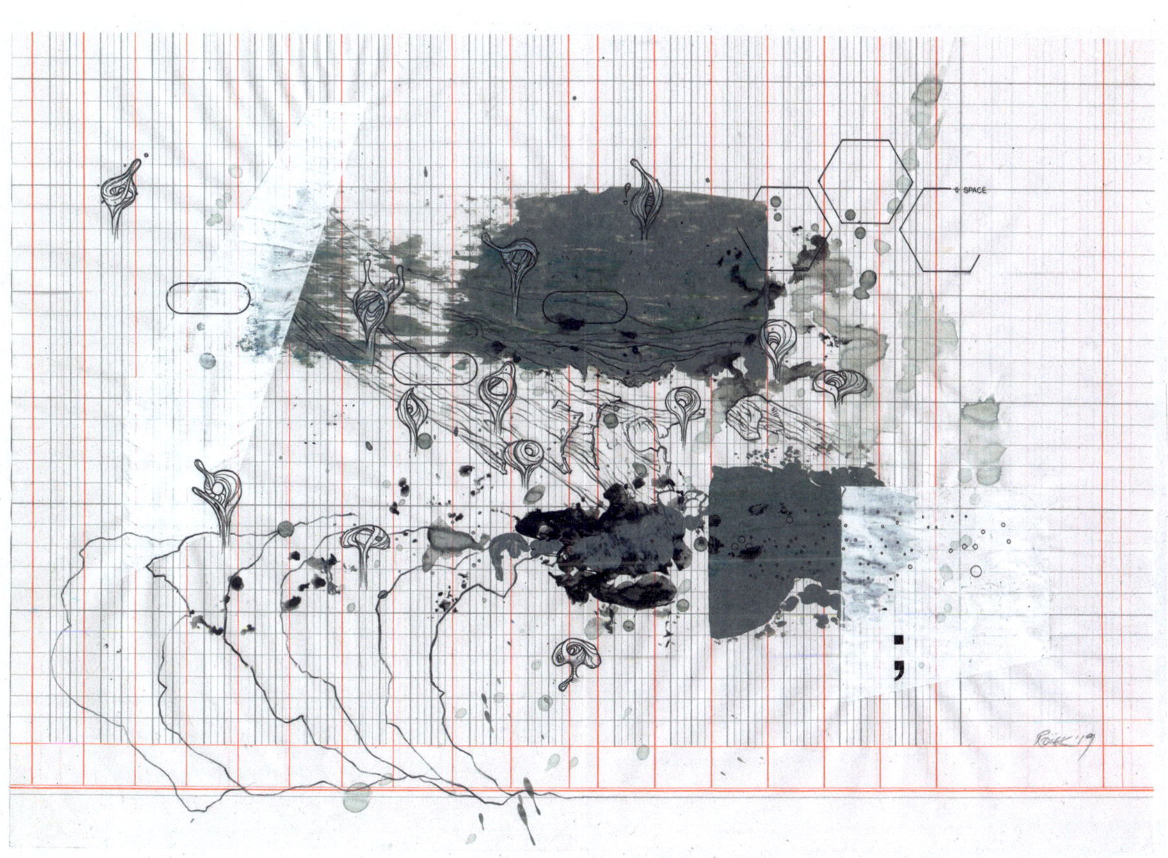
SPACE

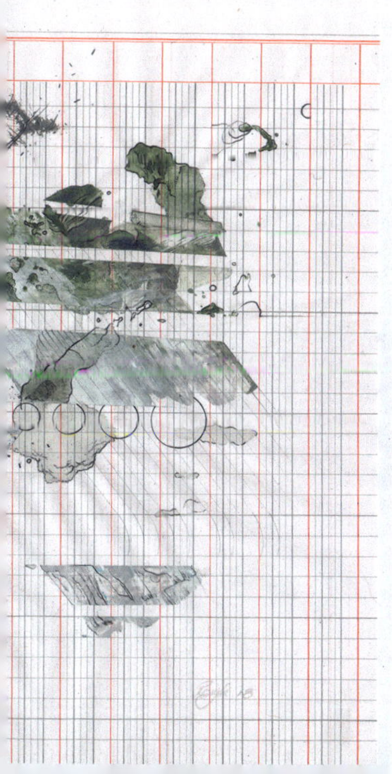

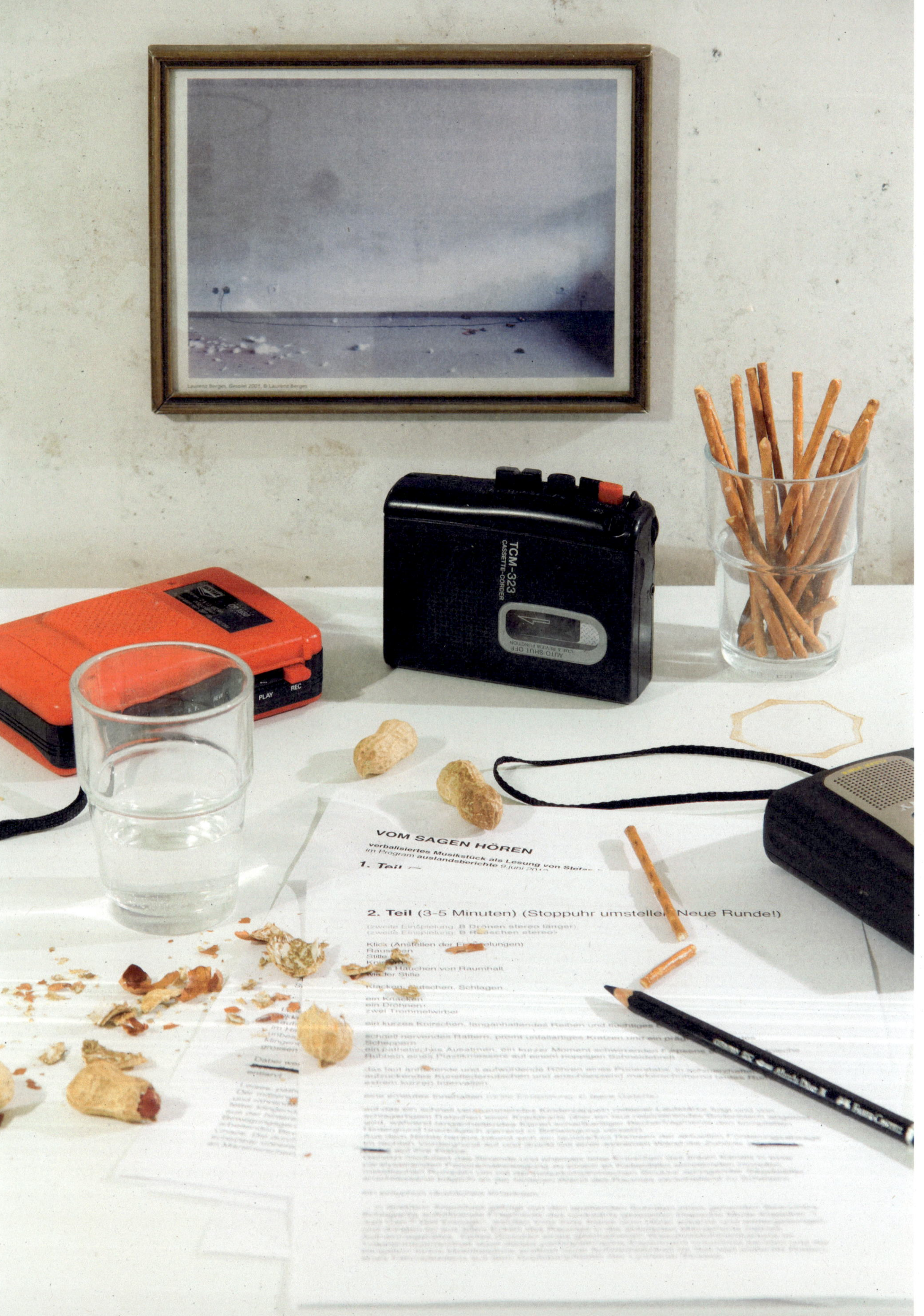

Laurenz Berges, Gmünd 2001, © Laurenz Berges
VOM SAGEN HÖREN
verbalisiertes Musikstück als Lesung von Stefan
im Program auslandsberichte 9 juni 20
1. Teil
2. Teil (3-5 Minuten) (Stoppuhr umstellen, Neue Runde!)
(zweite Einspielung: B Dröhnen stereo länger)
(zweite Einspielung: B Rauschen stereo?)
Klick (Anstellen der Einspielungen)
Rauschen
Stille
Knacken
ein Hauchen von Raumhall
Wieder Stille
Klacken, Rutschen, Schlagen
ein Knacken
ein Dröhnen
zwei Trommelwirbel
TCM-323
CASSETTE-CORDER
PLAY   REC

vom Sagen hören

2012–15

Text : Stefan Roigk

A Spoken Word Piece That Puts Sound Into Words Without Capturing It – A Performative Reflection at the Touchpoint of Notion and Sensory Experience

Translation : Jim Campbell

TEIL 1 7–9 Minuten
Stoppuhr anstellen

PART 1 7–9 minutes
start **stopwatch**

Zuerst ist das Nichts (Pause), ein unendlich weiter und von Leere überfüllter Raum, dessen Eigenresonanz mit einem kaum hörbaren Rauschen den Anfang dieser nun hörbaren Komposition bildet.

First there is nothing, the void (pause), an infinitely vast space packed full of emptiness, whose self-resonance, noise, barely audible, forms the beginning of this now audible composition.

Rauschen. Leise und verhalten, wie ein Blätterwald am nahen Campingplatz. Da die Fenster des im Herbstnebel stehenden Wohnmobils aufgrund der frischen Temperaturen geschlossen wurden, wirken die höheren Frequenzen des chaotischen Bewegungsspiels leicht gedämpft und das Klangbild einlullend kontemplativ. Einige Minuten lang scheint das Geräusch keiner Veränderung unterzogen. Es wird zum Teppich und verschwindet schließlich aus dem vorderen Fokus der Aufmerksamkeit.

Noise. Quiet and restrained, like a forest of leaves nearby at a campground. Since the windows of the camping van have been closed due to the cool temperature and the autumn mist, the higher frequencies from the chaotic interplay of movements appear slightly muted and lullingly contemplative. For several minutes, the noise does not seem to undergo any change. It becomes wallpaper effectively, ultimately vanishing from the anterior focus of attention.

In sehr offener Struktur setzen kratzende und durchaus voluminös klingende Geräusche kurzen Papierknüllens stark räumlich differenzierte Akzente in die bisher meditativ anmutende Endlosigkeit und durchbrechen den an das Ende einer Tonbandkassette erinnernden Klangraum. Damit durchstoßen sie nicht nur die bisherige Monofonie, sondern lenken den Wahrnehmungsfokus der Zuhörer:innen (also Ihre Aufmerksamkeit, meine Damen und Herren), direkt auf das sich nun langsam herausschälende Dolby Surround Arrangement des Sie nun völlig umschließenden Klangraumes.

Within a very open structure, quite voluminous scratching noises of a brief paper crumpling provide powerful accents, in a spatially differentiated fashion – inside an infinitude that previously felt meditative – and breach this sound space resembling the end of a tape cassette.
In doing so, they not only pierce through the previous monophony – they also shift the focus of the listeners' perception (that is to say, your attention, ladies and gentlemen) directly to the now gradually emerging Dolby Surround arrangement of the sound space that soon completely encompasses you.

Proportional zur steigenden Aufmerksamkeit erhöht sich der Anteil des Reißens und die Papiergeräusche enden oft scharf an der Grenze des Schmerzhaften.

The amount of ripping rises in proportion to the increasing attention, and the paper noises often cease only after very nearly exceeding the pain threshold.

Einspielung 1: »Leipziger Kaffee«

playback 1: »Leipzig Coffee«

Loses, stark räumlich klingendes Knacken erklingt kaum hörbar im Hintergrund. Das um 3 Oktaven gepitchte Bollern einer Alufelge umgreift den Tiefbassbereich rechts hinter der Lautsprecherbox und lässt den Raum aus Rauschen und Reißen für einen kurzen Moment im Hintergrund des Zimmers verschwinden. Das Knacken, welches gerade noch ein eher unbestimmtes Dasein fristete, vermengt sich nun zu einem sanften Schwarm aus digital klingendem Rascheln und bewegt sich mit seinen auf- und abschwellenden Spitzen in großen bogenförmigen Schleifen um den Klangraum herum. Dabei werden die unteren Frequenzbereiche mit Annäherung an die Lautsprecher mit einem Boss Octaver bis zur Verzerrung angehoben und die räumliche Präsenz in Ihrer Fiktion entlarvt.

Barely audible, loose, intensely spatial-sounding cracking intones in the background. The banging of an aluminum wheel, pitched down three octaves, encompasses the low-bass range on the right behind the loudspeaker, causing the space composed of static hum and ripping to disappear for a brief moment in the background of the room. The cracking, which, just a moment ago, was carving out a rather indeterminate existence, now gathers into a gentle swarm of digital-sounding rustling and moves with its rising and falling peaks about the sound space in large arching loops. As this unfolds, the lower frequencies are boosted to distortion by means of a Boss Octaver pedal as one approaches the loudspeakers, revealing the spatial presence as the fiction it is.

Leises, pathetisches Singen dringt aus einem vorbeifahrenden Auto. Der mittlerweile sehr konkrete Hintergrund aus am Flughafen Tegel landenden Flugzeugen und röhrenden Motorrädern ebnet den Weg für den leicht süßlichen Singsang des immer fetter klingenden und in riesigen Emo-Reverbflächen verkitschten Gesangsteppich, welcher aus der hintersten Ecke langsam, aber beständig an Raum gewinnt.

Soft singing, tinged with pathos, escapes from a passing car. The background, composed of planes landing at Tegel Airport and roaring motorcycles, paves the way for the slightly saccharine singsong of the progressively swelling vocal ambience, kitschily wrapped in enormous walls of emo-reverb, which, emerging from the rear-most corner, is slowly but steadily gaining ground.

Bewegungsgeräusche raschelnder Synthetikstoffe und murmelnde Gespräche der arbeitenden Bevölkerung werden hörbar und erfüllen das Geschehen mit menschlichem Chaos. Die durch Max-MSP per Zufall arrangierten Fieldrecordings suggerieren eine scheinbar unberechenbare Dynamik, welche durch die positiv leuchtende Stimmfläche in eine an Marienerscheinungen erinnernde Atmosphäre aus wärmender Geborgenheit gebettet wird.

Movement noises of rustling synthetic fabrics and murmuring conversations of the working population become audible, filling the action with human chaos. The field recordings, randomly arranged by using Max-MSP, suggest a seemingly unpredictable dynamic, which, due to the positively luminous tapestry of voices, is embedded in an atmosphere of warming reassurance recalling apparitions of the Virgin Mary.

Der hell schwingende Strahl aus Vokalen moduliert zu einem politonen Geflecht kurzer und in verschiedenen Tonhöhen angeordneter Loops und lässt den Fluss der Zeit versiegen.
Die scheinbar stagnierende Komposition durchfährt ein schwebender Moment betörend leuchtender Utopie.

Glockenartige Schwingungen überwuchern die restlichen Klänge und lähmen deine Aktivität für einen kurzen Moment des Innehaltens. Die Obertöne beginnen in langsamen Pulsen mantraartige Wiederholungen zu formen und den Hörer in einen tranceartigen Zustand zu versetzen. Durch die dabei geschlossenen Augen wird die subtile Veränderung der Klänge deutlich spürbar. Die immer wieder übereinandergleitenden Polyrhythmen werden allmählich flirrender. Durch die Reduktion der einzelnen Looplängen wirken die Klänge digitaler und metallischer. Gleichzeitig bewirken Phasenverschiebungen sowie die Modulation des Frequenzspektrums einen Verlust an Wärme und bescheren dem ehemals weichen Klang eine klirrende Oberfläche, welche ihre Raumqualität völlig verloren hat.

Die gerade noch beruhigenden Soundscapes sind nun zu einem schnell vibrierenden Schwirren umgeschlagen und reizen die obere Schädeldecke durch leichte Interferenzen und subtile Pulsveränderungen. Ein leichtes Kitzeln durchfährt den Knochen und lässt den Hörer in ruckartigen Kopfbewegungen die Augen epileptisch auf und zuflackern.

Blitze des eindringenden Lichtes durchfahren den Körper und, nach erneutem Eintreffen eines Anrufes auf dem am Ende des Schreibtisches liegenden Handys, dringen schnarrende Schwärme und das Röcheln einer entlüfteten Heizung aus der Küche in die Umgebung.

The brightly pulsating beam of vowels modulates into a polyphonic mesh of brief loops arranged at various pitches, causing the river of time to run dry.
The seemingly stagnating composition passes through a floating moment of beguilingly luminous utopia.

Bell-like oscillations overrun all other sounds and paralyze your activity for a brief moment of pause. In slow pulses, the overtones begin to form mantra-like repetitions, placing the listener in a trance-like state.Here, with eyes closed, the subtle change to the sounds can be felt clearly. The flickering of the polyrhythms, sliding repeatedly across one another, gradually becomes stronger. The reduction of the individual loop lengths gives the sounds a more metallic, digital feel. At the same time, the phase shifts and modulation of the frequency spectrum cause a loss of warmth, giving the formerly soft sound a clangorous surface, which has lost its entire spatial quality.

The soundscape, calming just a moment ago, has now flipped into a rapidly vibrating buzzing, stimulating the top of the skull through delicate interference patterns and subtle alterations in pulse. A slight tickling sensation runs through the bone and causes the listener to open and shut their eyes epileptically in fitful head movements.

Flashes of the penetrating light run through the body, and, after the cell phone lying on the edge of the desk repeatedly receives a call, buzzing swarms and the wheezing of a bled radiator press forth from the kitchen into the surroundings.

Das Schwirren der kurzen Samples moduliert zu einem schleifenden Rattern und aus der Nachbarwohnung werden lautstarke Fernsehgeräusche hörbar. Die unverständlich verzerrten und extrem dumpf durch die Wand dringenden Sprachfetzen vermengen sich mit dem Krächzen und Rauschen zu einem extrem kickenden Groove und schwappen in treibenden Kaskaden und explosionsartigen Wogen immer dröhnender über die mittlerweile zu monophon klirrenden Sinustönen verkommenen Sprachbearbeitungen.

Diese recht aufreibende Geräuschmontage wird nun zusätzlich durch kristallines, mit Neumann Mikrofonen aufgenommenes Bersten von Spanholzplatten angeheizt. Scheinbar mikroskopisch splittern die in extrem guter Qualität aufgezeichneten Holzspäne in vollem Dolby Surround Sound über deinen Kopf hinweg.

Ihr faszinierender Detailreichtum und der extrem räumliche Klang binden die völlige Aufmersamkeit des Hörers, sodass sich scheinbar unbemerkt fanfarenartige Geräusche im linken Mittelgrund aufbäumen und die Magengegend mit ausreichend darmstrapazierenden Tiefbassfrequenzen versorgen konnten. In galoppartigen Wogen stürmt diese pferdeartige Kavallerie des Dröhnens mit extrem anschwellender Lautstärke und gleichzeitig abnehmender Volumenamplitude den Vordergrund und erstickt die audiofilen Fantasien der High Fidelity Liebhaber augenblicklich in einem unerträglichen Brei aus Bass, Röhren und Brummen.

The whirring of the short samples modulates into a looping clattering while insistent television noise from the flat next door becomes audible. The incomprehensibly distorted and extremely muffled speech fragments penetrating through the wall blend with the rasping and humming to form an extremely pounding groove. In driving cascades and explosion-like surges, they slosh, with a swelling drone, over the processed speech fragments, which have, in the meantime, decayed into monophonic, clanging sinus tones.

Now, this quite grueling montage of noises is additionally heated up by the crystalline cracking of particleboard panels, captured with Neumann microphones. Seemingly microscopic, the wood chips, recorded in extremely high quality, splinter past your head in full Dolby Surround sound.

Their fascinatingly rich details and extraordinarily spatial sound capture the listener's full attention, so that fanfare-like noises rise up seemingly unnoticed in the left-hand middle ground, and are able to supply the stomach area with sufficiently gut-punishing low-end frequencies. In galloping surges, this horse-like cavalry of drones storms the foreground with an extreme swelling of the sound level and simultaneous ebbing of volume amplitude, immediately smothering the audiophile fantasies of high-fidelity lovers in an unbearable slur of bass, roaring and buzzing.

TEIL 2 3-5 Minuten
Stoppuhr umstellen (neue Runde)
Einspielung 2 : »Dröhnen« (stereo, länger)
+ »Rauschen« (stereo)

Klick. (einschalten der **Einspielungen**)

Rauschen.

Stille.

Knistern.

Leises Hauchen von Raumhall.

Wieder Stille.

Klacken, rutschen, schlagen.

Ein Knacken.
Ein Dröhnen.
Zwei Trommelwirbel.

Ein kurzes Knirschen, lang anhaltendes Reiben
und flüchtiges Bollern.

Schnell nervendes Rattern, prompt unfallartiges
Kratzen und ein prägnant sitzendes Scheppern.

Ein pathetisches Ausatmen.

Ein kurzer Moment schwirrenden Fiepsens
sowie das stoische Rubbeln eines Plastikmessers
auf einem noppigen Schneidebrett.

Das laut anhaltende und aufwühlende Röhren
eines Pürierstabs, in schmerzhaften Spitzen auf-
zuckendes Kunstlederrutschen und anschließend
markerschütternd lautes Rumpeln in extrem
kurzen Intervallen.

Einspielung 3 : »Leere Galerie«

PART 2 3–5 minutes
reset **stopwatch** (new round)
playback 2 : »Droning« (stereo, longer)
+ »Static Noise« (stereo)

Click. (turning on the **playback**)

Static noise.

Silence.

Crackling.

A soft touch of room reverberation.

Then silence again.

Clip-clop, slipping, slapping.

A snapping.
A roaring.
Two drumrolls.

A brief crunching, sustained rubbing and a
fleeting bit of banging.

Rapid, annoying rattling, swift scratching, as if
an accident, and a tersely executed clanking.

A melodramatic exhalation.

A brief moment of whirring squeaking as well as
the stoic rubbing of a plastic knife on the bumpy
surface of a cutting board.

The loud sustained and upsetting roar of an
immersion blender, sliding across leatherette,
flashing in painful peaks and finally bloodcurd-
lingly loud rumbling occurring at extremely
short intervals.

playback 3 : »Empty Gallery«

Ein erneutes Innehalten ...

... auf das ein schnell verstummendes Kinderzappeln mittlerer Lautstärke folgt und vom schlagartigen Ratschen einer Kreditkarte über ein laut resonierendes Bodenblech abgelöst wird, während lang anhaltendes Klirren scharfkantiger Becherfragmente den kompletten Hintergrund unerträglich zerrend in Schwingung versetzt.
Aus dem Nichts heraus bäumt sich ein lautstarkes Reißen der aktuellen Förderungsabsage im rechten Vordergrund auf und drückt mit einer extremen Wand die Zuhörer:innen (also auch Dich!) auf ihre Plätze.
Gehetzt moduliert das flirrende und ehemals leise Knirschen des linken Kanals in einer paralysierenden Panoramabewegung zu einem an Kellerdisco erinnernden monoton metallischen Rumpeln, um mit der pseudorhythmischen Struktur springender Sägeblätter anschließend kläglich an der hinteren Wand des Raumes zerschellend zu scheitern.

Ein polyfon räumliches Knacksen ...

... in direktem Anschluss gefolgt von den spaltenden Schritten eines gehenden Besuchers. Schlagartig aufblitzende Fragmente des rückwärts gespielten Depeche Mode Klassikers „Just Can't Get Enough", werden trotz ihrer Kürze vom Hörer erkannt und weitergesungen und dringen so aus allen Ecken des Raumes in die aktivierten Mikrofone meines Aufnahmegerätes. Tiefes Grunzen eines geschobenen Waschmaschinenkartons im Treppenhausnachhall lässt dieses partizipatorische Experiment voluminös bersten und der Klingelton Ihres Mobiltelefons eröffnet neue Aufmerksamkeit für das weit entfernte Rattern eines Fahrradreifens auf dem Kopfsteinpflaster der Lychener Strasse.

A renewed moment of pause ...

... followed by a quickly hushed medium-volume fidgeting of children, which makes way for the abrupt ratcheting of a credit card being scraped across a loudly resonating base plate, while a sustained jangling of sharp-edged cup fragments sets the entire background into vibration in an unbearably wrenching manner.
Out of the blue, a strident hand-shredding of the current funding rejection letter rises up in the foreground to the right, its extreme wall of pressure pressing the listeners (that means you too!) back into their seats.
Harried, in a paralyzing panorama motion, the shimmering, formerly soft crunching of the left channel modulates into a monotonous metallic rumbling recalling a basement nightclub, only to fail miserably in the end, smashing into the back wall of the room with the pseudo-rhythmic structure of rupturing sawblades.

A polyphonic three-dimensional cracking ...

... followed immediately by the chopping steps of a visitor on foot. Abruptly flaring fragments of the Depeche Mode classic „Just Can't Get Enough" (played backwards) are recognized and sung back by the listener in spite of their brevity, forcing their way from every corner of the room into the active microphones of my audio recorder. The deep grunting of a washing machine's carboard box being shoved around in the echoing stairwell causes this participatory experiment to burst voluminously, and the ringtone of the visitor's cell phone opens new awareness for the far-away clatter of a bicycle tire on the cobblestone pavement of Lychener Strasse.

TEIL 3 3–5 Minuten
Stoppuhr umstellen (neue Runde)
Einspielung 2 : ausschalten
Einspielung 4 : »Walkman mit
Raumaufnahmen« (unverstärkt)

Wasser eingießen, trinken, Etwast kauen

Machen Sie es sich gemütlich.

Nehmen sie einen tief entspannenden Atemzug und schließen anschliessend bitte Ihre Augen.

Stellen Sie sich ein leises und statisches Murmeln vor. Hören Sie, wie dieses Murmeln durch langsame Panoramabewegungen die Räume Ihres inneren Gebäudes ausformuliert und erfahrbar macht.

Stellen Sie sich darin bewegende Bassflächen vor. Sie wabern von einem Ort zum nächsten und befüllen das Volumen ihrer Vorstellungskraft.

Jetzt richten Sie ihre Aufmerksamkeit bitte auf die kleinen und niedlichen Knackser (Pupse), welche erst mono, dann stereo im räumlichen Nachhall gebrochen direkt mit einem auf schwarze Turnmatten herunterfallenden Bleistift in absoluter Stille ersticken.

(Die Gedanken sollen nun einfach für eine viertel Minute frei schweben ...)

15–sekündige **Pause**
(Essen und Trinken)

PART 3 3–5 minutes
reset **stopwatch** (new round)
turn off **playback 2**
playback 4 : »Walkman with room
recordings« (unamplified)

pour water, drink, chew something

Make yourself comfortable.

Take a deep relaxing breath and then please close your eyes.

Imagine a quiet and static murmuring sound. Listen to how this murmuring, through slow panoramic movements, elaborates the rooms of your inner building and opens them for you to experience.

Imagine bass surfaces moving around inside. They swirl from one place to the next and fill up the volume of your imagination.

Now, please direct your attention to the cute little pops (farts) which are, alongside a pencil, falling onto black gym mats, immediately snuffed out in absolute silence – first in mono , then in stereo – refracted in a spacious echo.

(Your thoughts should now simply be allowed to float freely for a quarter of a minute...)

15–second **pause**
(eating and drinking)

TEIL 4 3–5 Minuten
Stoppuhr umstellen (neue Runde)
ausschalten : »**Walkman**«
Einspielung 5 : »**Brummen**«
+ »**Beschreibungen**«

PART 4 3–5 minutes
reset **stopwatch** (new round)
turn off : »**Walkman**«
playback 5 : »**Humming Noise**«
+ »**Descriptions**«

Das extrem leisen Rauschen einer Laptopfestplatte.

The extremely quiet hum of a laptop hard drive.

Herunterfallende Wattebausche.

Falling cotton balls.

Das feine Geräusch eines platzenden Pickels, welcher bei jeder kleinsten Berührung unglaublich schmerzte und deshalb direkter Entfernung bedurfte.

The delicate sound of a popping pimple that caused incredible pain at the slightest touch and thus needed to be removed straightaway.

Leises Hauchen von Raumhall.

A quiet touch of room reverberation.

Wanddurchdringende Stimmen aus der Wohnung Ihrer Nachbarn.

Wall-penetrating voices from your neighbors' flat.

Vereinzeltes Knacken des Dielenbodens.

Scattered creaking of the floorboards.

Das Streicheln eines Kinderschokoladepapiers, nachdem der Riegel genüsslich mit ausdrücklich konzertantem Schmatzen verzehrt wurde.

Idly stroking a chocolate bar wrapper after the candy has been consumed with relish and an explicitly musical, performative smacking.

Durch die Schornsteinschächte transportiertes …
… Pianospiel.

Piano playing …
… transported through the chimney shafts.

An dieser Stelle möchte ich darauf hinweisen, dass die modulierenden Drones zwischenzeitlich polyfoner wurden und ein weites Feld aus kristallinen und weit verhallten Sinuswellen gebildet haben.

At this point, I would like to take the opportunity to point out that the modulating drones have become more polyphonic in the meantime and have formed a vast field of crystalline and long-fading sinus waves.

Ein lautes und tief wummerndes Radiobrummen von rechts hat Vorfahrt.

A loud and deeply booming radio hum has the right of way approaching from the right.

Einspielung 6 : »**SplitterEcho**«

playback 6 : »**SplitterEcho**«

Scharf knirschendes Rutschen und dröhnendes Rubbeln auf frisch gebohnertem Holz wird übertönt vom laut grölenden Rumpeln eines seit Tagen nicht mehr gefüllten Magens.

Eine extrem laute und völlig verzerrte Aufnahme der Tagesschau Titelmelodie mit sofort verstummendem Zirpen. Und direkt davor noch das Resonieren eines quietschenden Kamms auf einer hölzernen Zigarrenschachtel.

Einspielung 7 : »TapeCutUp«

Das Knacken, Rasseln und Scheppern einer alten und verkalkten Kaffeemaschine.

Wenn der Duft der guten Tasse schwarzen Kaffees an der Nase angelangt ist, verfügt das Knistern und Ächzen über seine höchste Klangdichte und der Hauptschalter des Gerätes wird umgelegt.

Warm aufgebackenes Krachen im Hintergrund, während wild das gestische Scratchen eines Schreibutensils auf Papier an eine unglaublich wichtige und schnell zu fixierende Idee erinnert.

Ein aufrührendes Grunzen, welchem die abfallende Anspannung der vierzehntägigen Stuhlgangblockade problemlos anzuhören ist.
Das Holpern einer Geschirrbürste über die leicht verschmutzte Gummifußmatte meiner scheidenden Nachbarin.
Knusprig in die Länge gezogene Messergeräusche. Schnell gefolgt vom hochscheppernden Gesäusel einer verführerischen Stimme im Hintergrund.

An einer Werkzeugbank schabend.

Plötzliches Ausrollen einer Tapetenrolle mit Furnierholzmuster.

Ein langgezogenes Brummen.

Sharply grating sliding and droning rubbing on freshly polished wood is drowned out by loud bellowing rumbling of a stomach that has not been fed for days.

An extremely loud and totally distorted recording of the opening theme to the nightly TV news with immediately muted chirps. And right before that the resonating sound of a comb squeaking on a wooden cigar box.

playback 7 : »TapeCutUp«

The clicking, rattling and clanking of a calcified old coffeemaker.

When the scent of a damn fine cup of (black) coffee reaches your nose, the crackling and groaning has attained its highest sonic density and the main button of the device is switched off.

Oven-baked banging in the background, while the wild gestural scratching of a pen on paper calls to mind an incredibly important idea that must be captured quickly.

An agitating grunting which readily discloses the seceding tensions of a two-week struggle with constipation.
The jolting of a dish scrubber across the lightly soiled rubber doormat of my parting neighbor.
Knife noises, drawn out crisply. Followed quickly by the intensely rattling rustle of a seductive voice in the background.

Scraping on a workbench.

The sudden unfurling of a roll of wallpaper, featuring a veneered wood pattern.

A long, drawn-out humming sound.

TEIL 5 2 Minuten
Stoppuhr umstellen (neue Runde)
alles ausschalten außer **»Brummen«**

Rauschen, Rauschen, Rauschen.

Hören Sie das Rauschen der Heizungsanlage?

Haben Sie es die ganze Zeit gehört?

Dabei war es doch permanent vorhanden ... Und durchströmte den Raum ständig mit mikrotonalen Schwingungen erfrischender Molekülen.

Und doch nehmen wir es kaum war; schenken ihm kaum Beachtung ...
lassen es ziehen, untergehen und ungeachtet im Nebenzimmer warten, bis auch der letzte vereinbarte Termin abgearbeitet wurde.

Wie auch das Rauschen im Kopf.

Dieses kleine und diffizile Sausen, das uns manchmal ereilt in der Nacht und im Stress. Und John zu Unglaublichem verholfen hat.

Dieses Rauschen ist ein ständiger Begleiter, kein dunkler, nein, ein konstanter Freund im Leben.

Und wir ...

Wir schieben ihn weg, vielleicht aus Gewohnheit oder aus Angst. Und trotzdem spendet es Zuspruch und Gewissheit:

Denn wenn er fehlt,

sind wir Tod.

PART 5 2 minutes
reset **stopwatch** (new round)
turn off **everything** except **»Humming Noise«**

Noise, noise, noise.

Can you hear the noise of the heating system?

Have you been hearing it the whole time?

In fact, it was constantly present ... Continuously flooding the room with microtonal vibrations of refreshing molecules.

And still, we hardly perceive it; we pay little to no attention to it ...
allowing it to recede, to be drowned out and wait unconsidered in the room next door until the last appointment has also been crossed off the list.

Just like the noise in our heads.

This difficult little buzzing that befalls us sometimes in the night or when we're under stress. And which empowered John to do incredible things.

This noise is a constant passanger, not a dark one, no, a steady friend in life.

And we ...

We push it away, perhaps out of habit, or fear. And yet it gives us solace and certainty:

For when it is absent,

we are dead.

CD - version / voice (reading) with manual sound actions and live playback of sound-recordings / 20 – 30 minutes / a studio recording of "vom Sagen hören" was published on "Worte wie Schall und Raum" (CD + 8 A5 postcards) in 2016 by Revolver Publishing / 32:07 / CD 1 – track 14

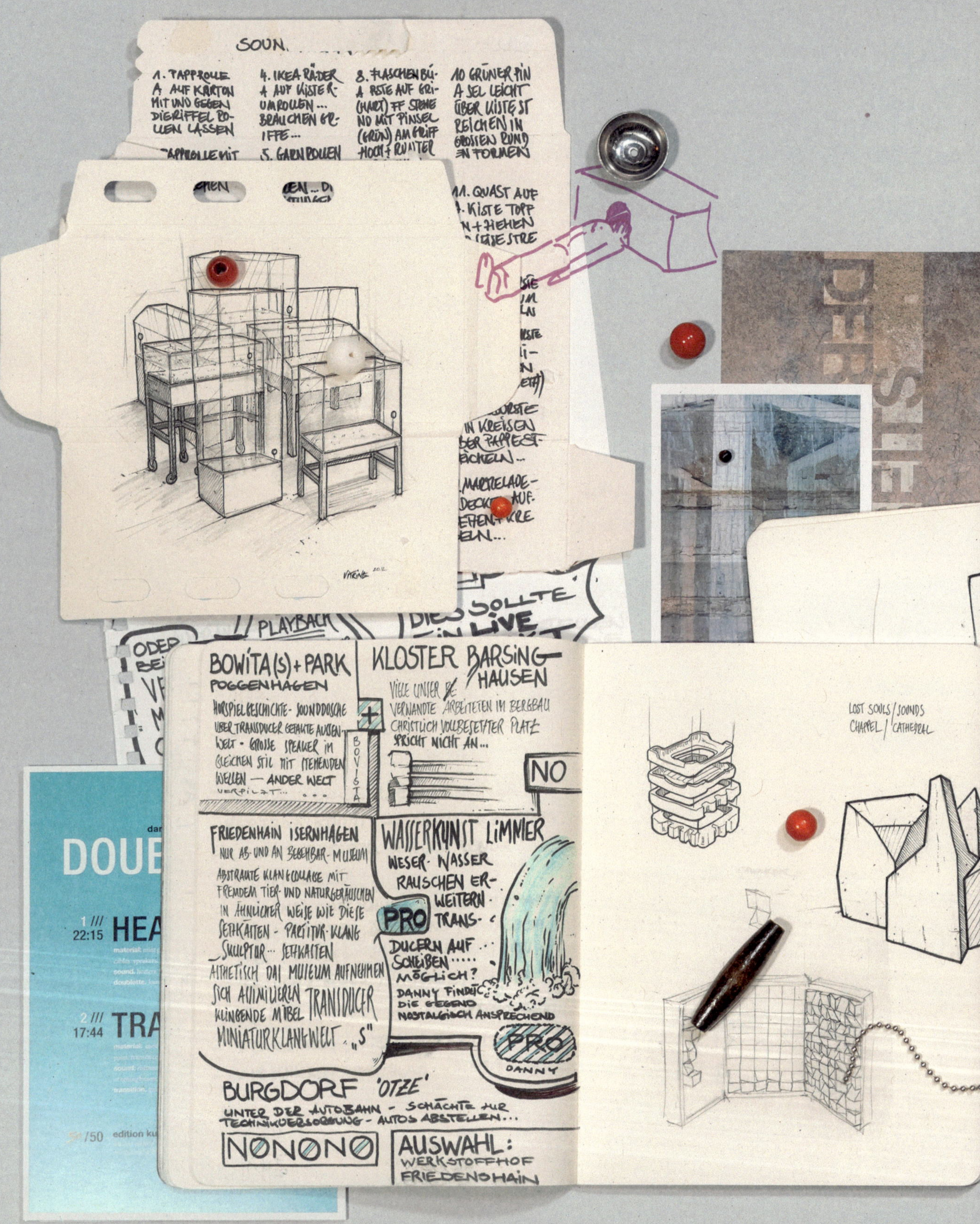
SOUN
1. TAPPROLLE
A AUF KARTON
MIT UND GEGEN
DIE RIFFEL ROL-
LEN LASSEN
4. IKEA RÄDER
A AUF LISTER-
UMROLLEN ...
BRAUCHEN GR-
IFFE ...
8. FLASCHENBÜ-
A RSTE AUF GRI-
(HART) FF STEHE
ND MIT PINSEL
(GRÜN) AM GRIFF
HOCH + RUNTER
10 GRÜNER PIN
A SEL LEICHT
ÜBER LISTE ST
REICHEN RUND
EN FORMEN
5. GARN ROLLEN
11. QUAST AUF
KISTE TOPP
PLAYBACK
DIES SOLLTE
IN LIVE
BOWITA(S) + PARK
POGGENHAGEN
HÖRSPIELGESCHICHTE - SOUNDDUSCHE
ÜBER TRANSDUCER GETAKTE AUSSEN-
WELT - GROSSE SPEAKER IM
GLEICHEN STIL MIT STEHENDEN
WELLEN — ANDER WELT
VERPILZT...
BOVITA
KLOSTER BARSING-
HAUSEN
VIELE UNSER BE
VERWANDTE ARBEITETEN IM BERGBAU
CHRISTLICH VOLLBESETZTER PLATZ
SPRICHT NICHT AN ...
NO
FRIEDENHAIN ISERNHAGEN
NUR AB- UND AN SEHENBAR - MUSEUM
ABSTRAKTE KLANGCOLLAGE MIT
FREMDEM TIER- UND NATURGERÄUSCHEN
IN ÄHNLICHER WEISE WIE DIESE
SETZKASTEN - PARTITUR-KLANG
SKULPTUR... SETZKASTEN
ÄSTHETISCH DAS MUSEUM AUFNEHMEN
SICH ASSIMILIEREN TRANSDUCER
KLINGENDE MÖBEL TRANSDUCER
MINIATURKLANGWELT „S"
WASSERKUNST LIMMER
WESER-WASSER
RAUSCHEN ER-
WEITERN
PRO TRANS-
DUCERN AUF
SCHEIBEN ......
MÖGLICH?
DANNY FINDET
DIE GEGEND
NOSTALGISCH ANSPRECHEND
PRO
DANNY
BURGDORF 'OTZE'
UNTER DER AUTOBAHN - SCHÄCHTE ZUR
TECHNIKERÜBERLAGERUNG - AUTOS ABSTELLEN...
NONONO
AUSWAHL:
WERKSTOFFHOF
FRIEDENSHAIN
LOST SOULS / SOUNDS
CHAPEL / CATHEDRAL
DOUB
DOUBLE
HEA
22:15
TRA
17:44
/50 edition ku

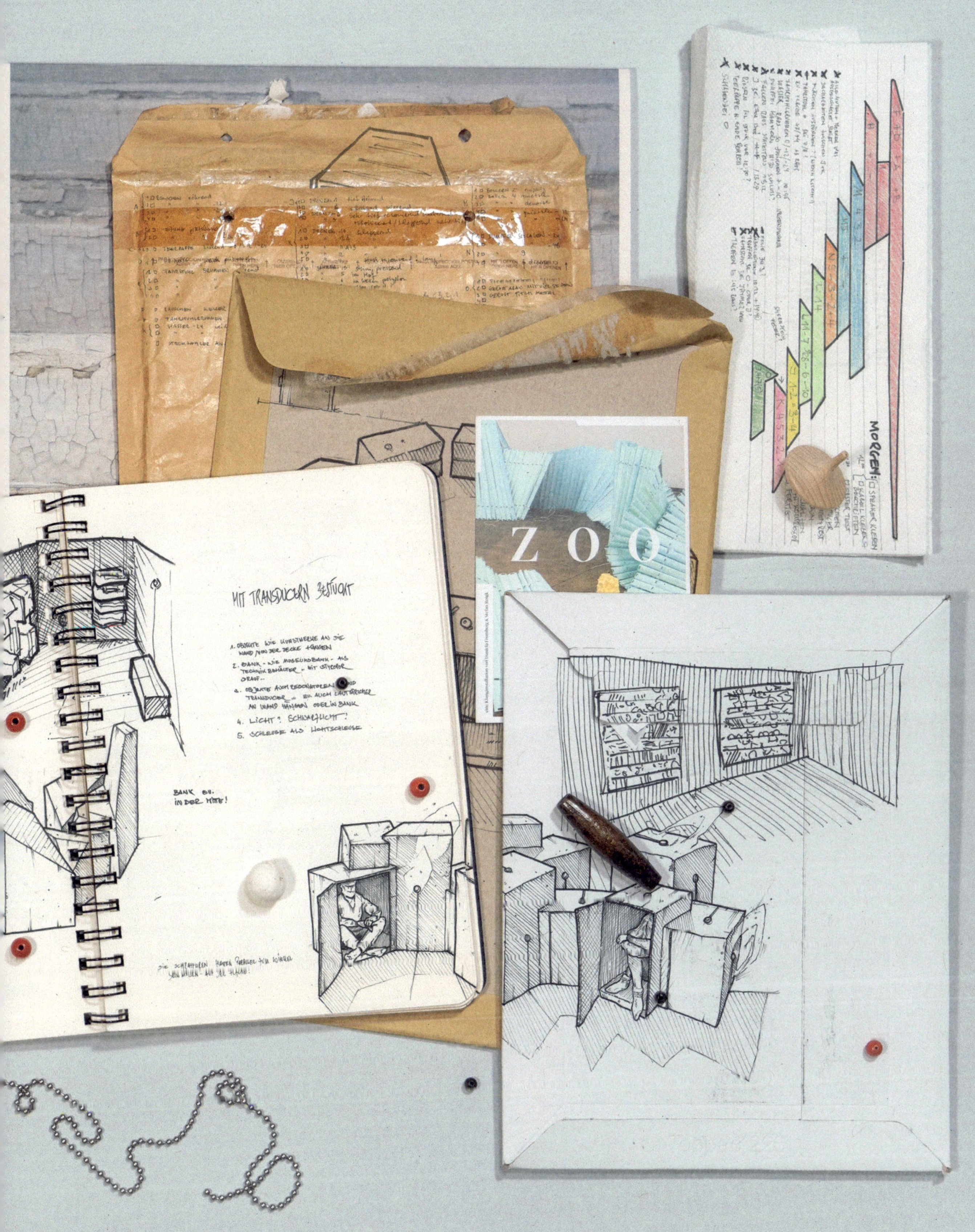
ZOO
MIT TRANSDUCERN BESTÜCKT
BANK SO.
IN DER MITTE!
MORGEN

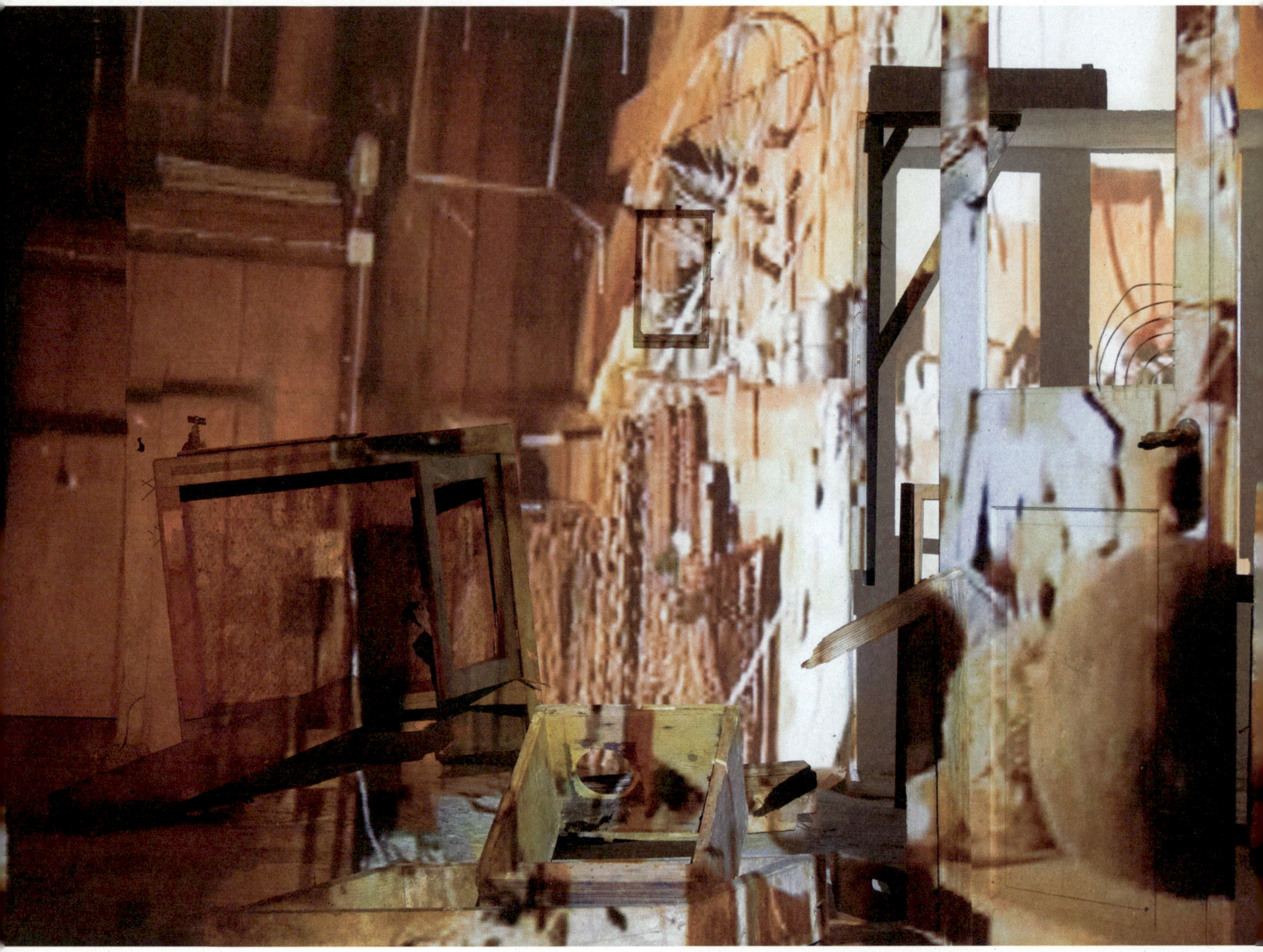

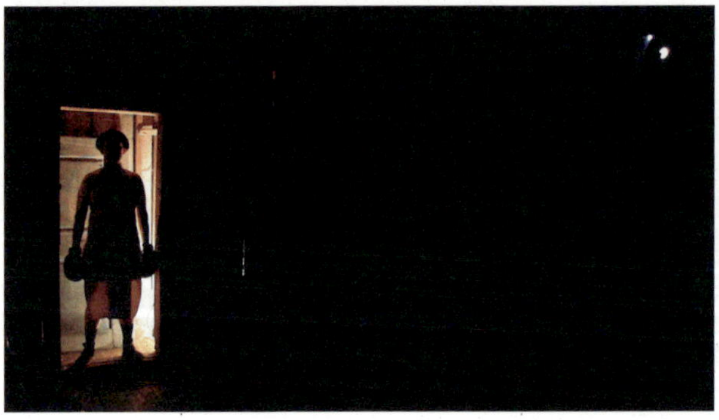

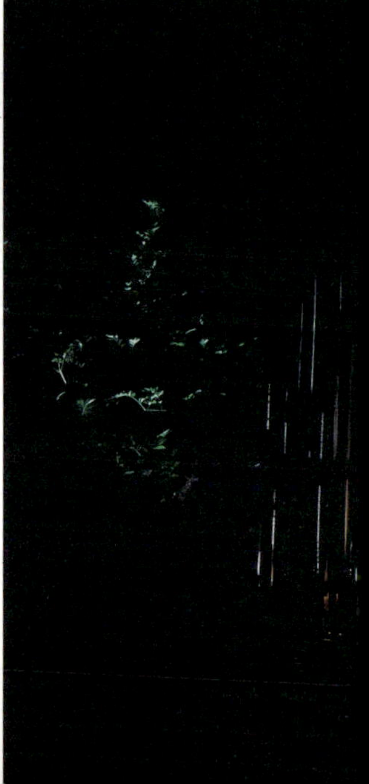

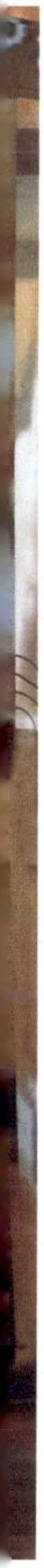

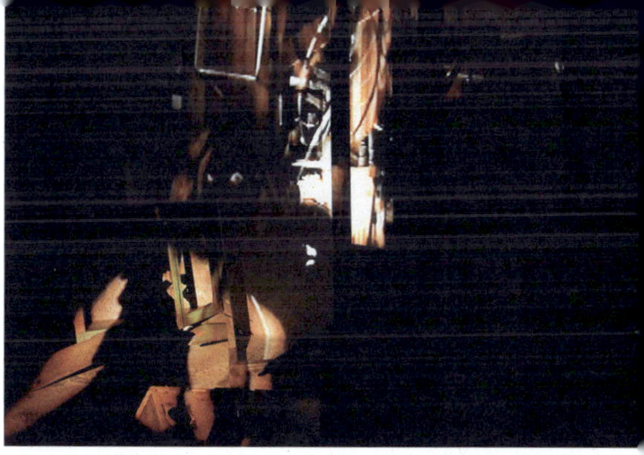

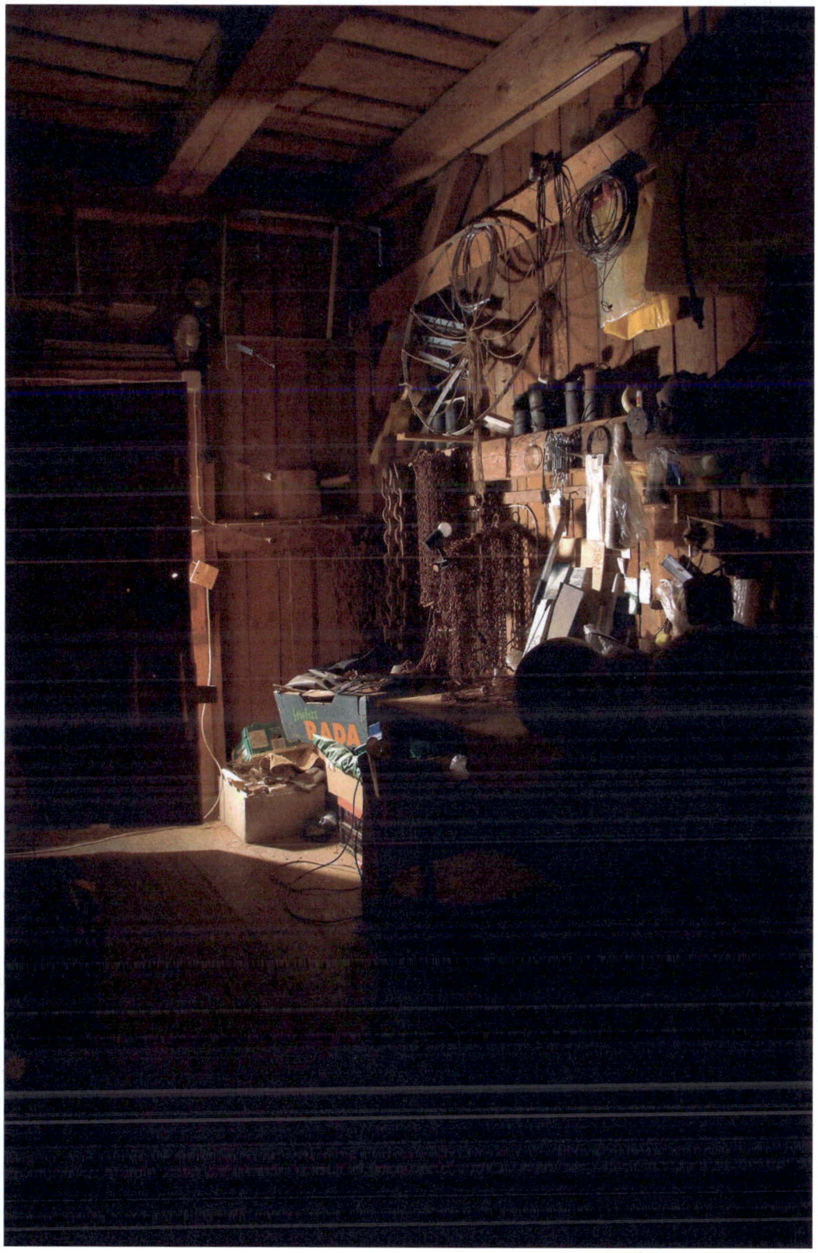

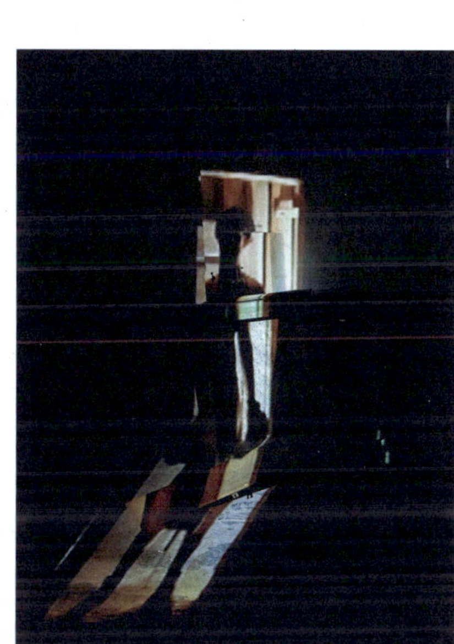
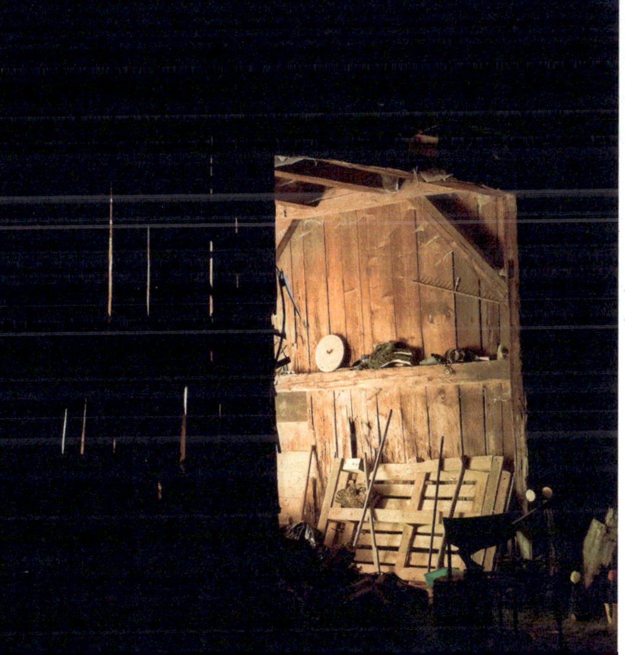

Video :
full HD **/** loop (9:00)

Installation :
light reflections **/** video projection on arranged furniture fragments and construction materials **/** 400 x 250 x 200 cm

Sound :
2-channel acousmatic composition **/** balloon noises, vocal fragments and everyday atmospheres **/** an edited version of the soundtrack has been published as "Blowing Up the Master's Workshop" **/** 16:57 **/** CD 1 – track 2

Beside the Liquid Mirror (Casting a Shadow Is Worth It)

2011

experimental film and video installation
in co-operation with Daniela Fromberg

» the Inhabitants of This Liminal World Appear to Interact With One Another in the Most Urgent Manner, Although the Narrative Remains Deliberately Ambiguous

"Beside the Liquid Mirror (Casting a Shadow Is Worth It)" is based on the projected images and soundscape of the video-sound installation "Liquid Mirror Casting (by a Charred Palace)" and is inspired by the collage "Das Schlafzimmer des Meisters (es lohnt sich darin eine Nacht zu verbringen)" by Max Ernst.

Employing a fixed camera position, the video shows a dark, deconstructivist architecture made of construction materials and old furniture, on which almost motionless nighttime stills were projected. Through the searching light movements and sudden light changes of this video material, a scene full of spatial illusions and dream-like visions is displayed from out of nowhere, only to disappear in the next moment.

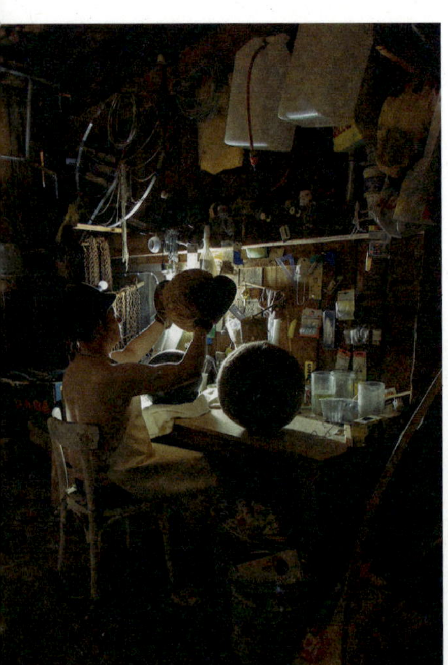

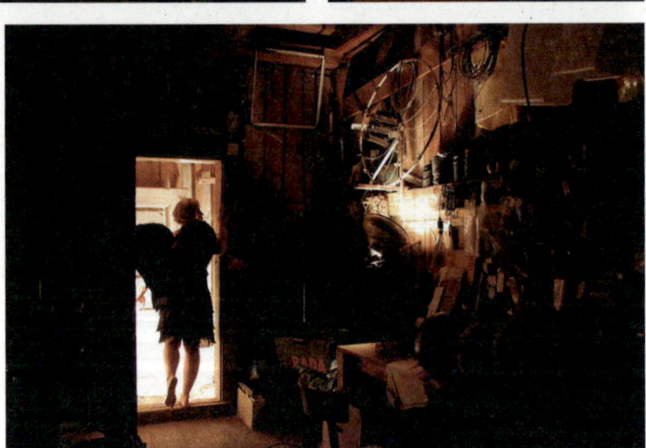

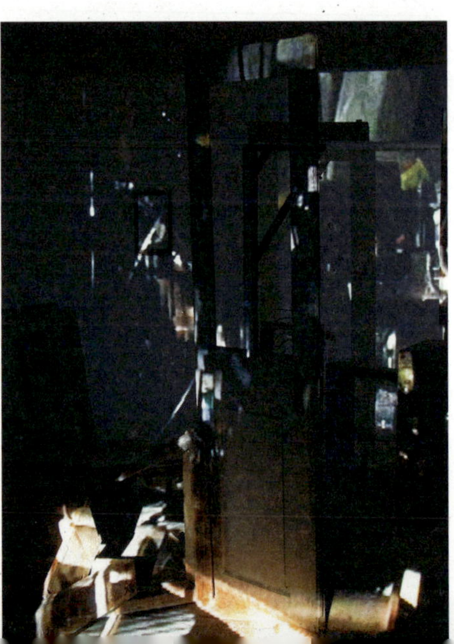

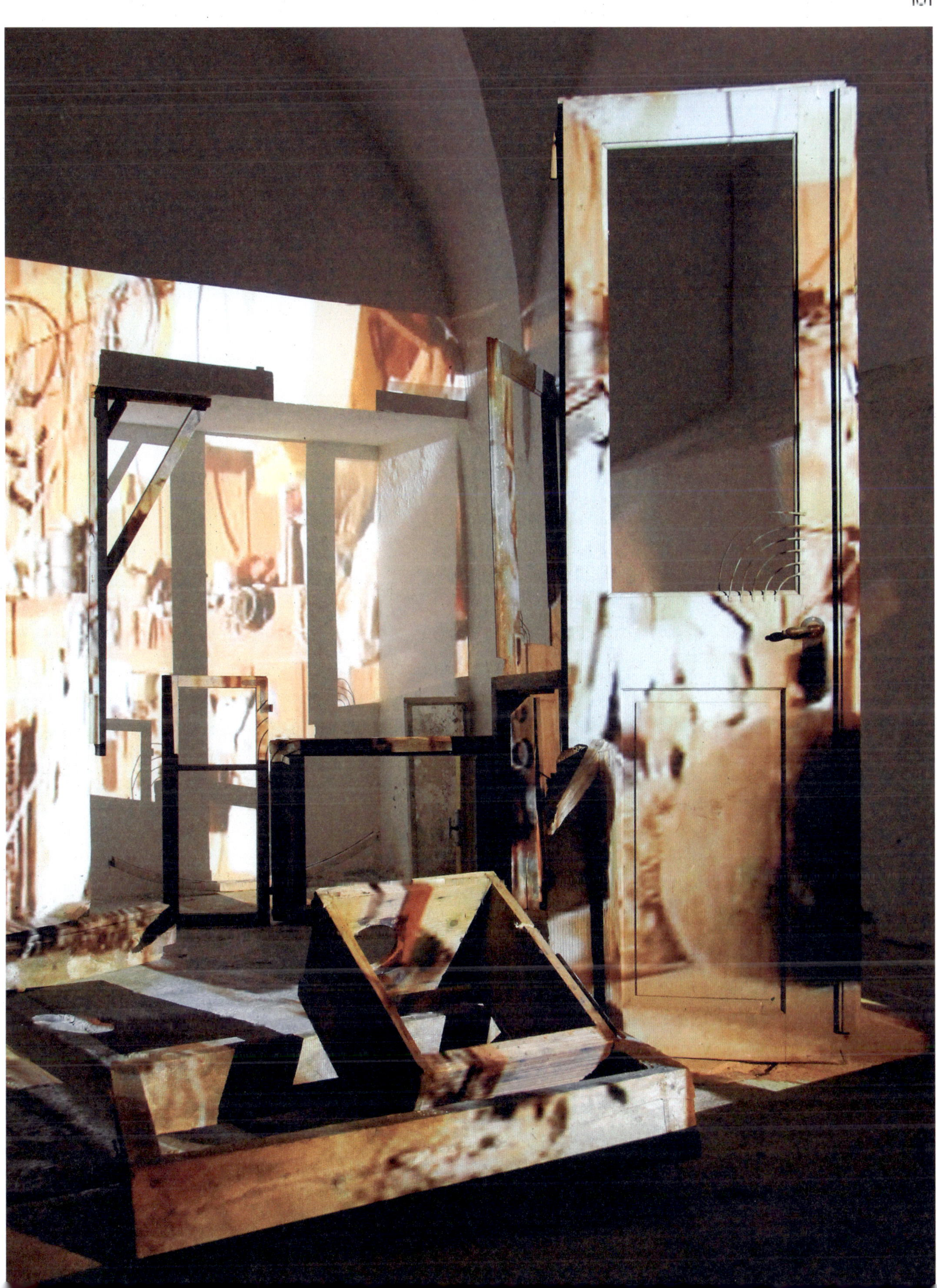

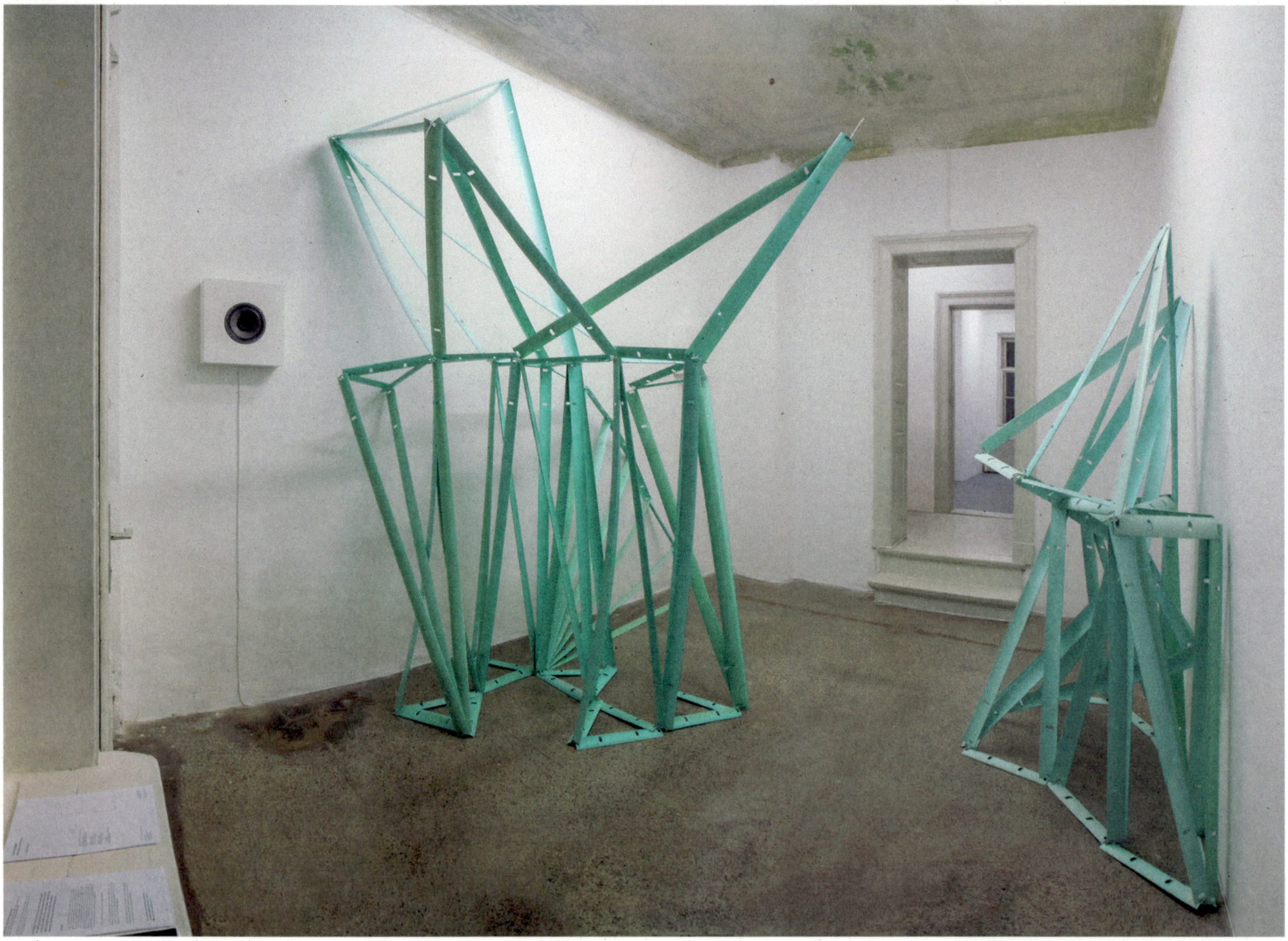

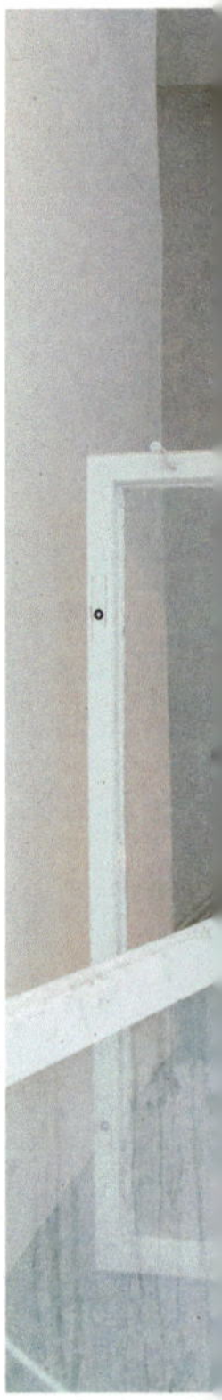

Heat

2012

mixed-media sound installation
in co-operation with **Daniela Fromberg**

**» the Longing for a Heated
Apartment Turns Out to Be a Wet
Dream of a Classicist Economy**

Objects :
mint-green window-blind slats,
cable ties, medium-density
fiberboard, acrylic paint, power
outlets, full-range loudspeakers,
cables and playback equipment **/**
300 x 450 x 300 cm
(size variable)

Sound :
4-channel acousmatic
composition **/** immersive
soundscapes **/** dripping water,
humming radiators, droning
fans and noises from the actions
of a chimney sweep **/** 2 loops
(30:00 + 60:00) **/** CD1 – track 17

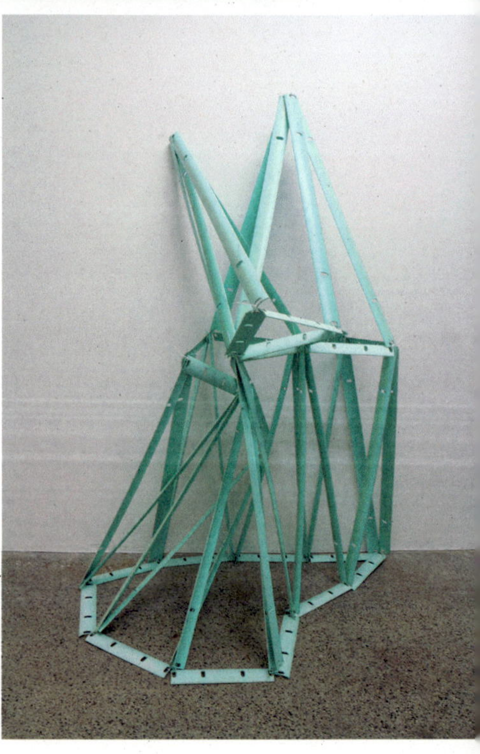

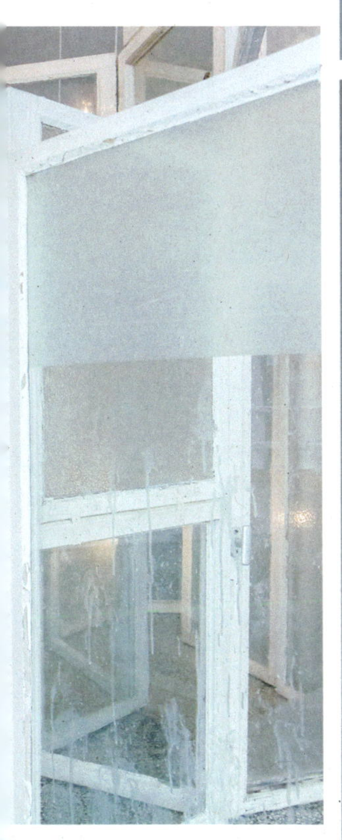

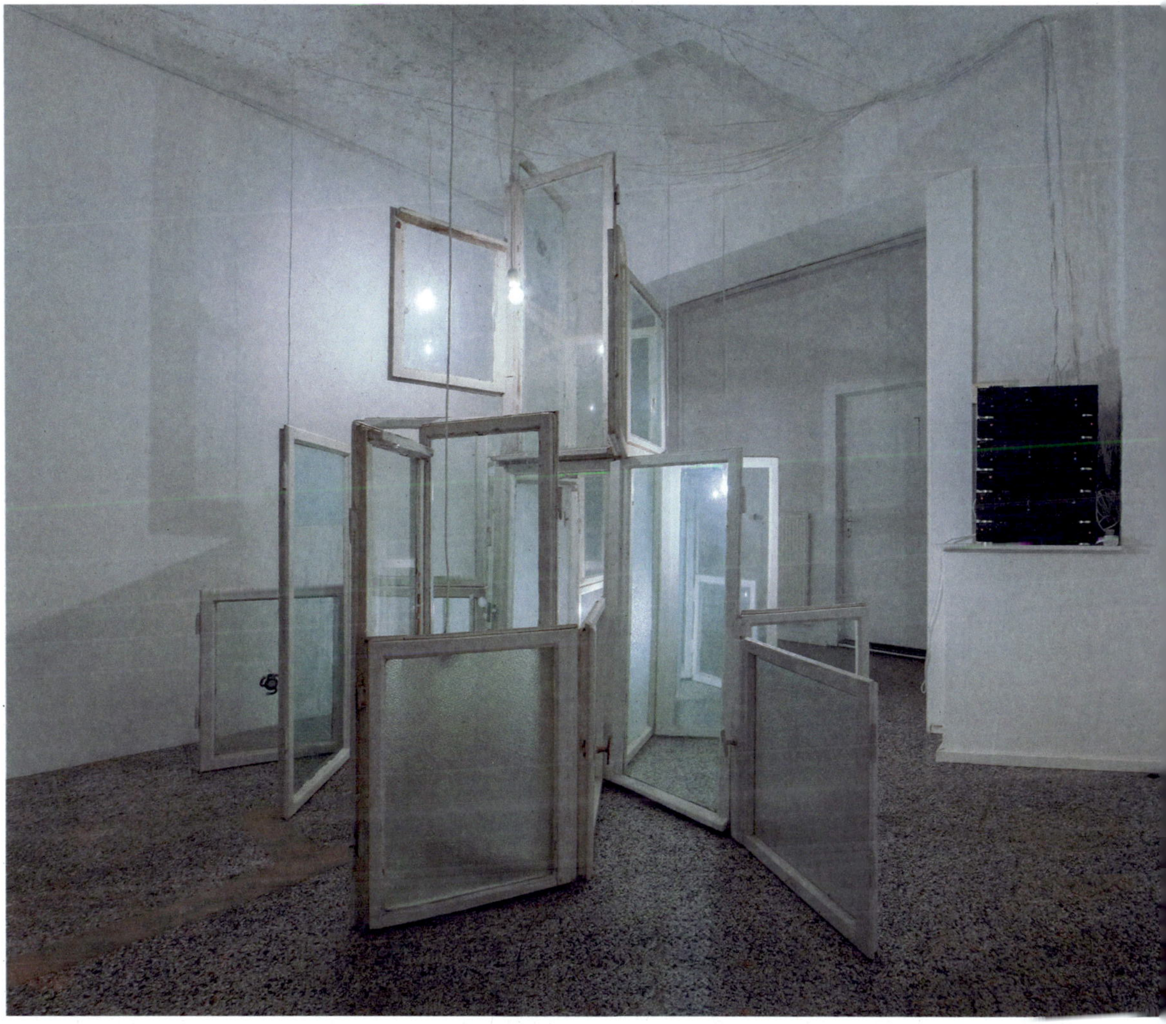

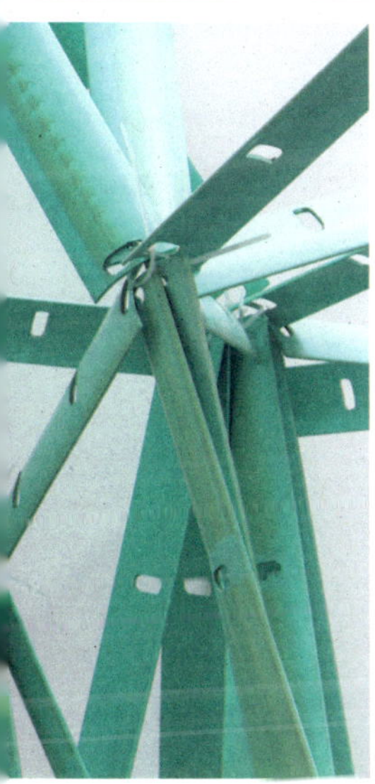

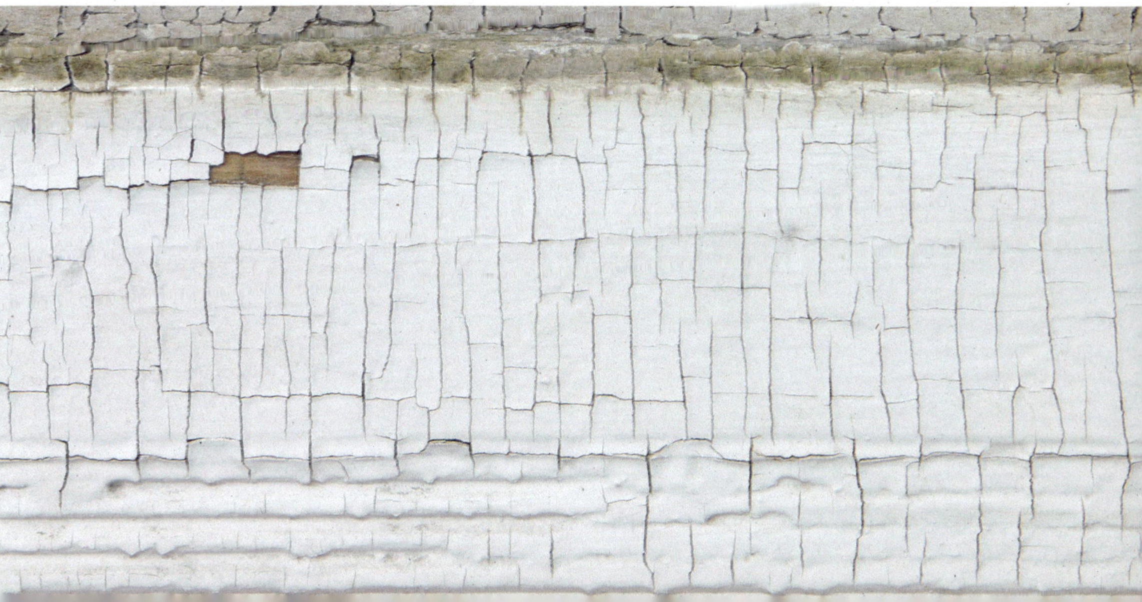

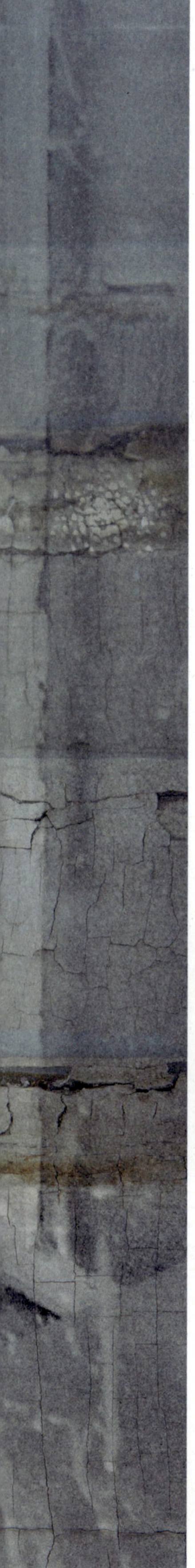

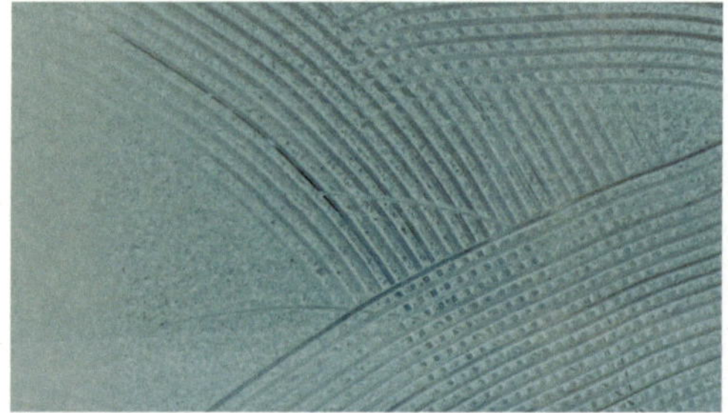

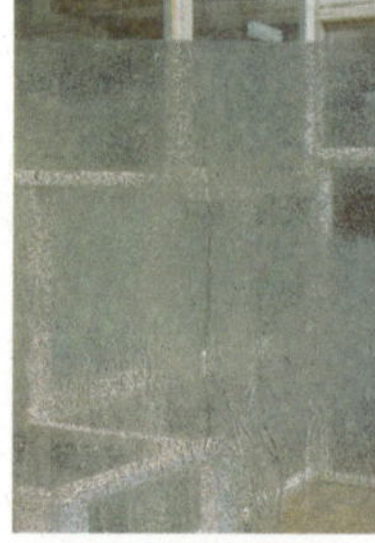

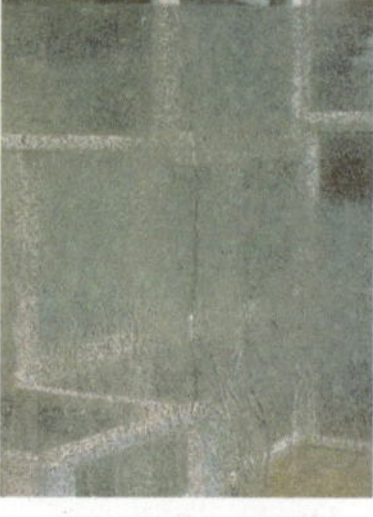

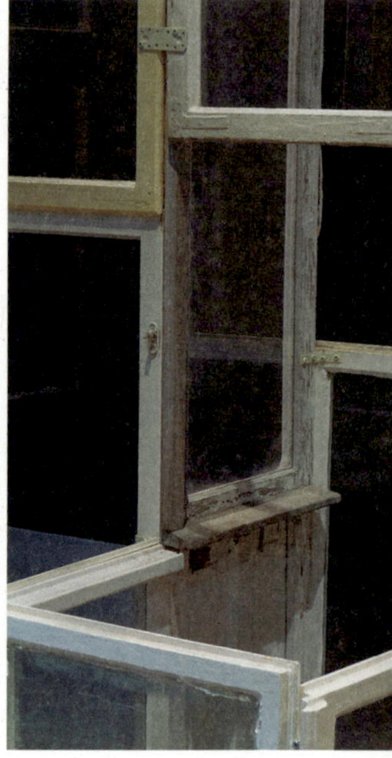

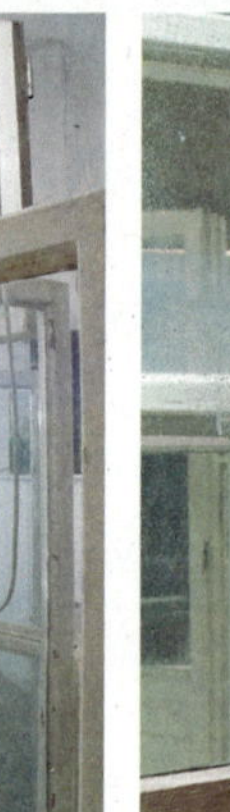

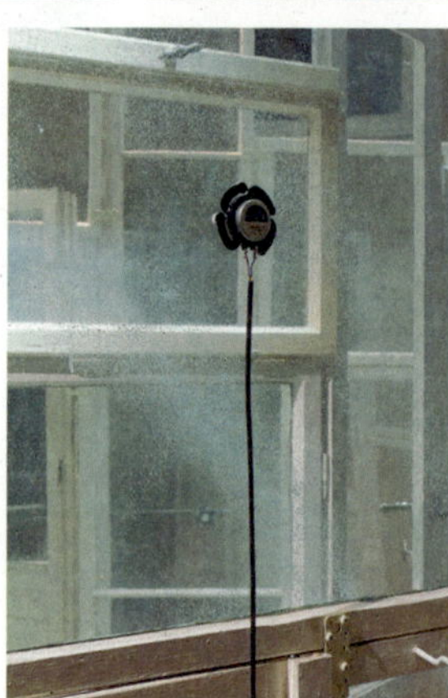

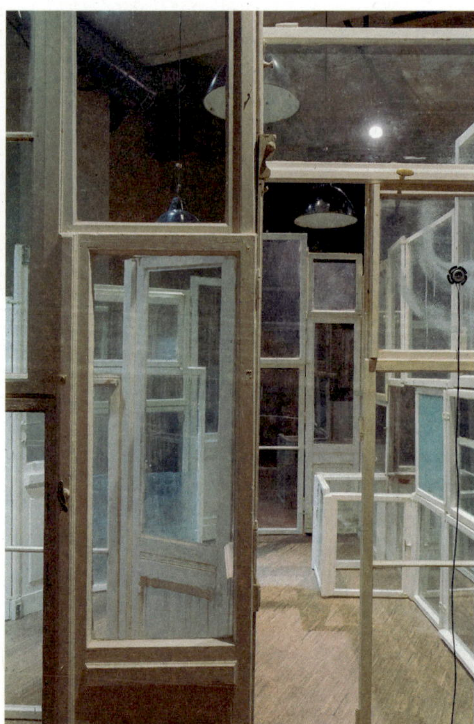

Unfamiliar Home

2018

mixed-media sound installation
in co-operation with Daniela Fromberg

» on the Acoustic Effects of
Gentrification and Modernization of
Inhabited Tenement Buildings

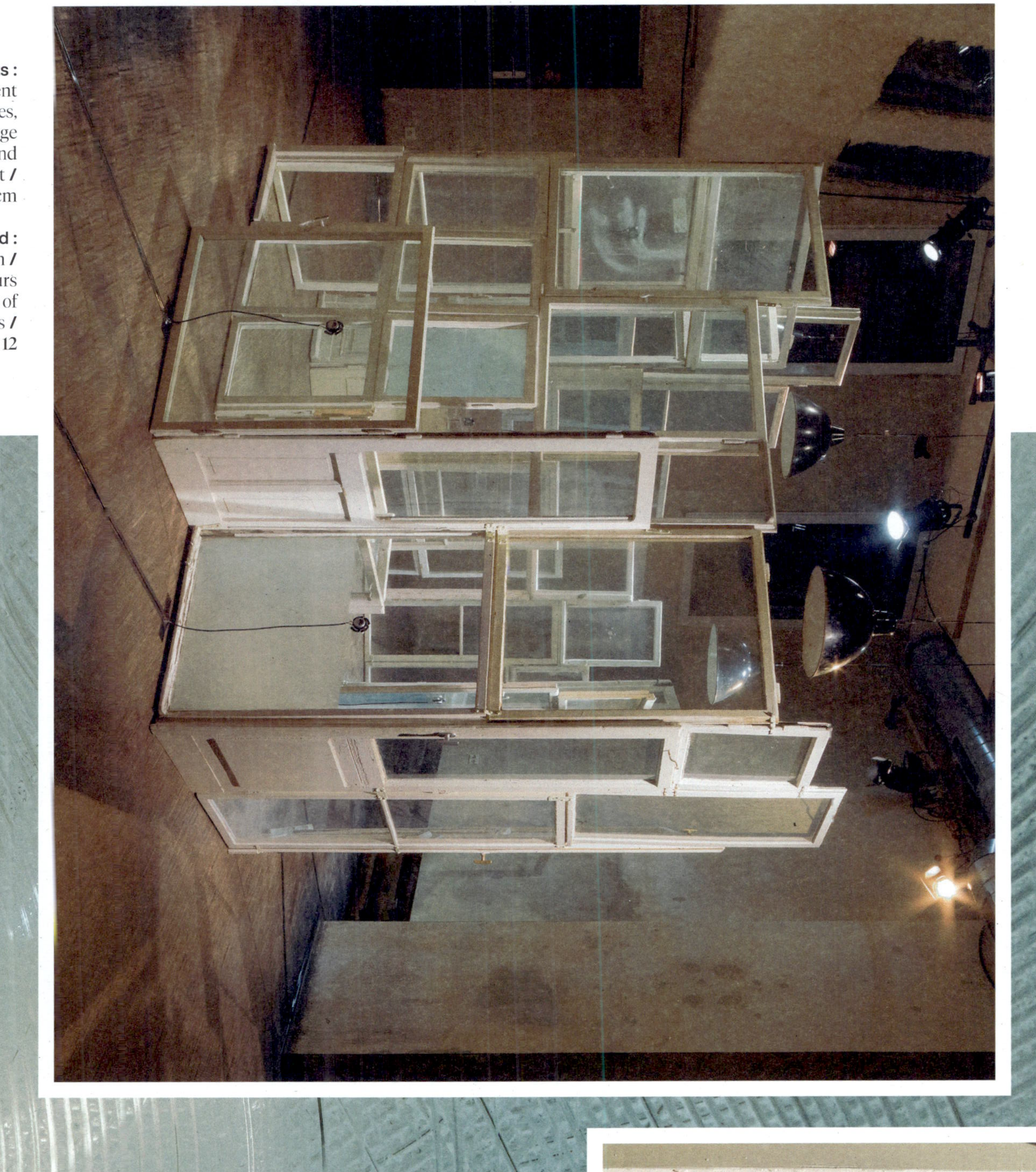

Objects :
pre-WWII apartment
windows, refir, lampshades,
transducers, full-range
loudspeakers, cables and
playback equipment /
450 x 550 x 350 cm

Sound :
12-channel composition /
audio collage of 400 hours
of audio recordings of
construction site noises /
loop (20:44) / CD 2 – track 12

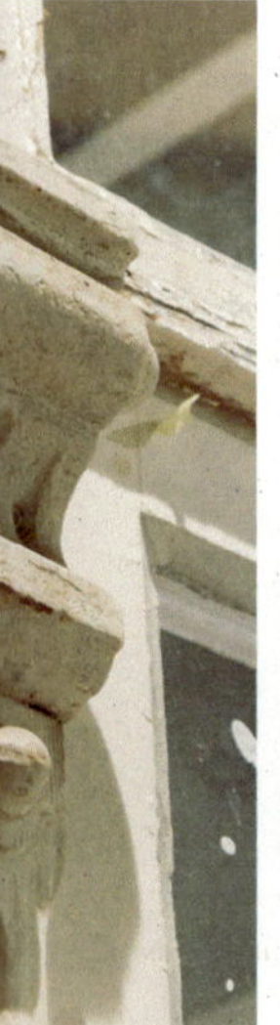
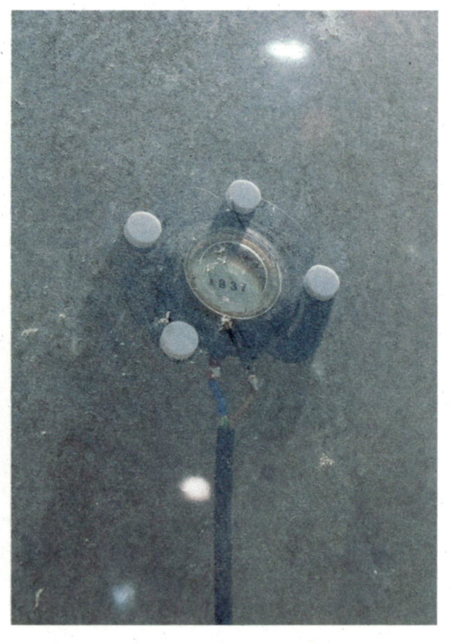
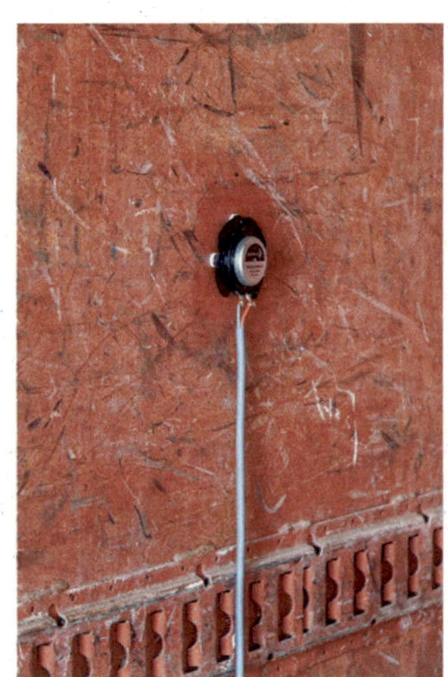
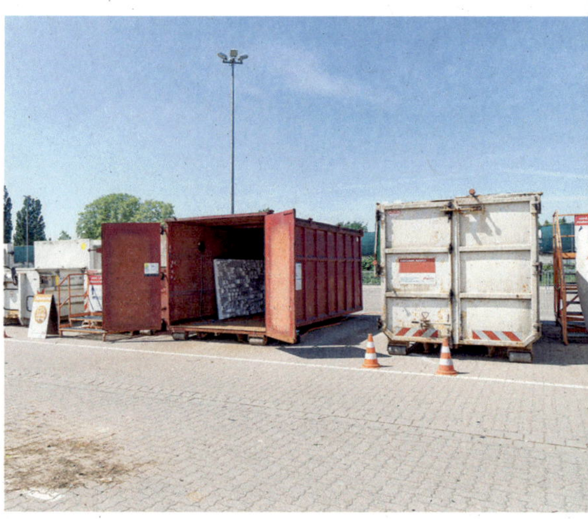

Kabinett des industriellen Elends

2021

site-specific sound installation
in co-operation with Daniela Fromberg
**» a Swan Song to the Lost Souls
of electronic scrap**

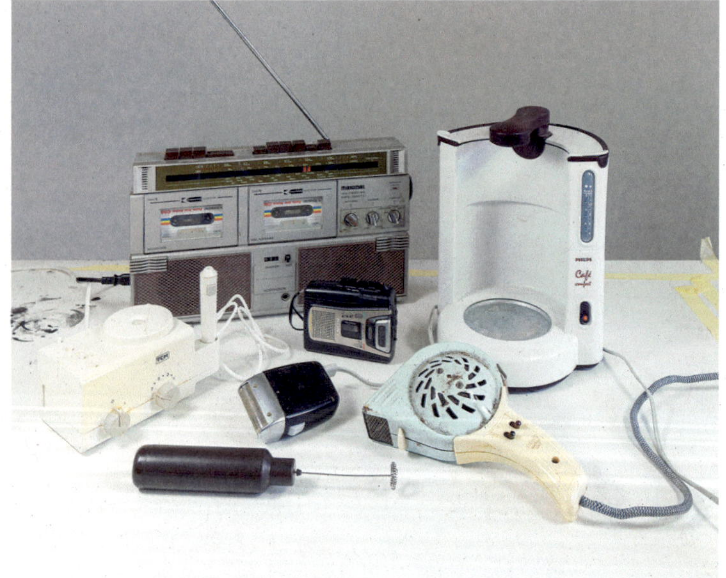

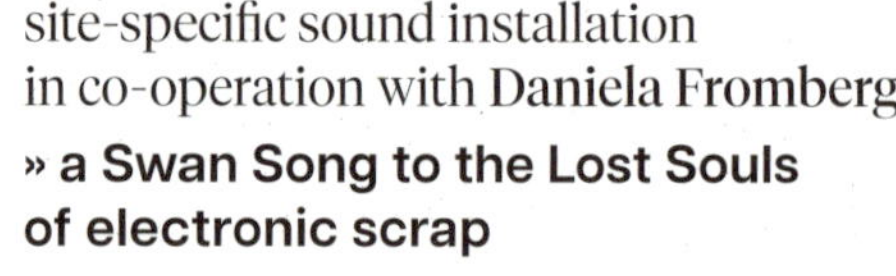

Objects :
light polystyrene packaging,
adhesive, medium-density
fiberboard, lacquer, magnets,
sound transducers, cables
full-range loudspeakers and
playback equipment **/**
650 x 250 x 250 cm

Sound :
8-channel acousmatic
composition **/** noises from
defective electronic devices
and sounds derived from
the container surface **/**
loop (13:42) **/** CD 2 — track 9

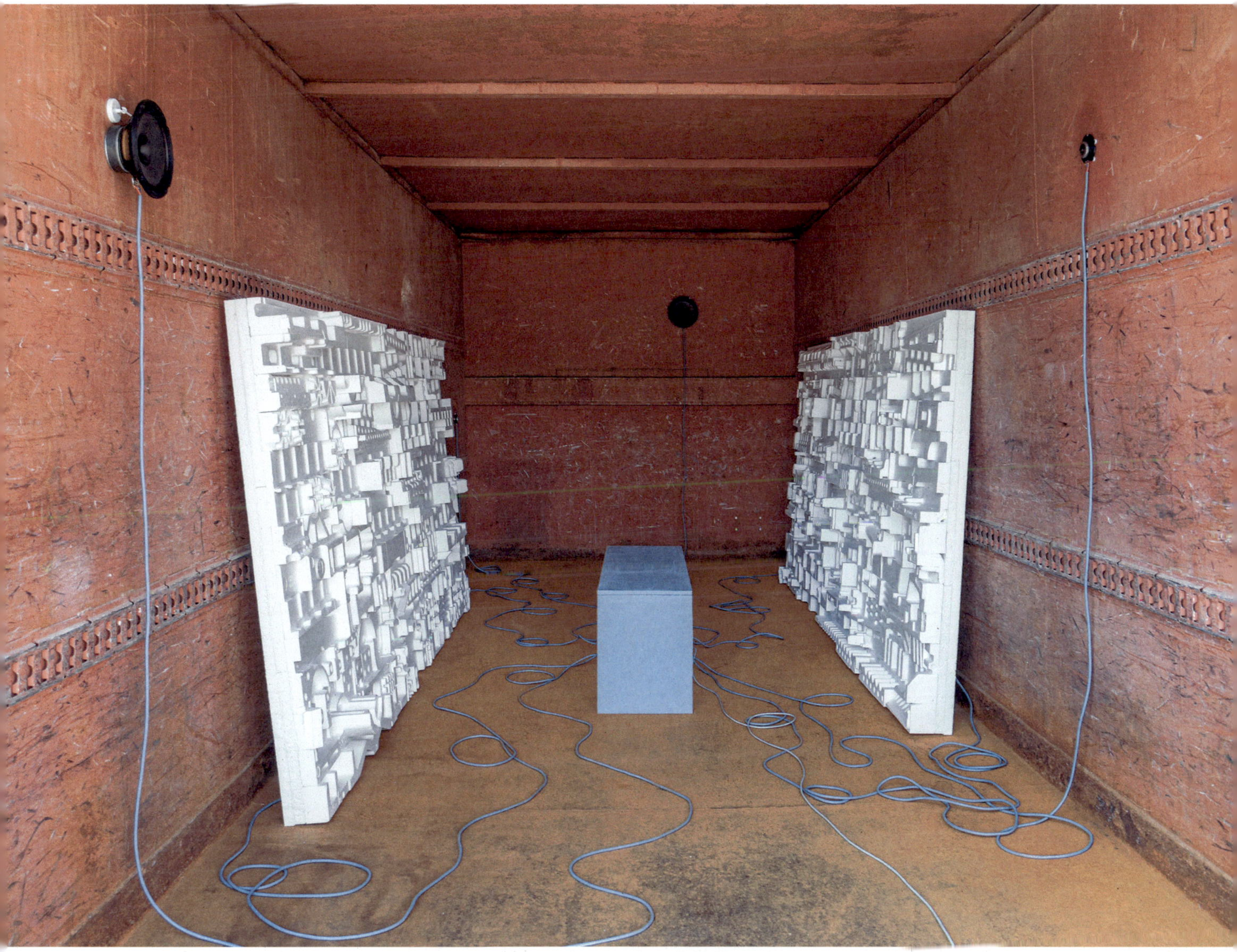

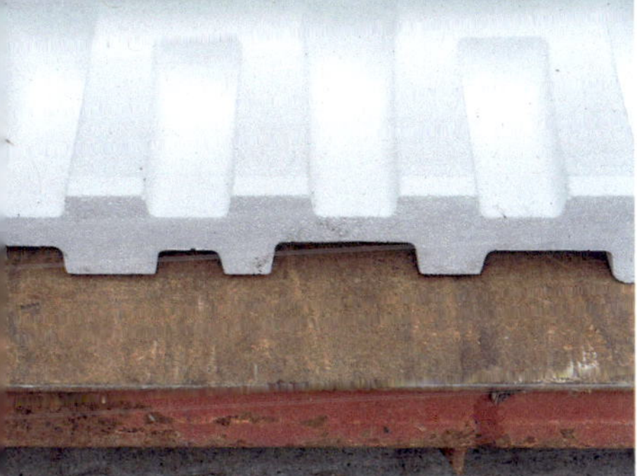

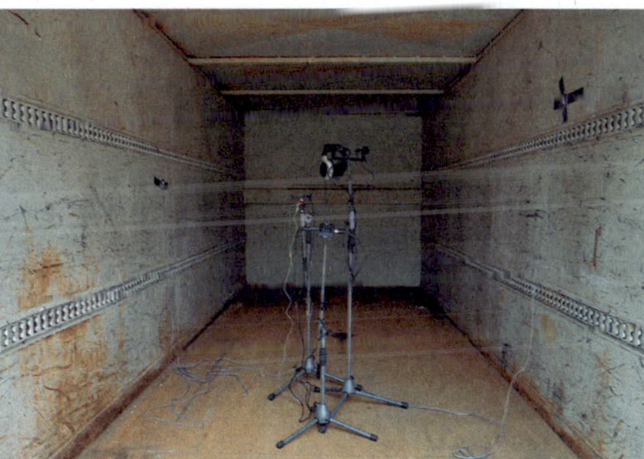

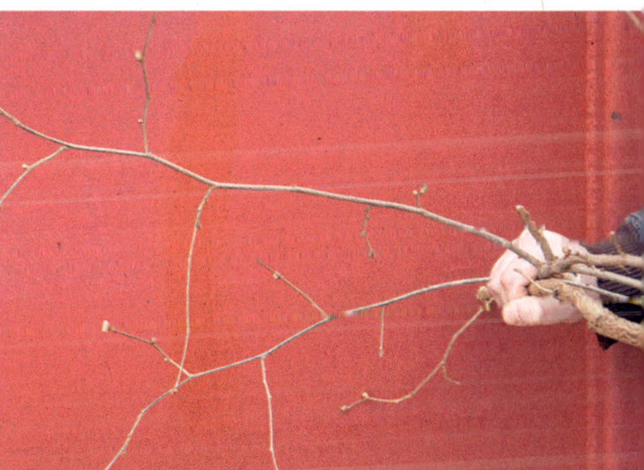

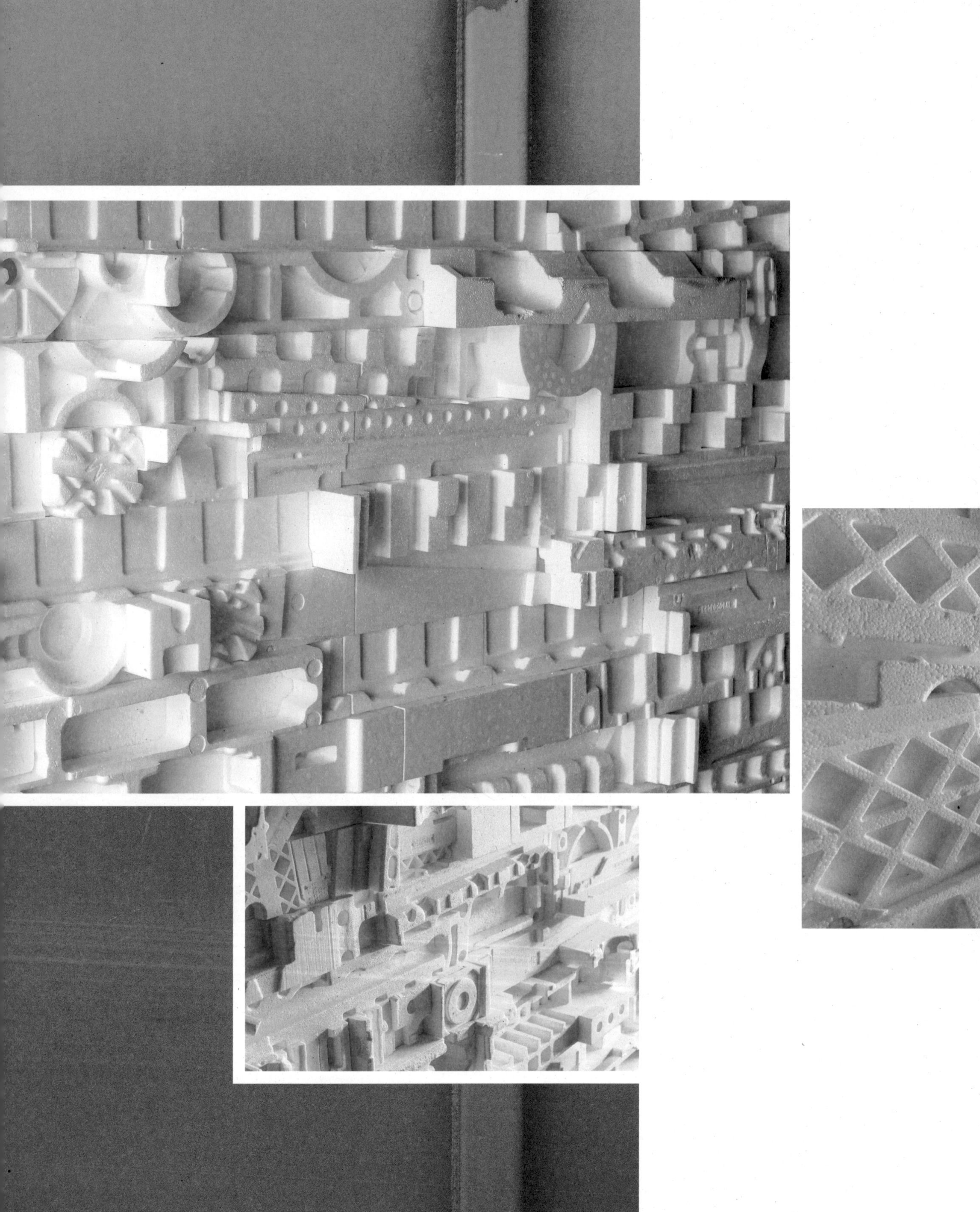

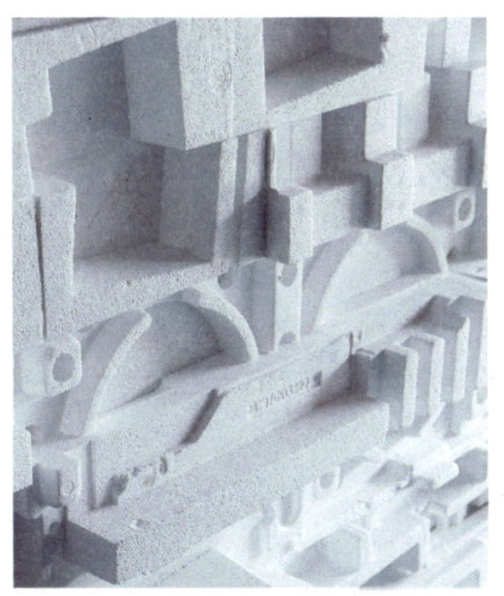
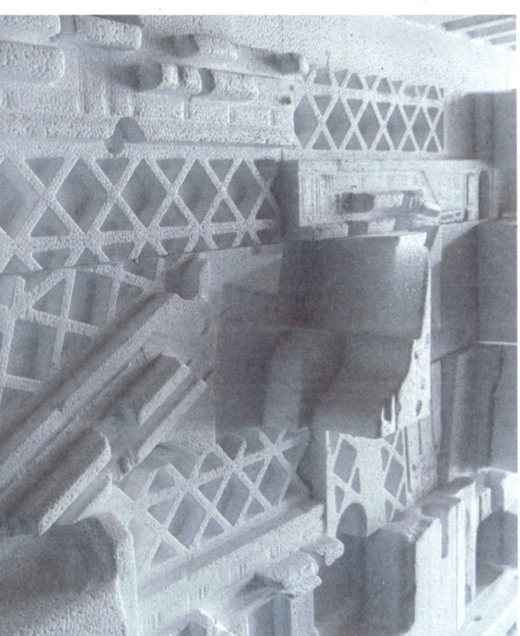
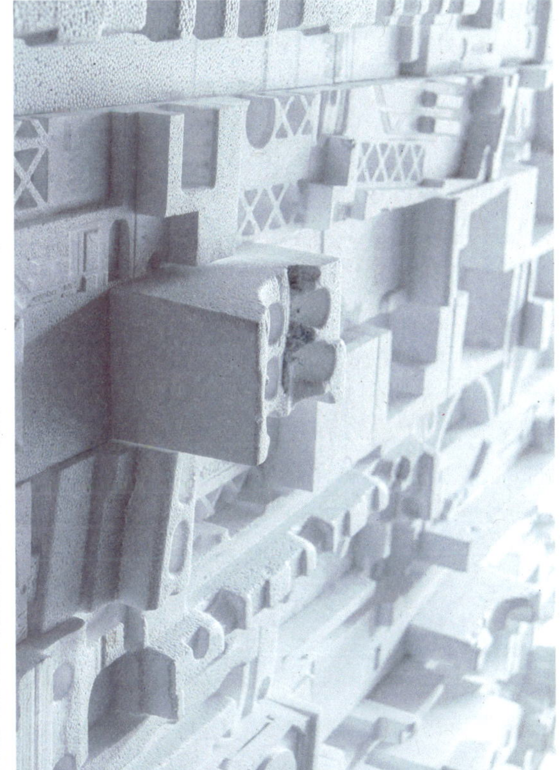
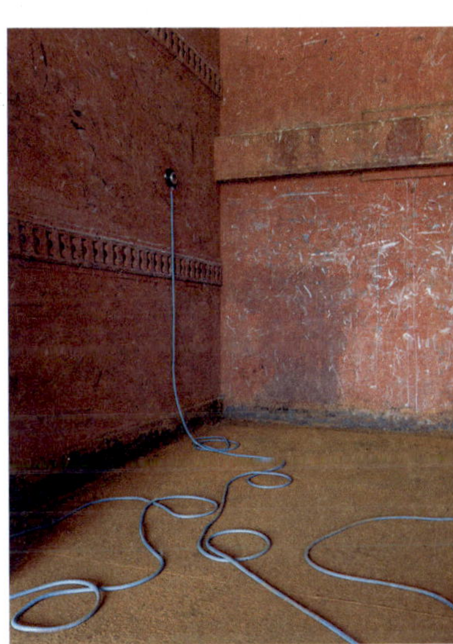
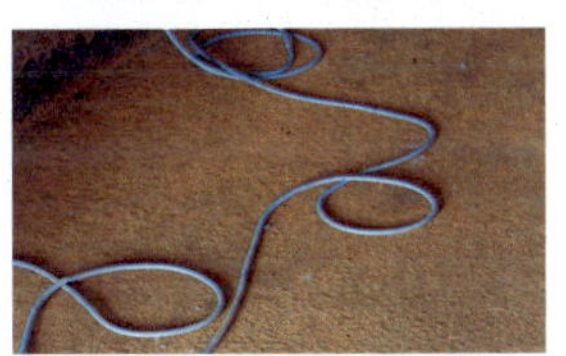
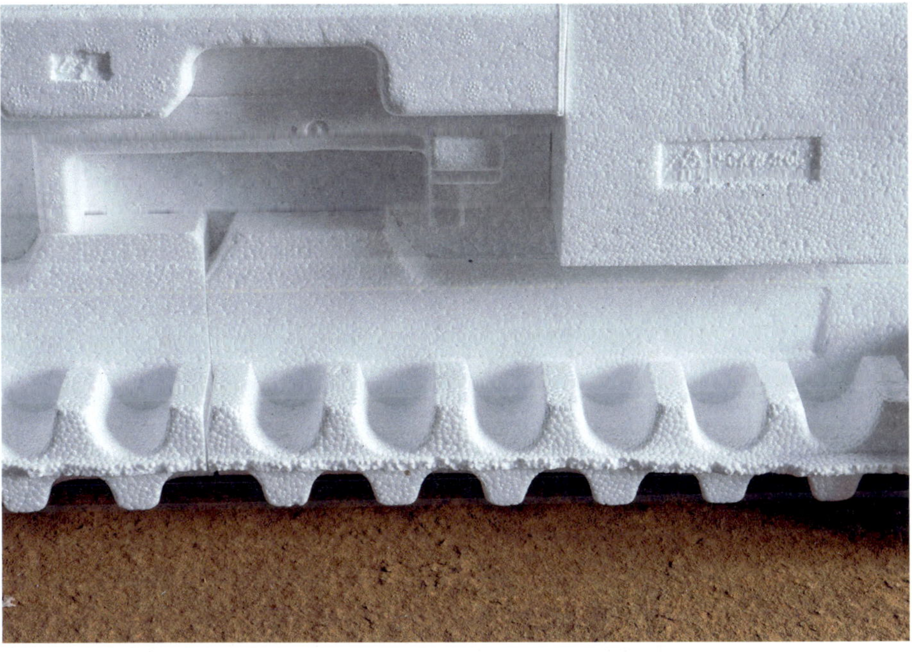

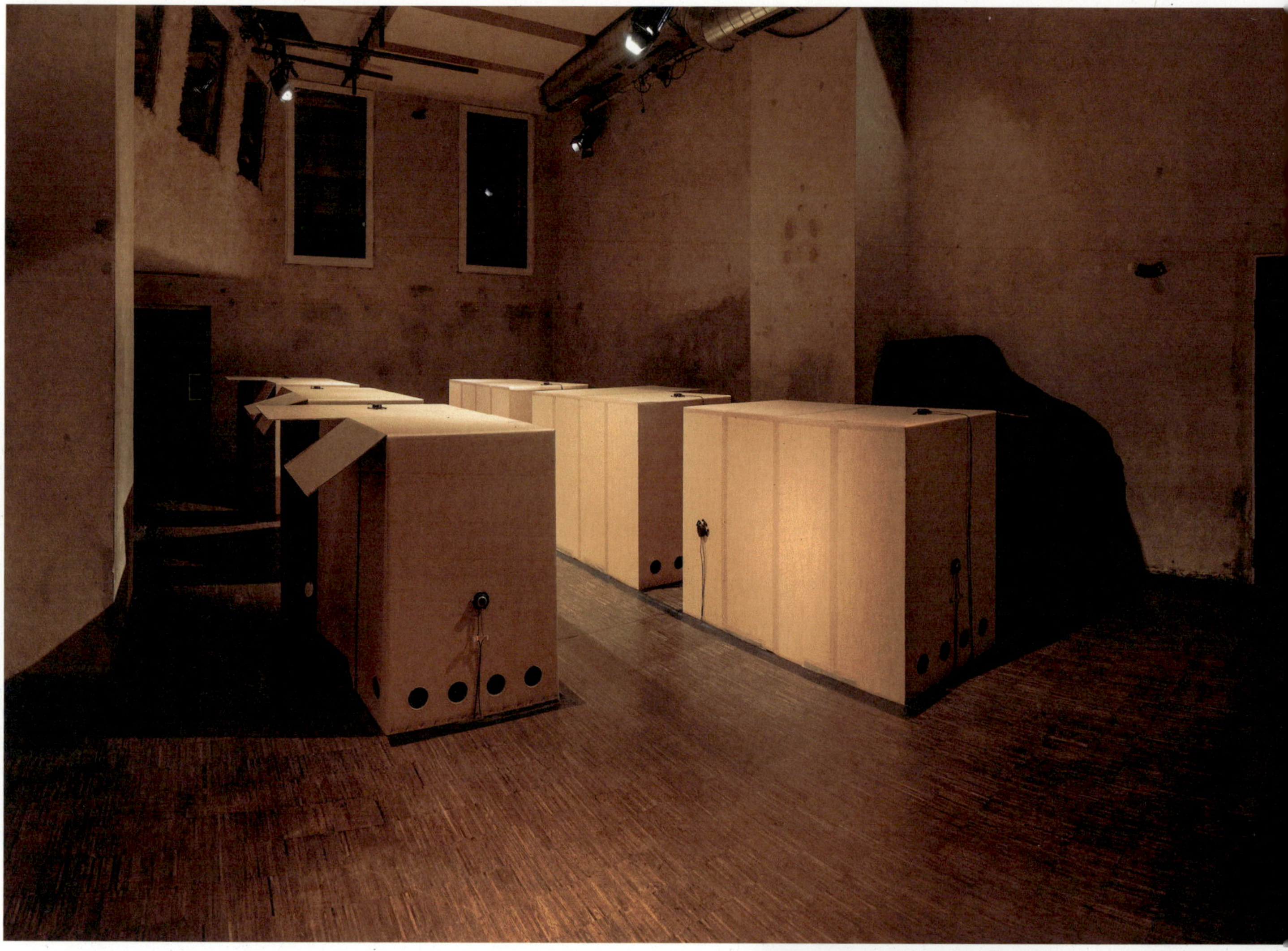

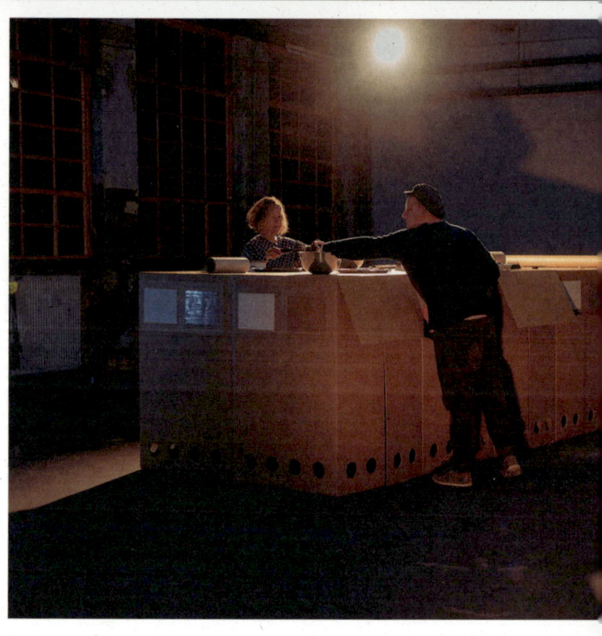

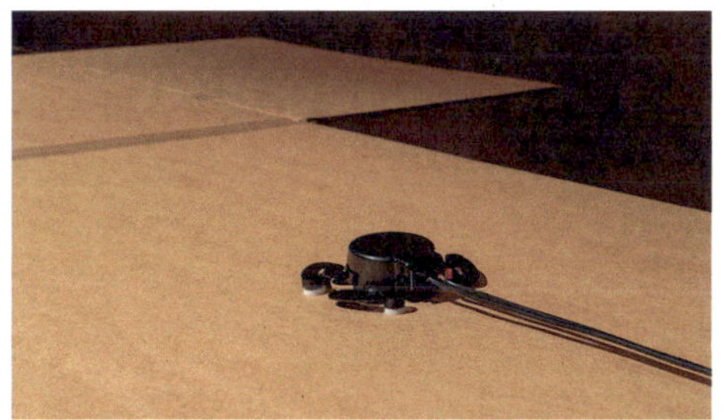
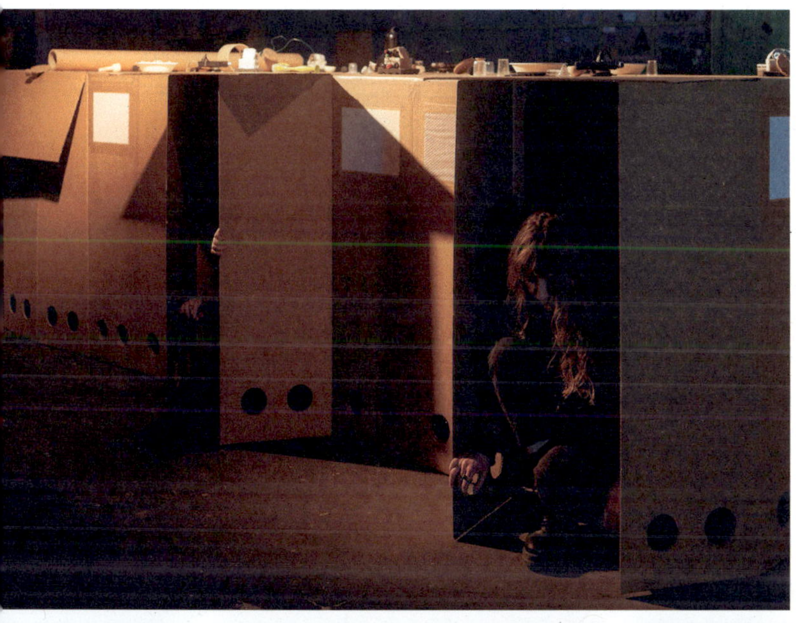
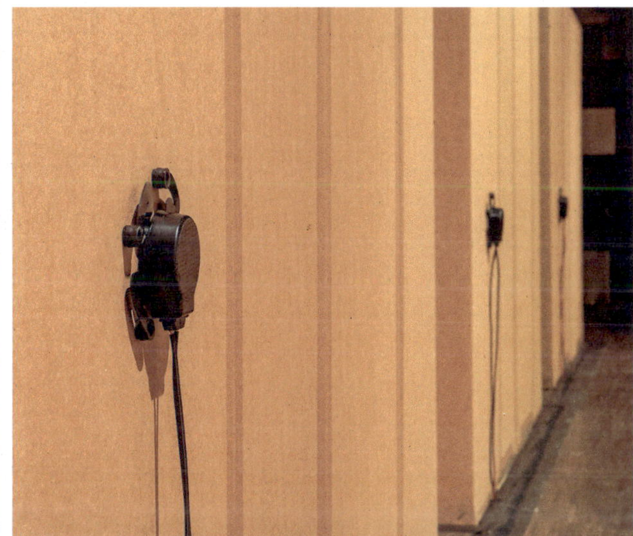
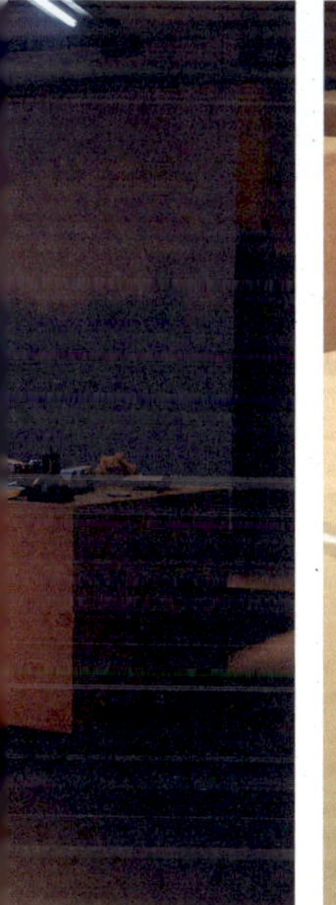
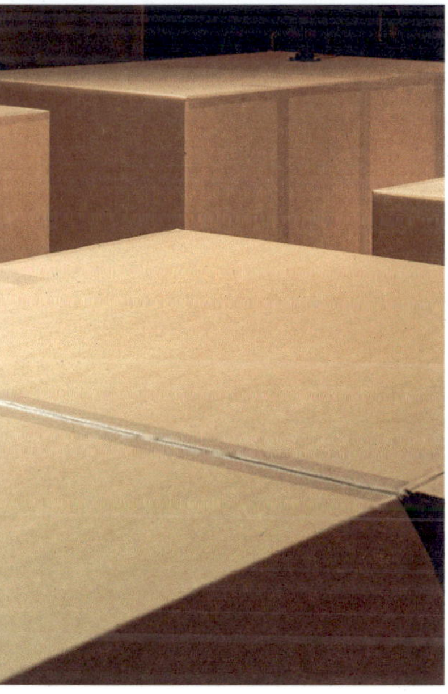
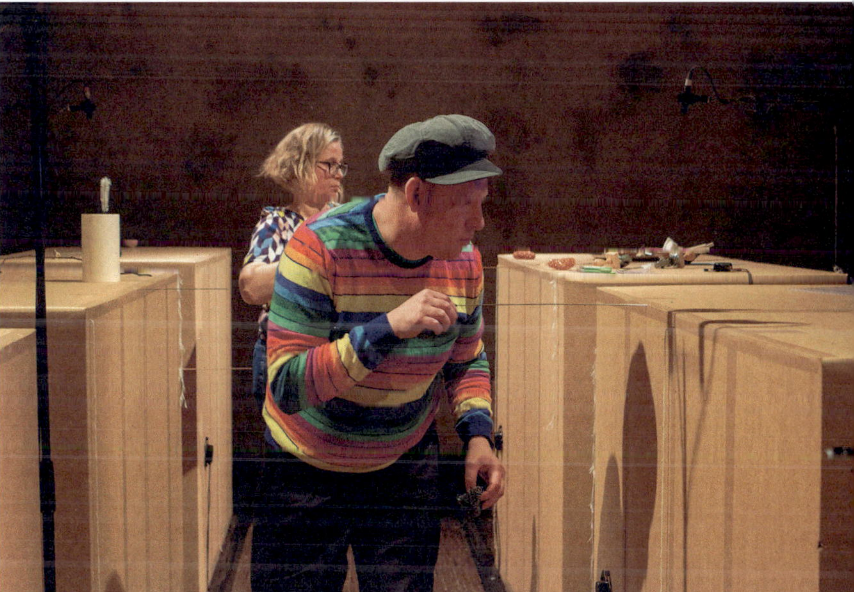

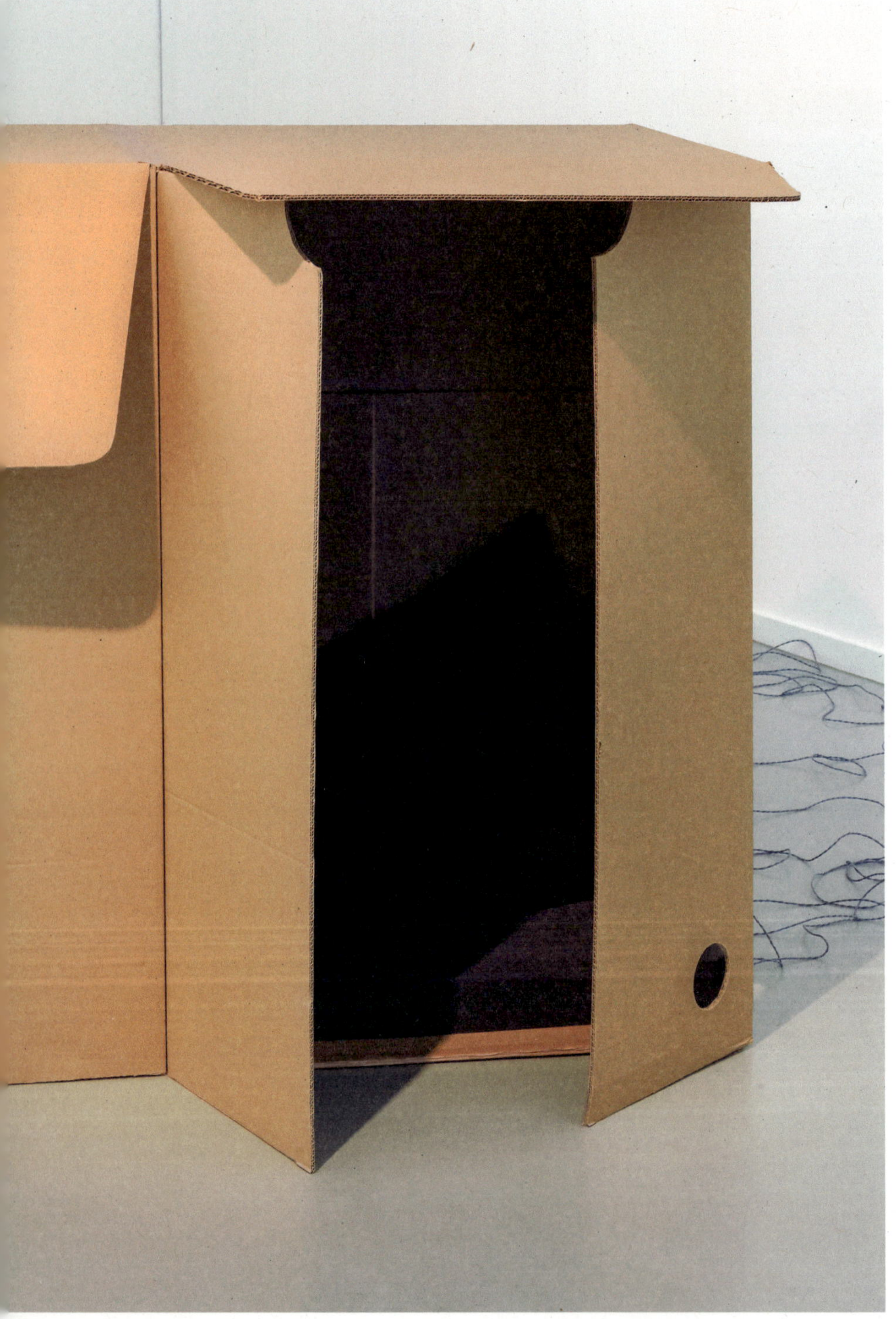

Objects :
palette cartons, fabric tape,
foam rubber, cushions,
carriage bolts, Wago clamps,
sound transducers, cables
and playback equipment **/**
160 x 80 x 120 cm each
(set-up variable)

Sound :
4-channel acousmatic
composition and concert for
2 performers **/** dynamic sound
actions with yarn, combs,
branches, bottle brushes, dish
scrubbers, carboard cores,
cleaning sponges, gyro,
copper bars, milk frothers,
trays, surface brushes, metal
bowls and cans, superballs,
leafstalks, wide brushes,
structural foil, whisks, plastic
forks, yoghurt cups, suction
cups, wooden spheres,
plastic cups **/** loop (18:16) **/**
CD 1 − track 7 + 10 **+**
CD 2 − track 15

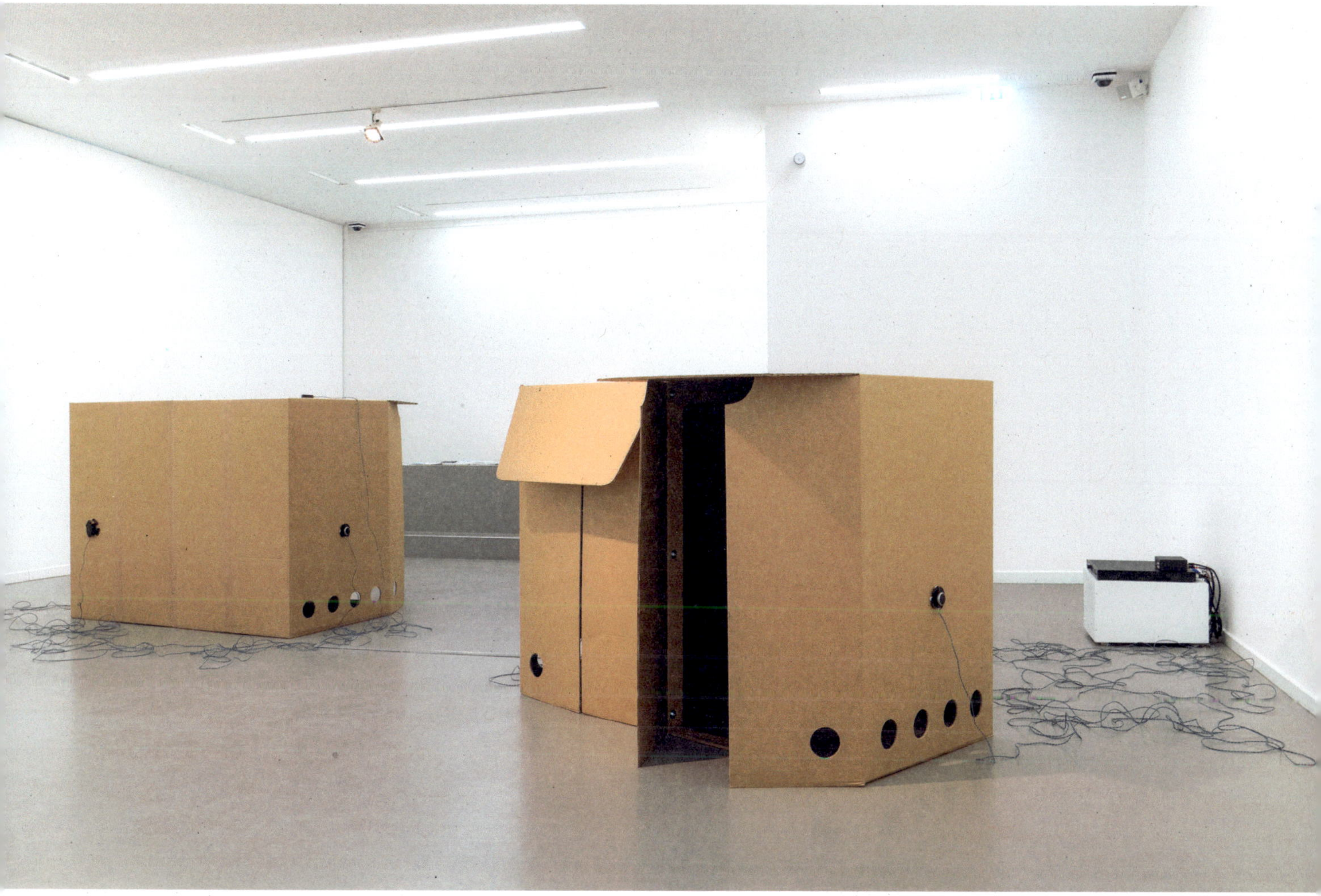

Jenseits
der Wand

2021

mixed-media sound installation
and concert for 2 performers
in co-operation with Daniela Fromberg

**» the Simultaneity of Proximity
and Isolation in Urban Living
Arouses a Detective-Like Curiosity
(One Literally Bathes in Sound)**

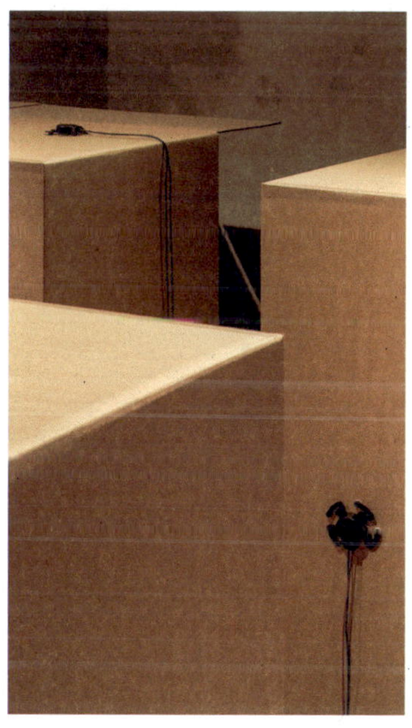

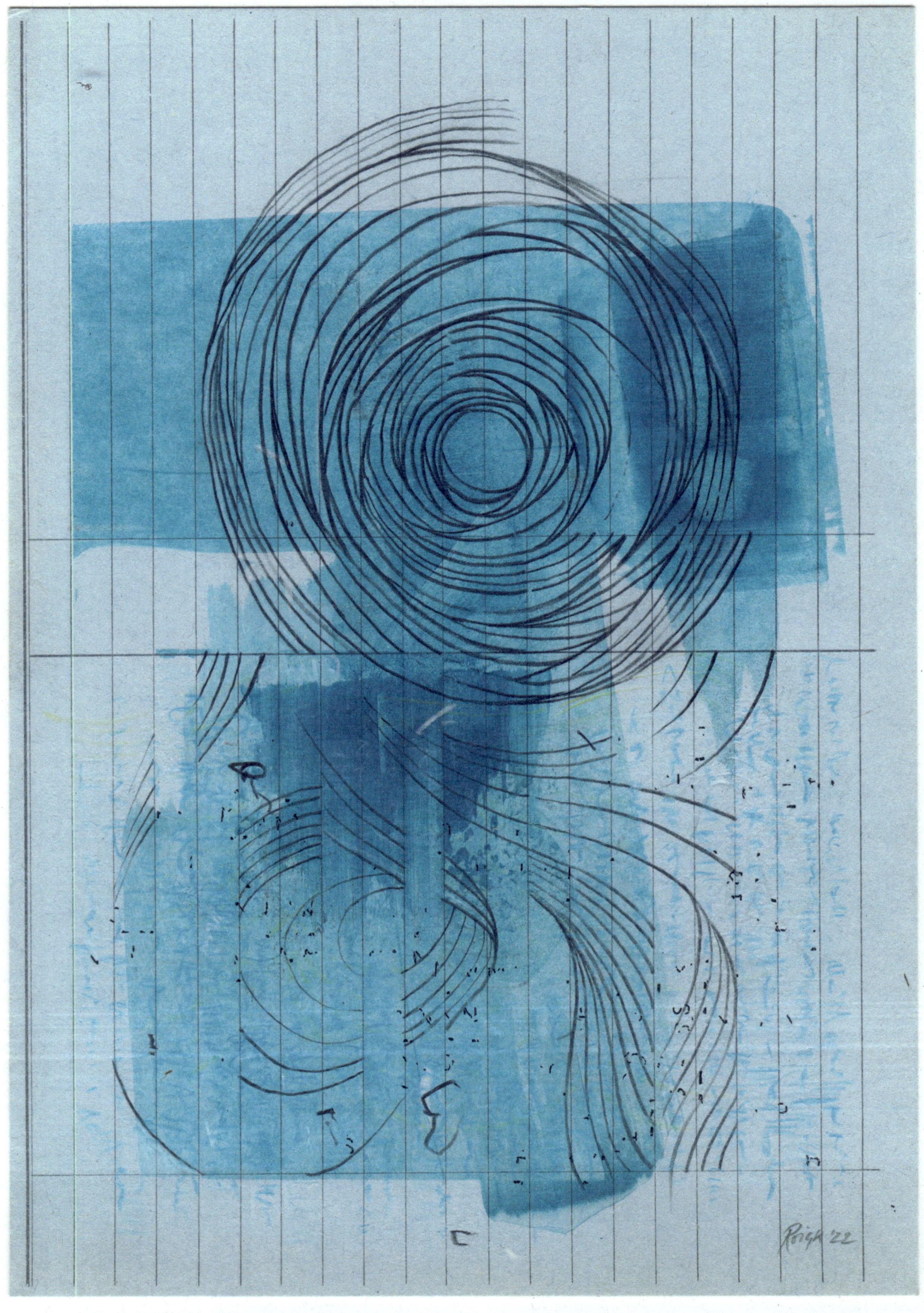

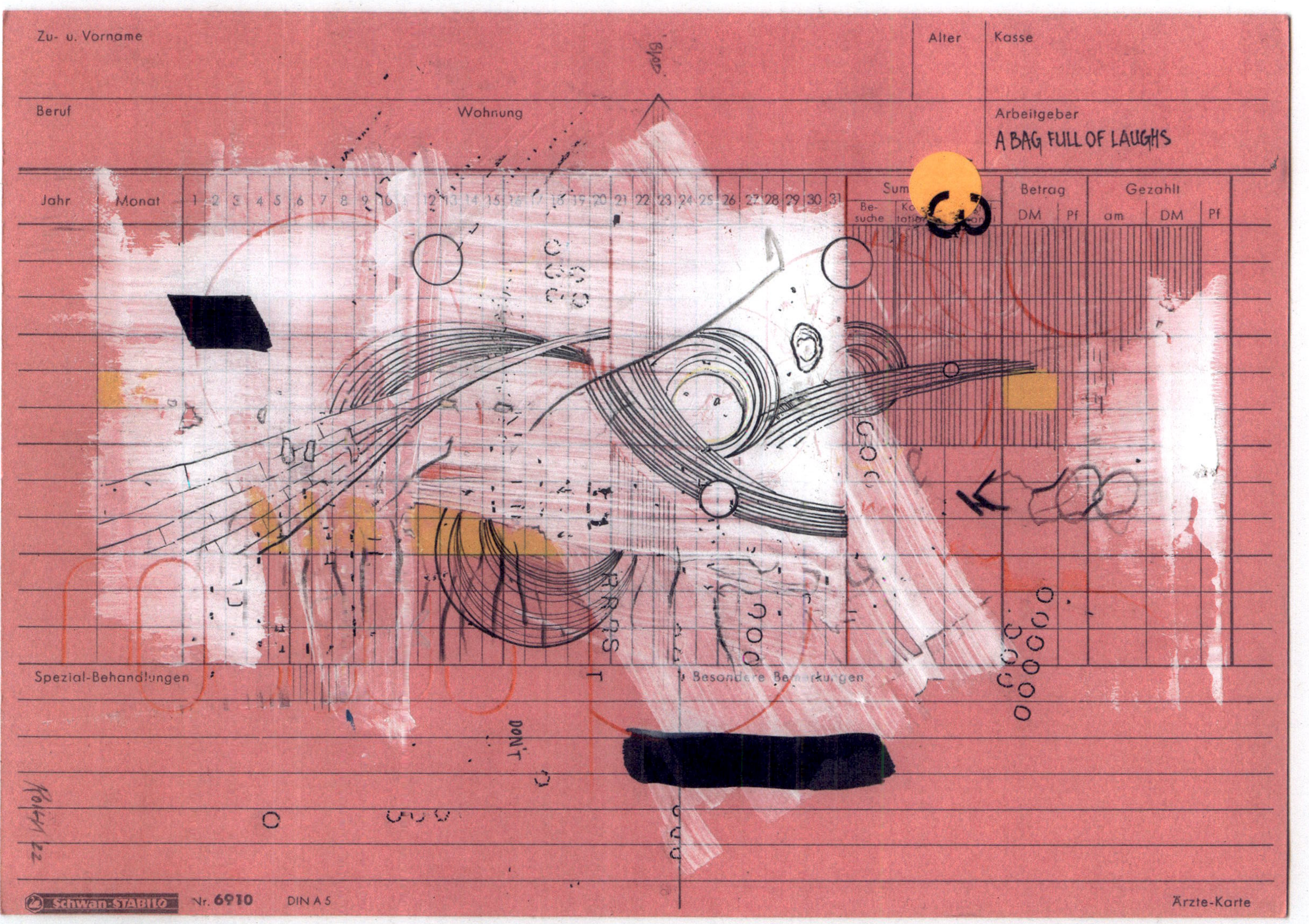
Zu- u. Vorname
Alter
Kasse
Beruf
Wohnung
Arbeitgeber
A BAG FULL OF LAUGHS
Jahr
Monat
1 2 3 4 5 6 7 8 9 10 11 12 13 14 15 16 17 18 19 20 21 22 23 24 25 26 27 28 29 30 31
Summe
Be-
suche
Ko.-
tation
Betrag
DM Pf
Gezahlt
am
DM Pf
Spezial-Behandlungen
Besondere Bemerkungen
DON'T
Schwan-STABILO
Nr. 6910
DIN A5
Ärzte-Karte

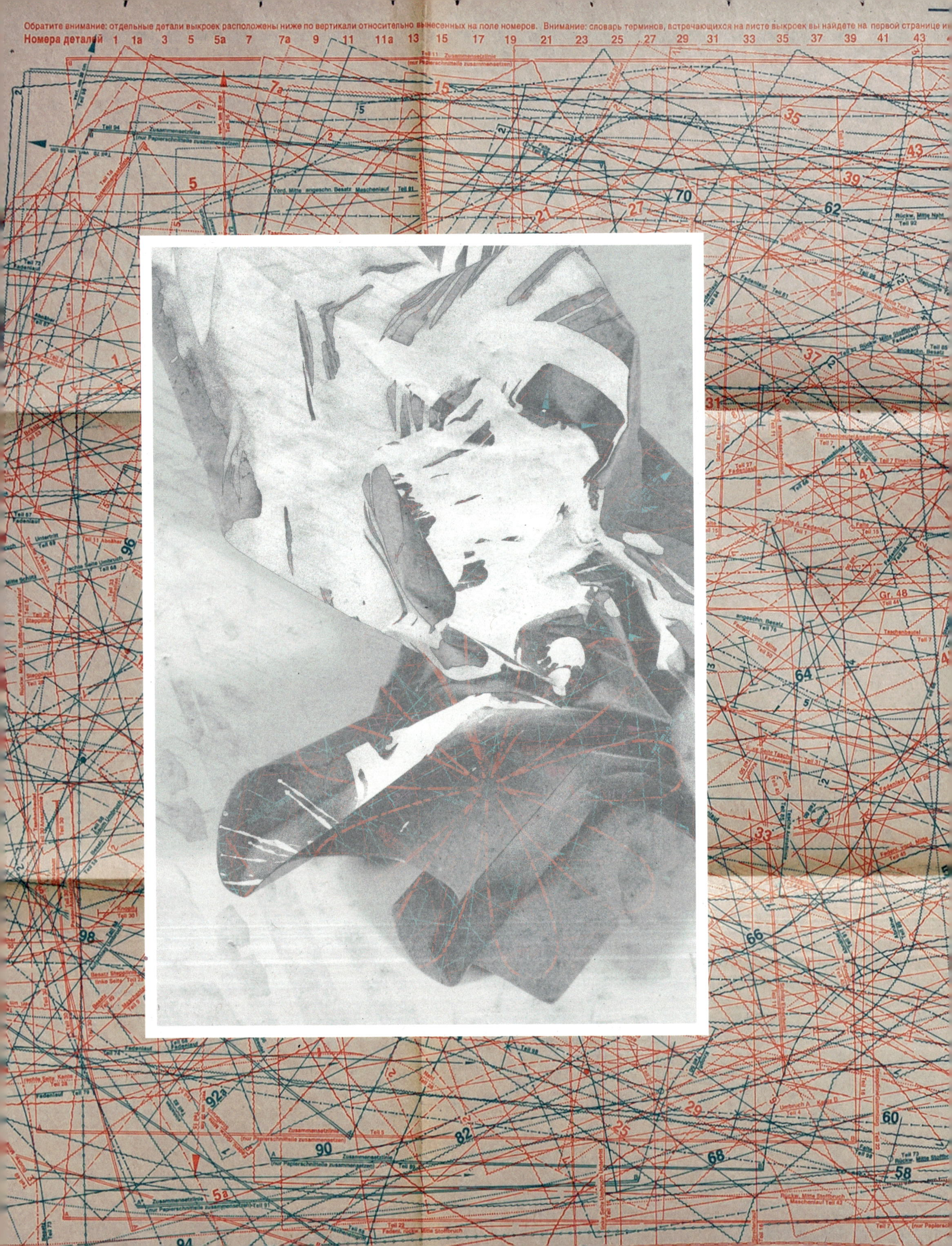

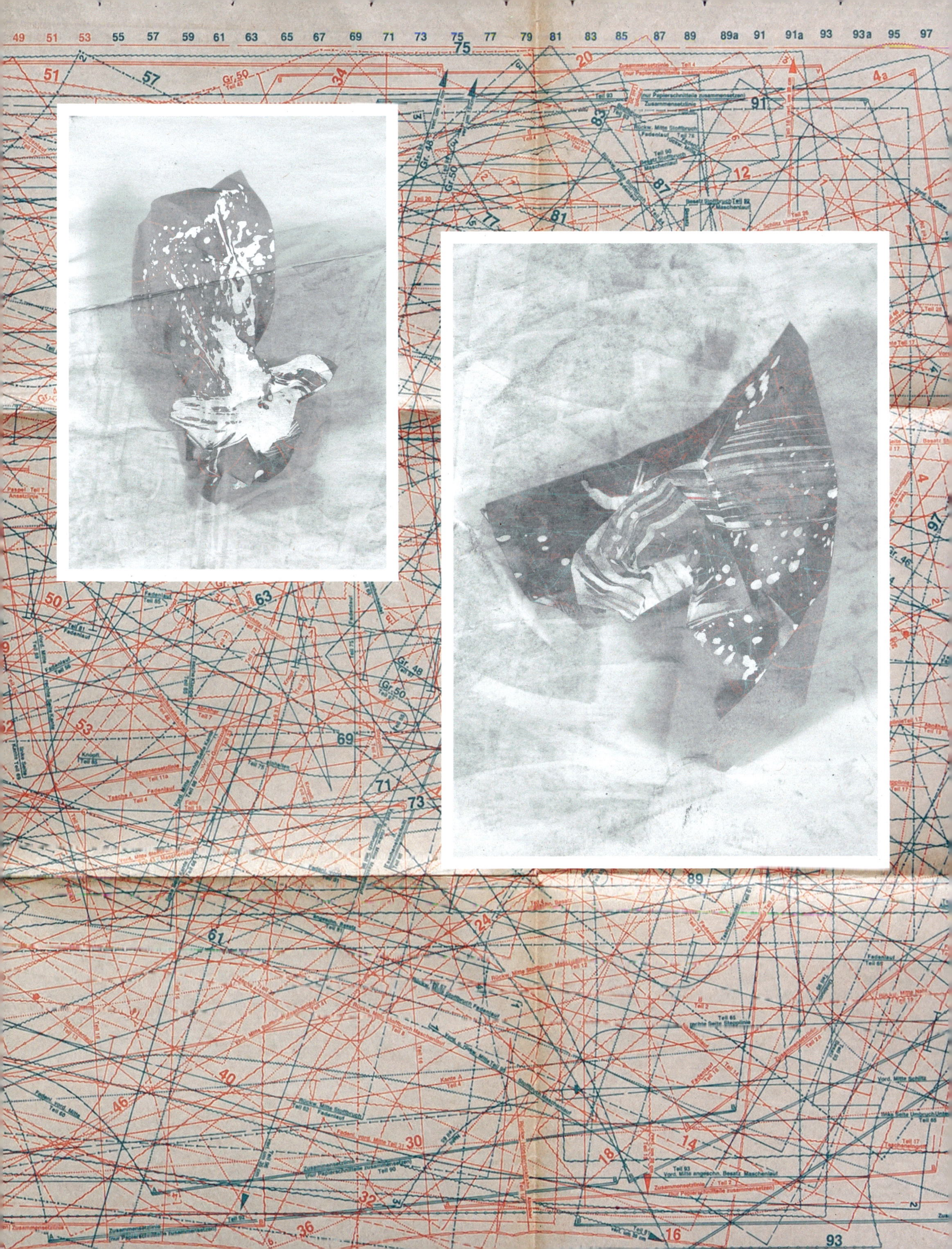

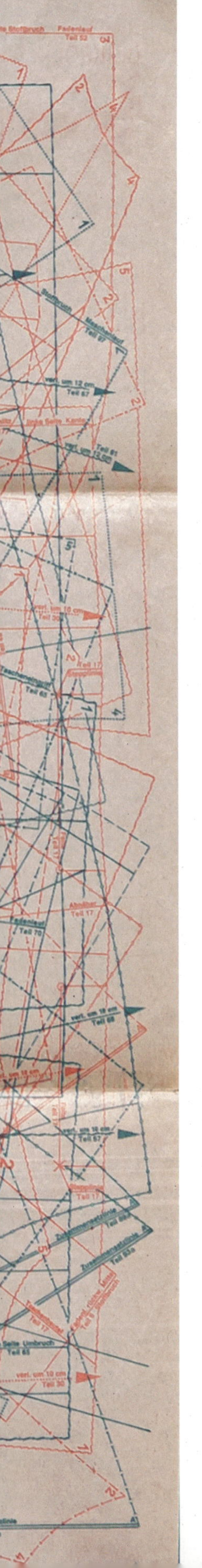

Traces—Of

ongoing artistic research project
» **Artistic Investigations Into
the Reconstruction of an
Electro-Acoustic Composition**

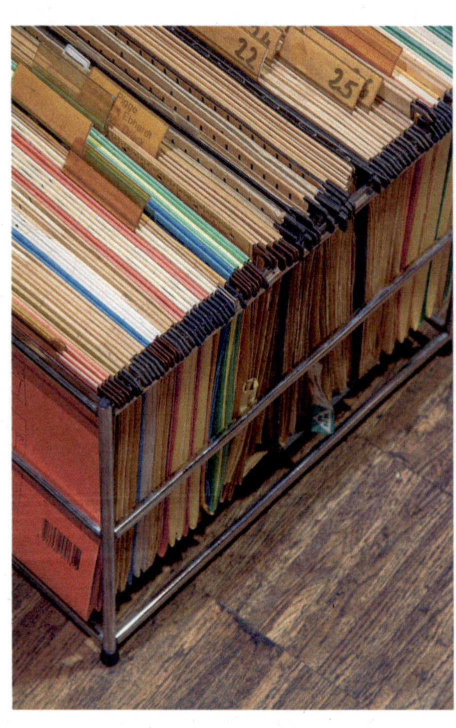

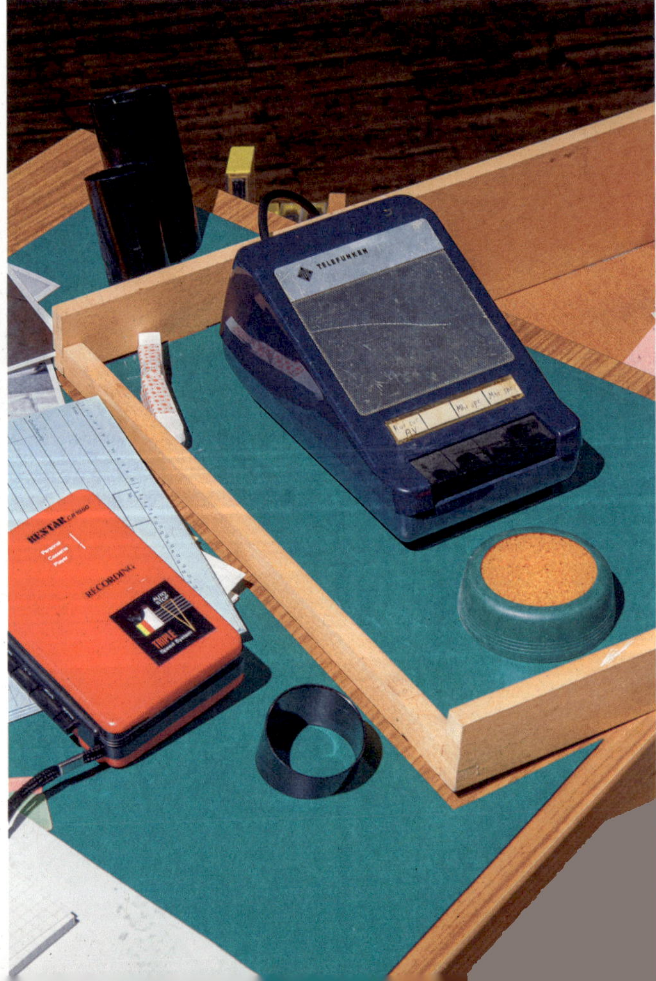

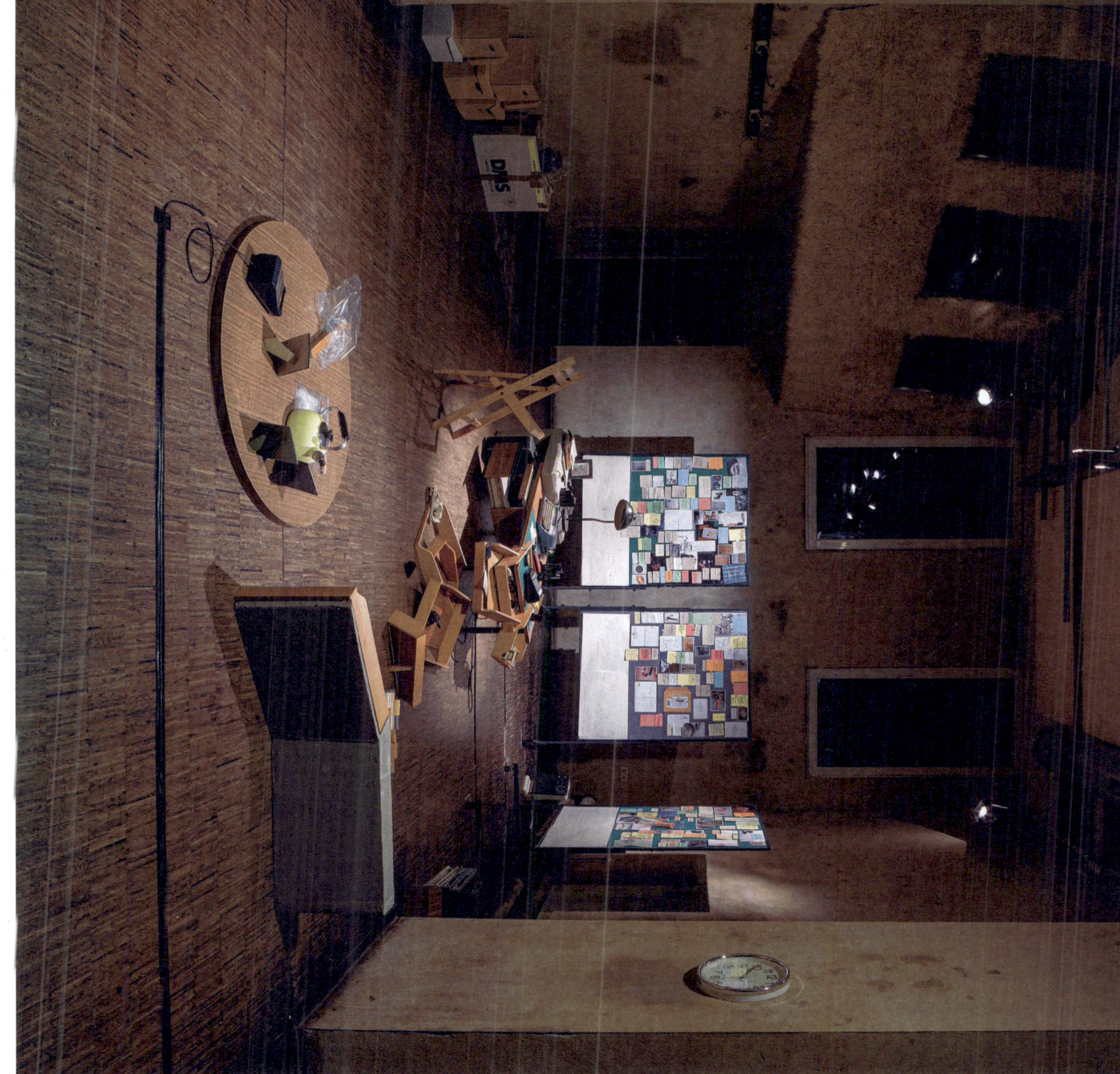

Objects :
modified desk with
deconstructed drawers,
polystyrene, tile adhesive,
intercoms, pin boards, cards
with interview fragments,
written notes on interviews,
objects suspected of being
sound sources, photographs
of supposed noise producers,
pencil cups, office
paraphernalia, hanging files,
desk lamp and fan (each
modified with loudspeakers),
vintage hi-fi loudspeakers,
full-range loudspeakers
and playback equipment
/ 500 x 400 x 200 cm
(set-up variable)

Sound :
8-channel / aleatoric
arrangement / recordings
of noises of the original
composition re-enacted
concretely during the
interviews: film atmospheres,
making coffee, closing jars,
pouring water, pushing and
pulling, radio static, opening
shuttered cabinets, fan
and mouth noises / loop
(60:00) / CD 1 – track 12 +
CD 2 – track 13

underlying composition /
7:23 / CD 2 – track 16

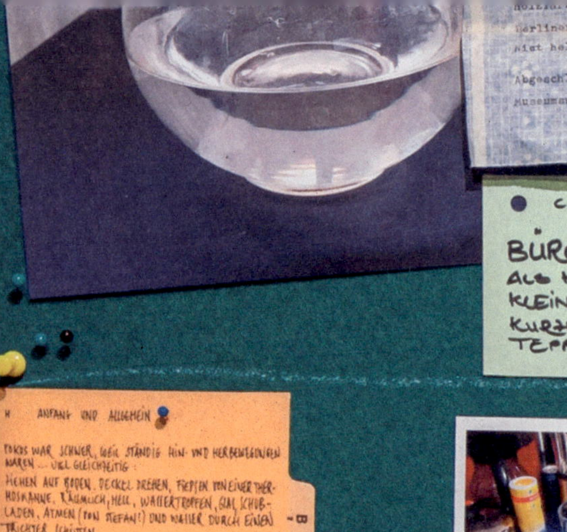

Berliner Altbau 8-12 m2
Miet hell - Gemütlichkeit oder
Verschanzen?

Abgeschlossen, max. kleines Fenster

Museumswohnung in der Dunckerstrasse

C TEIL 1
BÜROCONTAINER
ALS HANDLUNGSORT
KLEIN - ZWECKGEBUNDEN
KURZER HALL!
TEPPICHBODEN

G Beschreibung der ersten Lokalität:
Eher dunkel... viel Schatten, wie ein Keller
oder Geheimlabor... wie bei Frankenstein
Sehr filmisch... und es gab ein Dröhnen im
(Dröhnen!) Hintergrund, sehr dunkel... in
der ersten Hälfte sehr präsent

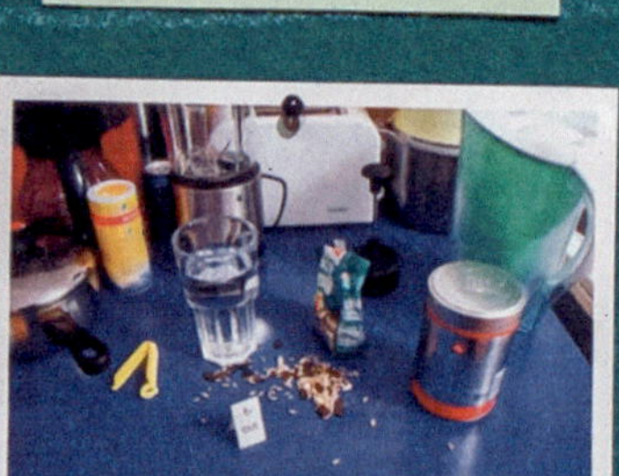

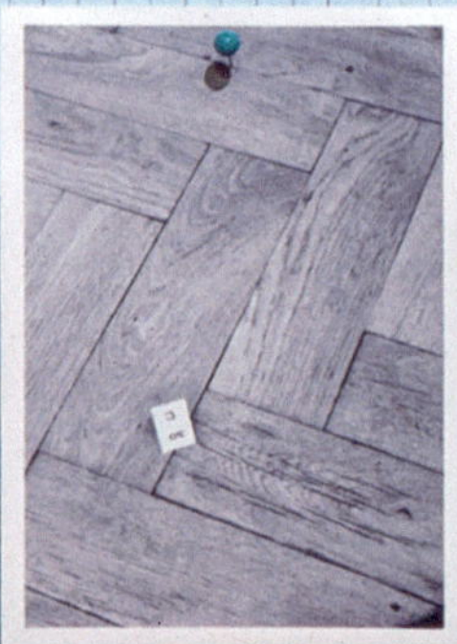

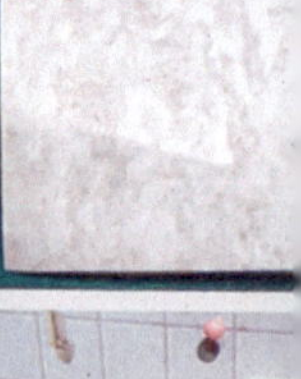

H ANFANG UND ALLGEMEIN
TOREG WAR SCHWER, WEIL STÄNDIG HIN- UND HERBEWEGUNG
WAREN ... VIEL GLEICHZEITIG
...CHEN AUF BODEN, DECKEL DREHEN, FIEPEN TON EINER THER-
MOSKANNE, RÄUMLICH, HELL, WASSERTROPFEN, GAS SCHUB-
LADEN, ATMEN (VON STEFAN) UND WASSER DURCH EINEN
TRICHTER SCHÜTTEN

GLOCKE - ANFANG KIRCHENHALL BZW. KIRCHENRAUM

EIN SCHENKEN MIT STRAHL, WIE PINKELN, WIE MIT
EINEM TRICHTER - UND ES GAB DECKEL ZUSCHRAUBEN
DER DECKEL WAR EHER PLASTIK ALS METAL

DANN EIN TISCHEN MIT THERMOSKANNE - DACHTE
ANFANGS ES WÄRE MIT DEM MUND GEMACHT

I 1/3 ANFANG
ES BEGINNT ALLE MIT EINEM GONG, WIE TAGESSCHAU,
UND IM KOPF WAR ES SOFORT EINE PERSON MIT DINGEN
BESCHÄFTIGT, SCHIEBEN, VERPACKEN, KONTINUIERLICH BESCHÄFTIGT
BIS ZUR ZWEITEN TÜRKLINGEL - ZWEITES TÜRKLINGELN MIT
SUMMER. NICHT NUR NATÜRLICHE GERÄUSCHE, SONDERN
SPHÄRISCHER SPANNUNGSAUFBAU -
VIELLEICHT AUCH SCHON ROTE WARE EINSCHENKEN, RIETEN
NICHT PER SE BEDROHLICH, ABER AUFBAUENDE SPANNUNG
BIS ZUM LETZTEN DRITTEL FINDET ALLES IN EINEM LANGEN RAUM
OHNE PUTZ AN DEN WÄNDEN, MIT GROBEN DIELEN, RAUEN WÄNDEN
UND UNGEMÜTLICHER ATMOSPHÄRE STATT

D "TEIL 1"
STARKES PANNING LINKS/RECHTS
GANZ KLAR RÄUMLICH DRINNEN UND
DRAUSSEN / ANFANG / ...
ESPRESSOKANNE AUF HERD, KUGELN,
SCHUBLADEN AUS HOLZ MIT ROLLEN,
DER ESPRESSO ZIEHT UND ZISCHT,
NICHT RÖCHELN, EHER RAUSCHEN,
AUF DEM BODEN HIN- UND HERWISCHEN
EINE KLANGSCHALE... ODER TOPF

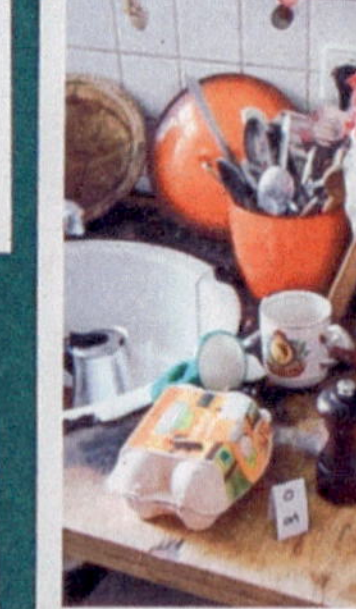

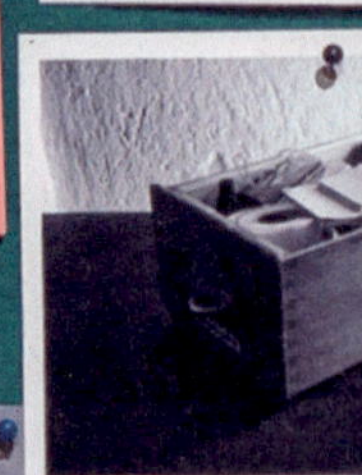

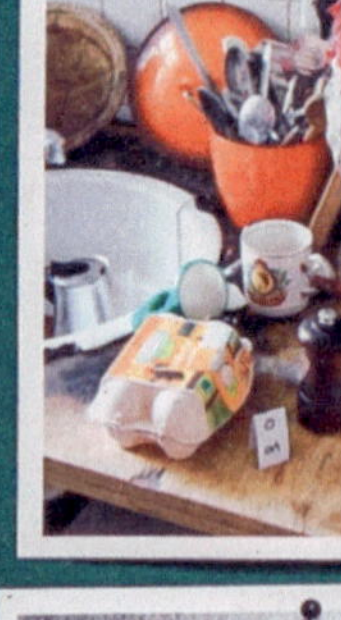

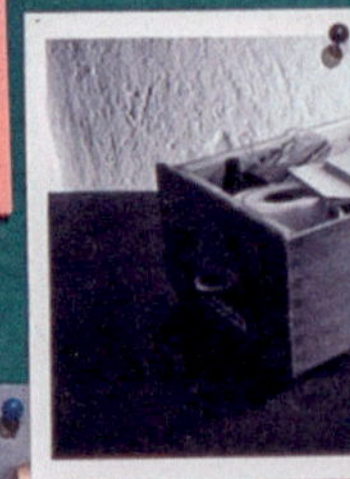

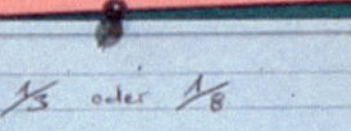

B 1/3
IN TÜR REINGEHEN MIT
KLIRRENDEM VORHANG
- IN KÜCHE. DA WURDE
DANN WAS GEMACHT.
- DURCH EINEN PLASTIK-
VORHANG GEHEN UND
DANN NACH RECHTS IN
DIE KÜCHE ABBIEGEN.

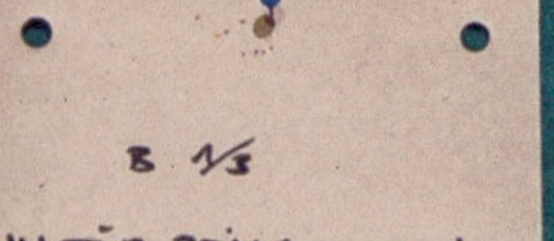

C TEIL A
KONKRETE GERÄUSCHE
AUSSCHIEBEN, WIE BAUKLÖTZE
UMFALLEN - UNTEN, RECHTS
HINFALLEN, RELATIV SCHARF
UND DANN ETWAS FEINER
AUSGESCHÜTTETES...
SPÄTER BEIM ATMEN INTENSIVER
ABER EHER KURZ

F ERSTER TEIL
ETWAS KONKRETES, HAUSHALTSWAREN
WIEDERKEHREND, ILLUSTRATIV - EIN-
NEHMEND. VERTRAUTHEIT, BRILLIA
IST KLAR UND KRÄFTIG.
DANN ENTFERNT SICH DIE SITUATI-
ON, WIRD ABSTRAKTER / GERÄUSCH-
HAFT MUSIKALISCH GEBROCHEN UND
VOM ILLUSTRATIVEN GELÖST
ES WIRD EINE UNBEKANNTE,
FREMDE KLANGLANDSCHAFT
UNVERTRAUT - DIESE BEIDEN E.-!
BENEN OSZILLIEREN HIN- UND HER.

B 1/8 oder 1/8
ES WURDE WASSER UMGEFÜLLT
ODER RAUSGEGOSSEN
GEFÜLLT, TRÖPFELND
SCHON EHER (SEHR FRÜH)

C TEIL A
DANN ABFOLGE VON SOUNDS
BÜCHSENVERSCHLUSS, STÜHLE
SCHIEBEN, SCHUBLADEN
ÖFFNEN, AUSGIESSEN, LEISE
VERRICHTUNGEN, EVENTUELL
SCHRITTE, DOSENÖFFNEN
RUMKRAMEN USW.
GERÄUSCH IMMER MIT GEGEN-
GERÄUSCHEN, IMMER ZWEI BIS
DREI GEGENEINANDER AUS
GESPIELT!

E Erster Teil
Also die Küche ist der Ort. Fängt mit Gong an
kleine Teile oder Ähnliches fallen runter...
Wasser tropft, wird eingefüllt, gefiltertes Ge-
räusch...harmonisch, passte gut zusammen...
Tee oder Wasser kochen...
Teekessel und Luftballon Quietschen...beim
Zusammendrücken... Luft raus...
später dann ein Teekessel mit Pfeife
oder Milchschäumen, essbar, auch Astgeräusche
In der Küche räumen, Hin- und Herräumen
Kessel mit Pfeife und oder wie Zünden des Gas-
Gasherds

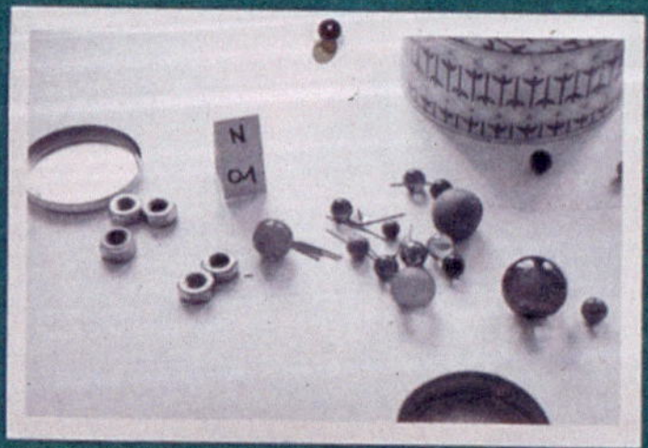

Spektrogramme der aqua...
(1 Teil - Luft)

B 1/8
GERÄUSCH NICHT VON PERSON
GEMACHT... BEOBACHTET!
BRETCHEN SCHIEBEN
AUF ANDERE BRETTCHEN
GEGENSTÄNDE BEWEGT
AUF EINER KÜCHENZEILE
MANCHMAL WAREN AUCH
MEHRERE ZUGLEICH!
JEMAND IST DIE GANZE
ZEIT AKTIV...

A ANFANG
GONG
AM ANFANG TAGESSCHAUGONG
FERNSEHER LÄUFT IM HINTER-
GRUND UND JEMAND MACHT
WAS NEBENBEI, SCHAUT NICHT
FERN - BEKOMMT ES NICHT MIT!

K ANFANG
EINGANGS IST DA EIN GONG
WIE BEI DEN NEWS
ZEITLICHE EINORDNUNG ETWA
ACHT UHR MORGENS ODER
ABENDS ODER AUCH ZEHN

B 1/3
Zischen, Piepsen, so, wie wenn
meine Nebenhöhlen aufgehen!
Nach 40-50 Sekunden
- Erleichterung pur!-
sehr sehr lang................

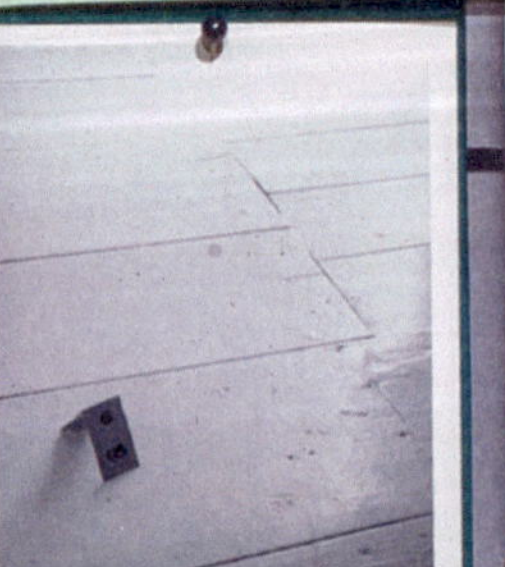

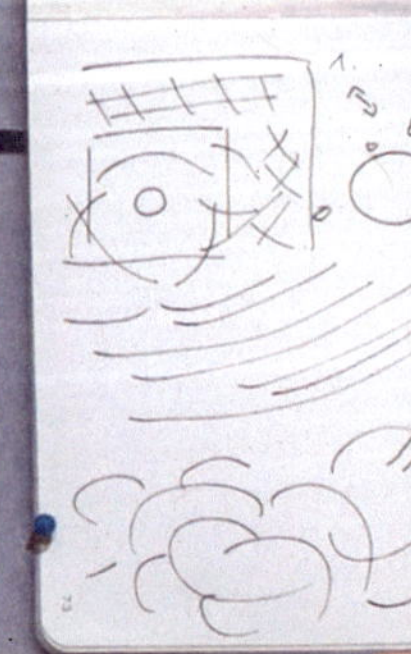

C TEIL 1
THEATERGONG
ALS ZEICHEN!

D teil 1
TAGESSCHAUGONG;!

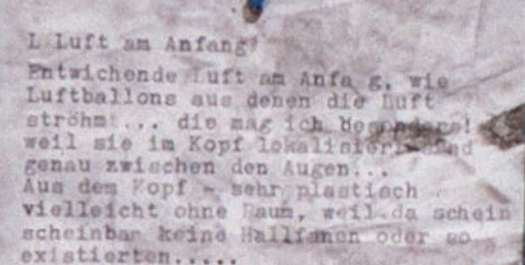

L Luft am Anfang?
Entwichende Luft am Anfang, wie
Luftballons aus denen die Luft
strömt... die mag ich besonders!
weil sie im Kopf lokalisiert und
genau zwischen den Augen...
Aus dem Kopf - sehr plastisch
vielleicht ohne Raum, weil da schein-
scheinbar keine Hallfahnen oder so
existierten.....

M WOHNRAUM - KÜCHE
MÜCKE - MIT GROSSEM DURCHHALTEVER-
MÖGEN - DIE TONAL CHROMATISCH ABFÄLLT
VERÄNDERT SICH - SUMMEN UND SIRREN

I ANFANG
MARKANT...

C TEIL A
MUSIKALISCHER
HINTERGRUNDAKKORD
MODULIERTES BRUMMEN
WIRD INTENSIVER UND VON
2. GERÄUSCHFLÄCHE
UNTERSTÜTZT

J ANFANG
WÄRME,
GESTALT
STANZ-
GEN KL...
VERBIND...

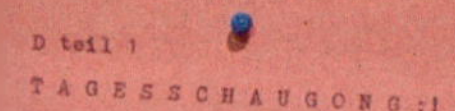

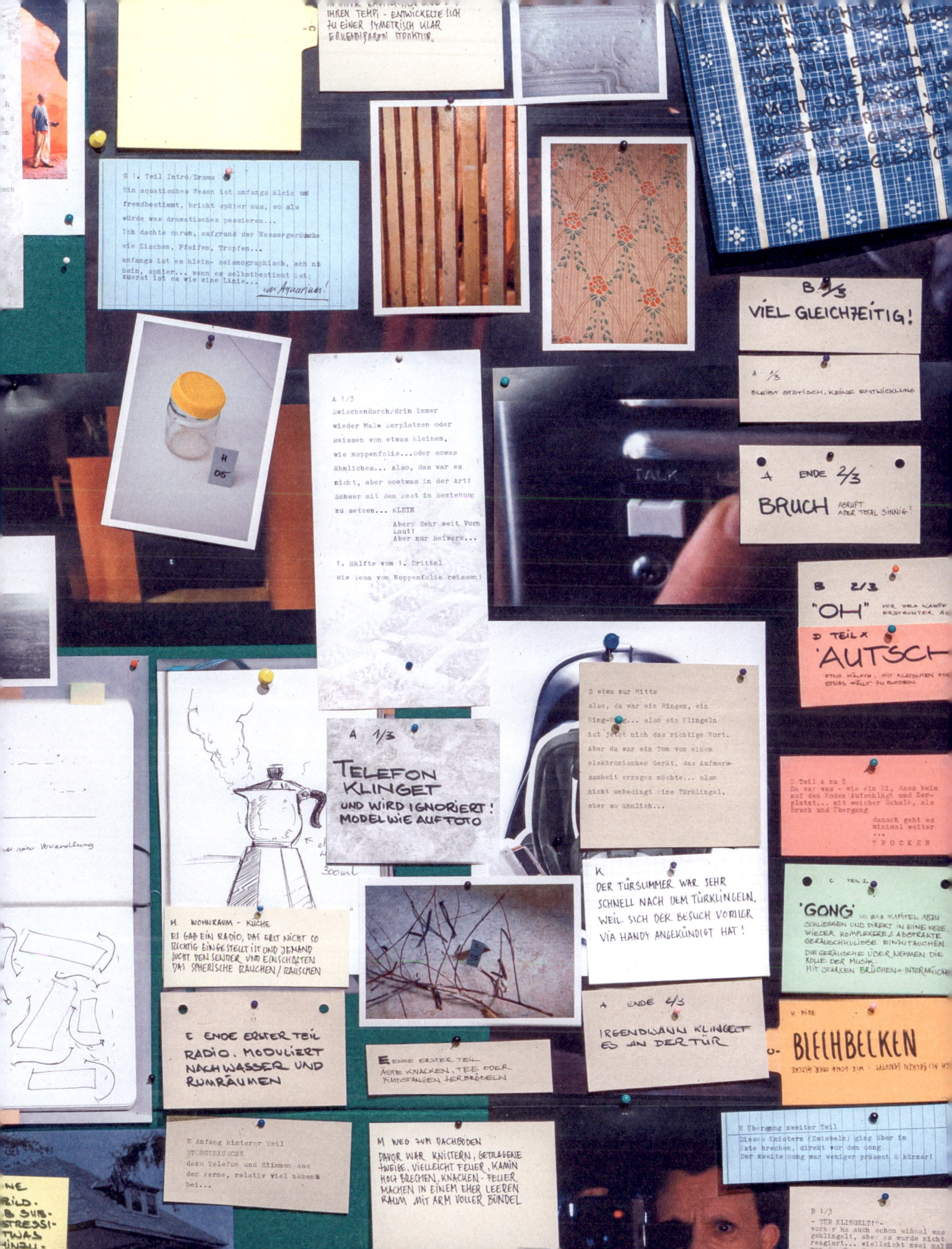

G 1. Teil Intro/Drama
Ein aquatisches Wesen ist anfangs klein und fremdbestimmt, bricht später aus, so als würde was dramatisches passieren...
Ich dachte daran, aufgrund der Wassergeräusche wie Zischen, Pfeifen, Tropfen...
anfangs ist es klein- seismographisch, ach nö nein, später... wenn es selbstbestimmt ist; zuerst ist es wie eine Linie...
im Aquarium!

A 1/3
Zwischendurch/drin immer wieder Mal* zerplatzen oder Reissen von etwas kleinem, wie Noppenfolie...oder sowas Ähnliches... Also, das war es nicht, aber soetwas in der Art! Schwer mit dem Rest in beziehung zu setzen... KLEIN
Aber Sehr weit Vorn
Laut!
Aber nur Beiwerk...
1. Hälfte vom 1. Drittel wie Tema von Noppenfolie reissen!

B 1/3
VIEL GLEICHZEITIG!

A 1/3
BLEIBT STATISCH, KEINE ENTWICKLUNG

A ENDE 2/3
BRUCH ABRUPT ABER TOTAL SINNIG

B 2/3
"OH" VOR DEM KAMPF ERSTAUNTER AU
D TEIL X
'AUTSCH'
ETWA HÄLFTE, MIT KLATSCHEN ODER ETWAS FÄLLT ZU BODEN

G etwa zur Mitte
also, da war ein Ringen, ein Ring-Ring... also ein Klingeln ist jetzt nich das richtige Wort. Aber da war ein Ton von einem elektronischen Gerät, das Aufmerksamkeit erregen möchte... also nicht unbedingt eine Türklingel, aber so ähnlich...

K
DER TÜRSUMMER WAR SEHR SCHNELL NACH DEM TÜRKLINGELN, WEIL SICH DER BESUCH VORHER VIA HANDY ANGEKÜNDIGT HAT!

A ENDE 1/3
IRGENDWANN KLINGELT ES AN DER TÜR

A 1/3
TELEFON KLINGELT UND WIRD IGNORIERT! MODEL WIE AUF FOTO
300 ml

M WOHNRAUM - KÜCHE
ES GAB EIN RADIO, DAS ERST NICHT SO RICHTIG EINGESTELLT IST UND JEMAND SUCHT DEN SENDER UND EINSCHALTEN DAS SPHERISCHE RAUCHEN / RAUSCHEN

E ENDE ERSTER TEIL
RADIO, MODULIERT NACH WASSER UND RUMRÄUMEN

E ENDE ERSTER TEIL
ÄSTE KNACKEN, TEE ODER ZIMTSTANGEN ZERBRÖCKELN

D Teil A zu B
Da war was - wie ein Ei, dass beim auf den Boden Aufschlägt und zerplatzt... mit weicher Schale, als Bruch und Übergang
danach geht es minimal weiter
...
TROCKEN

C TEIL 2
'GONG' UM DAS KAPITEL ABZU SCHLIESSEN UND DIREKT IN EINE NEUE WIEDER KOMPLEXERE / ABSTRAKTE GERÄUSCHKULISSE EINZUTAUCHEN.
DIE GERÄUSCHE ÜBERNEHMEN DIE ROLLE DER MUSIK.
MIT STARKEN BRÜCHEN + INTERAKTION

H MITE
BLECHBELKEN

E Übergang zweiter Teil
Dieses Knistern (Zwiebeln) ging über in Äste brechen, direkt vor dem Gong
Der zweite Gong war weniger präsent & kürzer!

E Anfang hinterer Teil
STÖRGERÄUSCHE
dazu Telefon und Atismen aus der Ferne, relativ viel neben bei.

M WEG ZUM DACHBODEN
DAVOR WAR KNISTERN, GETRAGENE ZWEIGE, VIELLEICHT FEUER, KAMIN HOLZ BRECHEN, KNACKEN - FEUER MACHEN IN EINEM EHER LEEREN RAUM, MIT ARM VOLLER BÜNDEL

B 1/3
- TÜR KLINGELT! -
vorher hat auch schon einmal was geklingelt, aber es wurde nicht reagiert... vielleicht war es

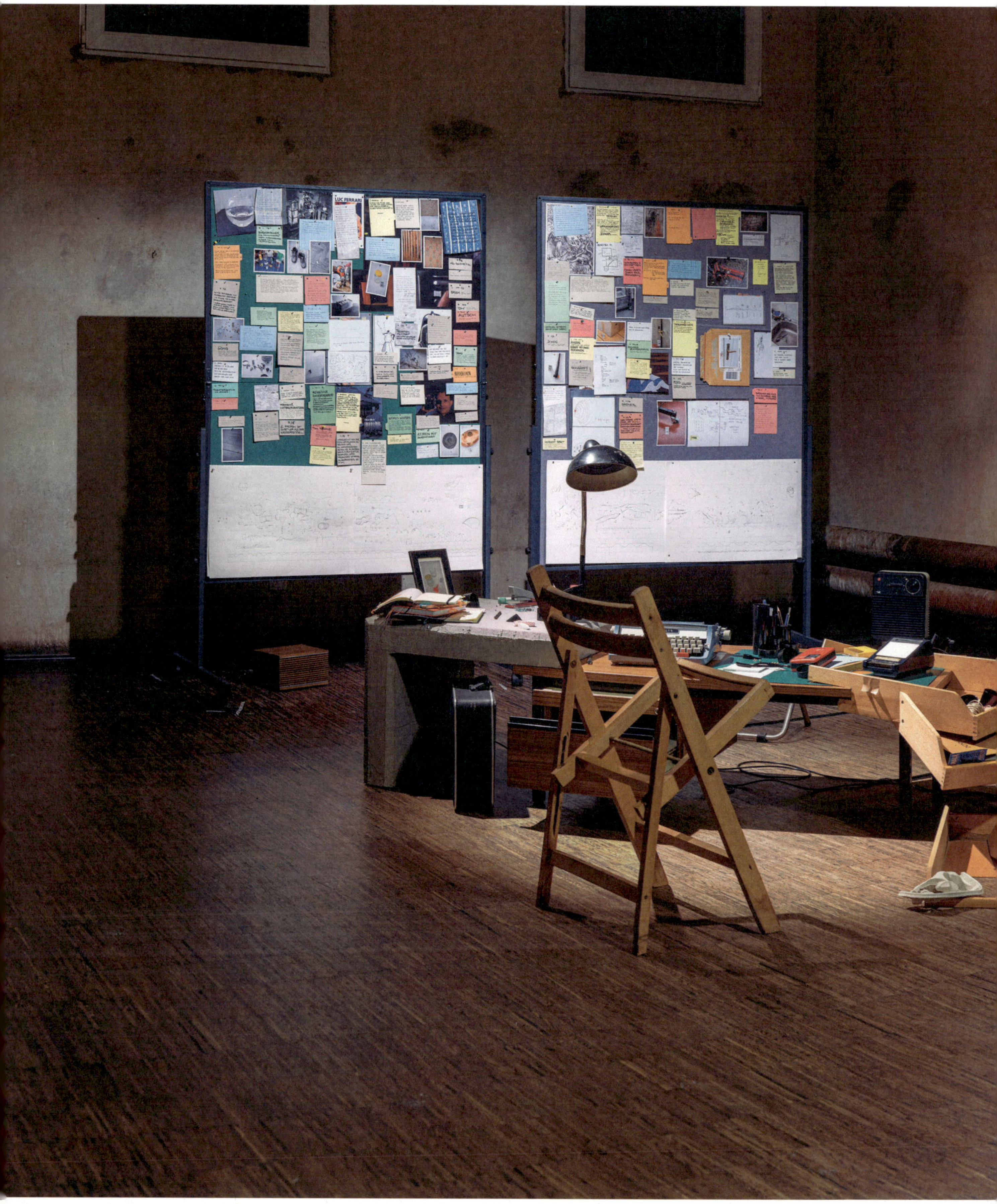

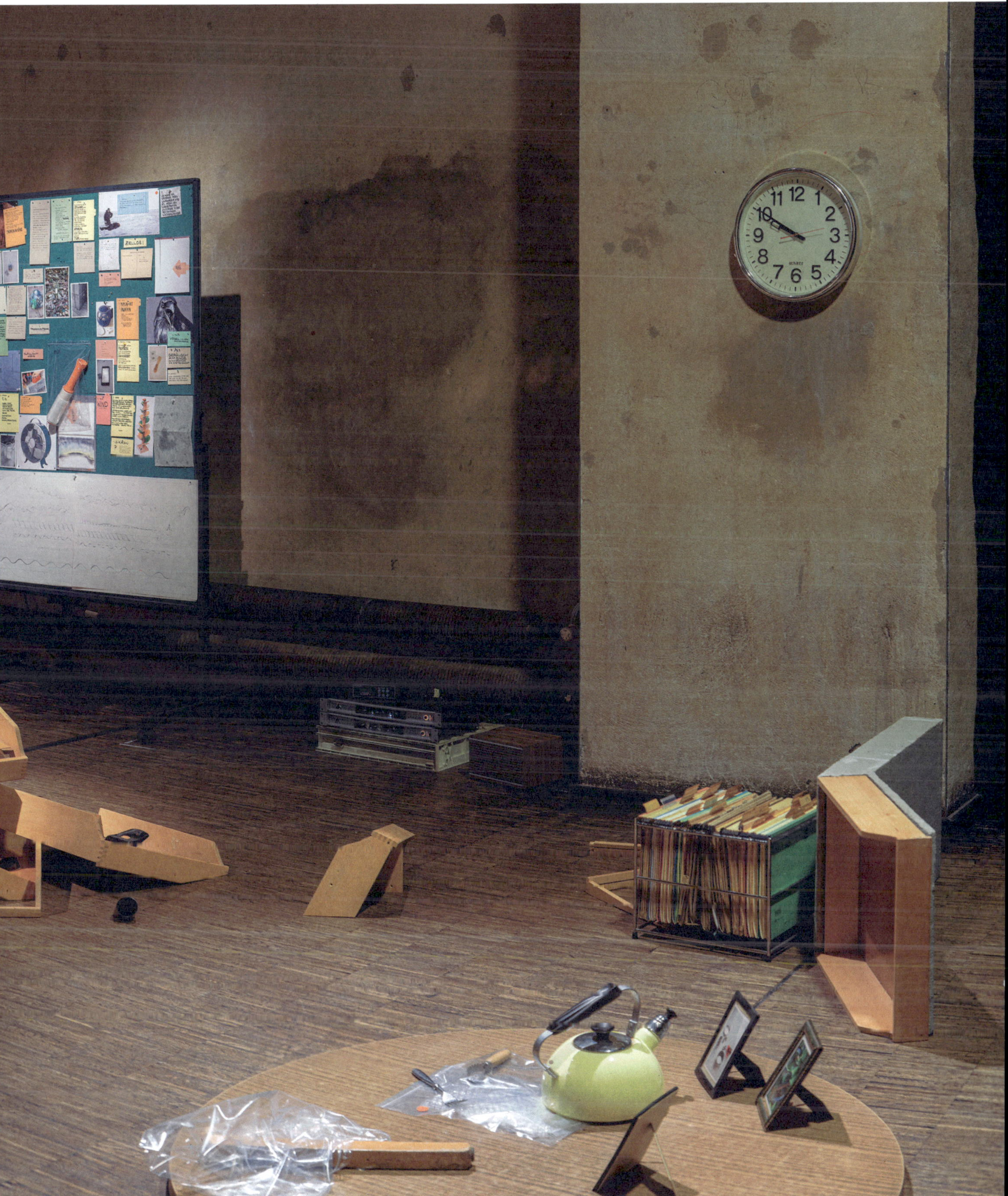

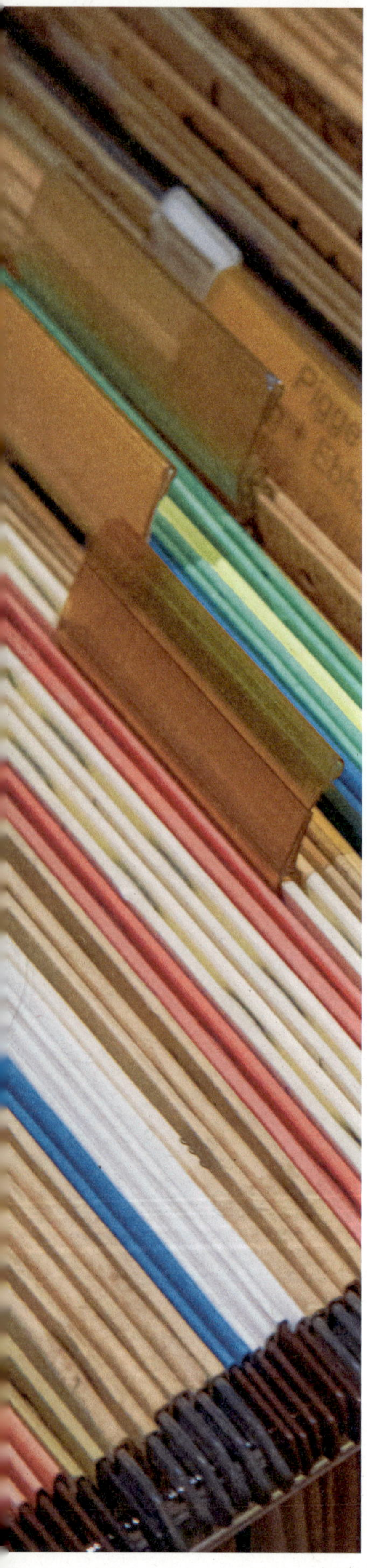

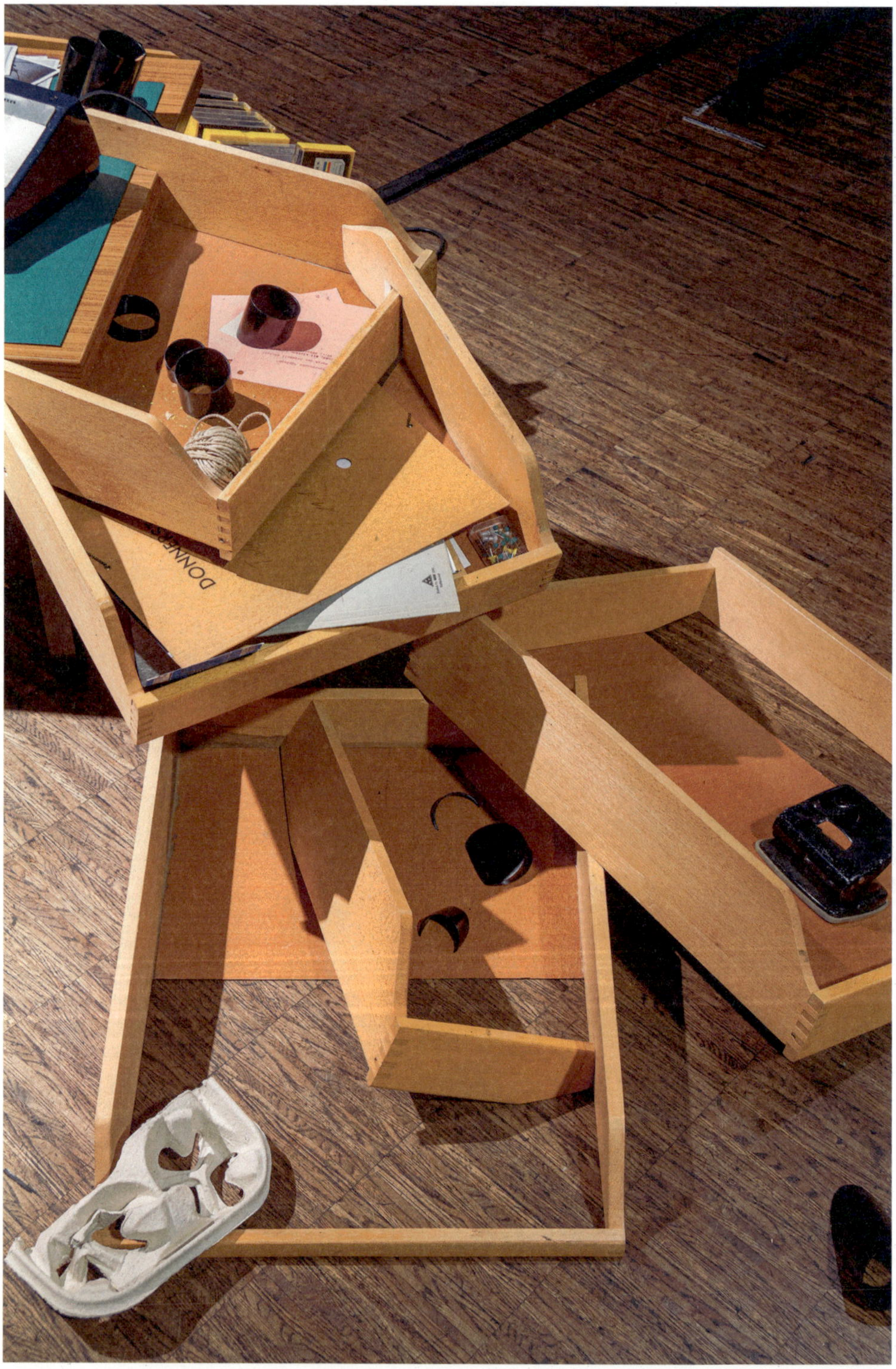

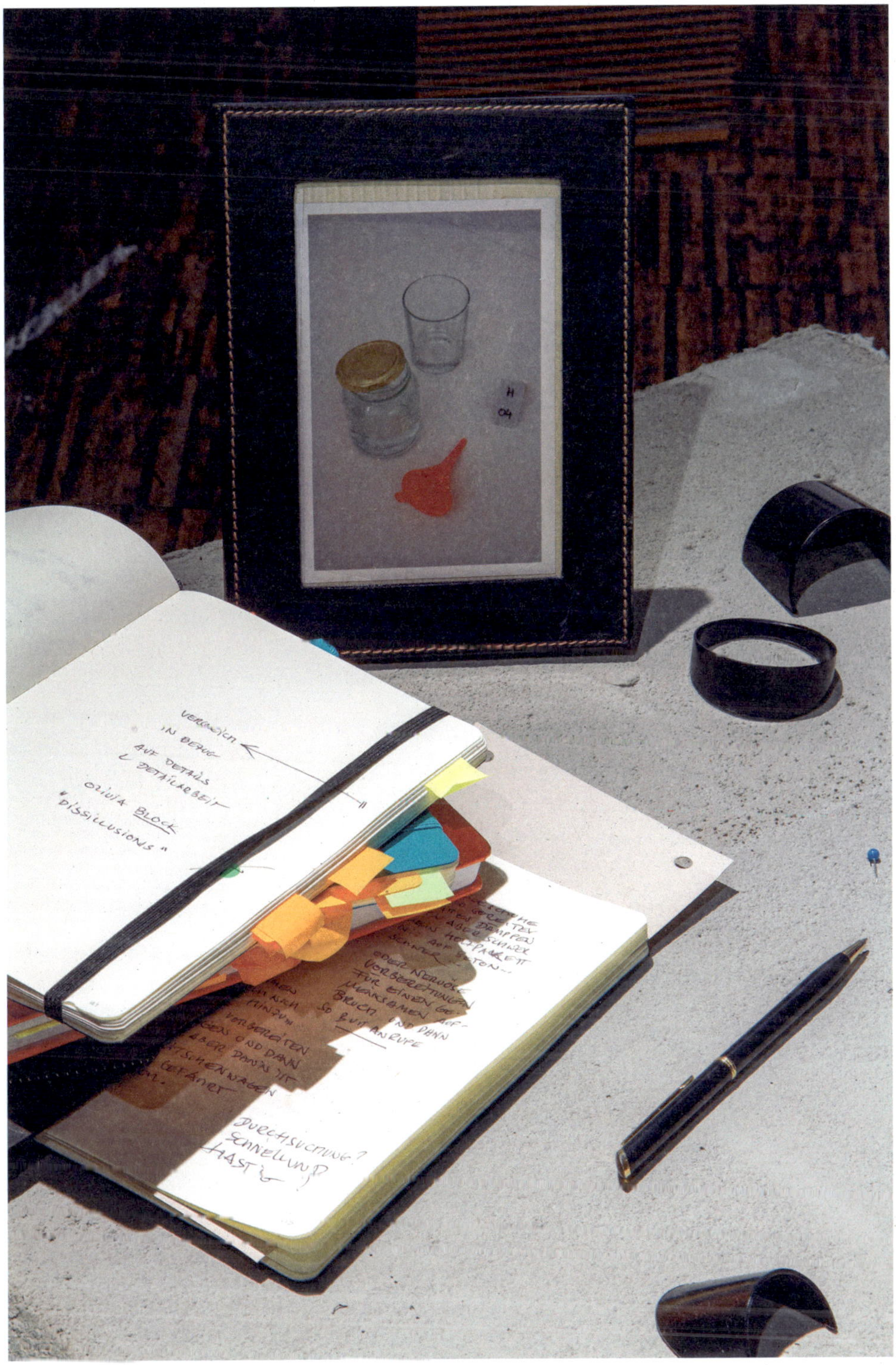

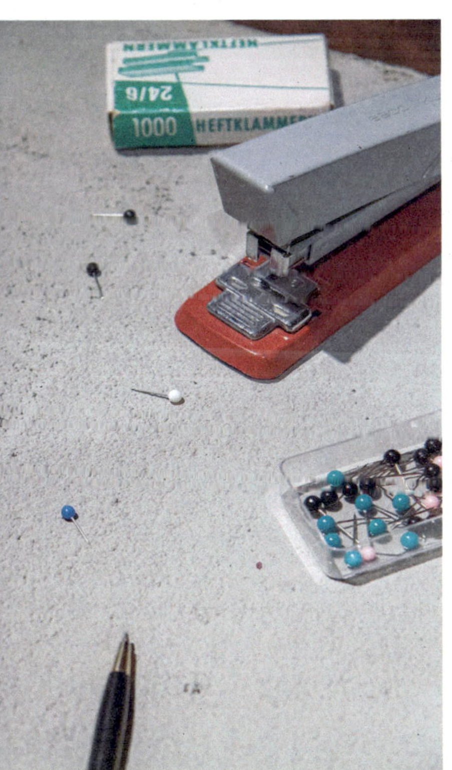

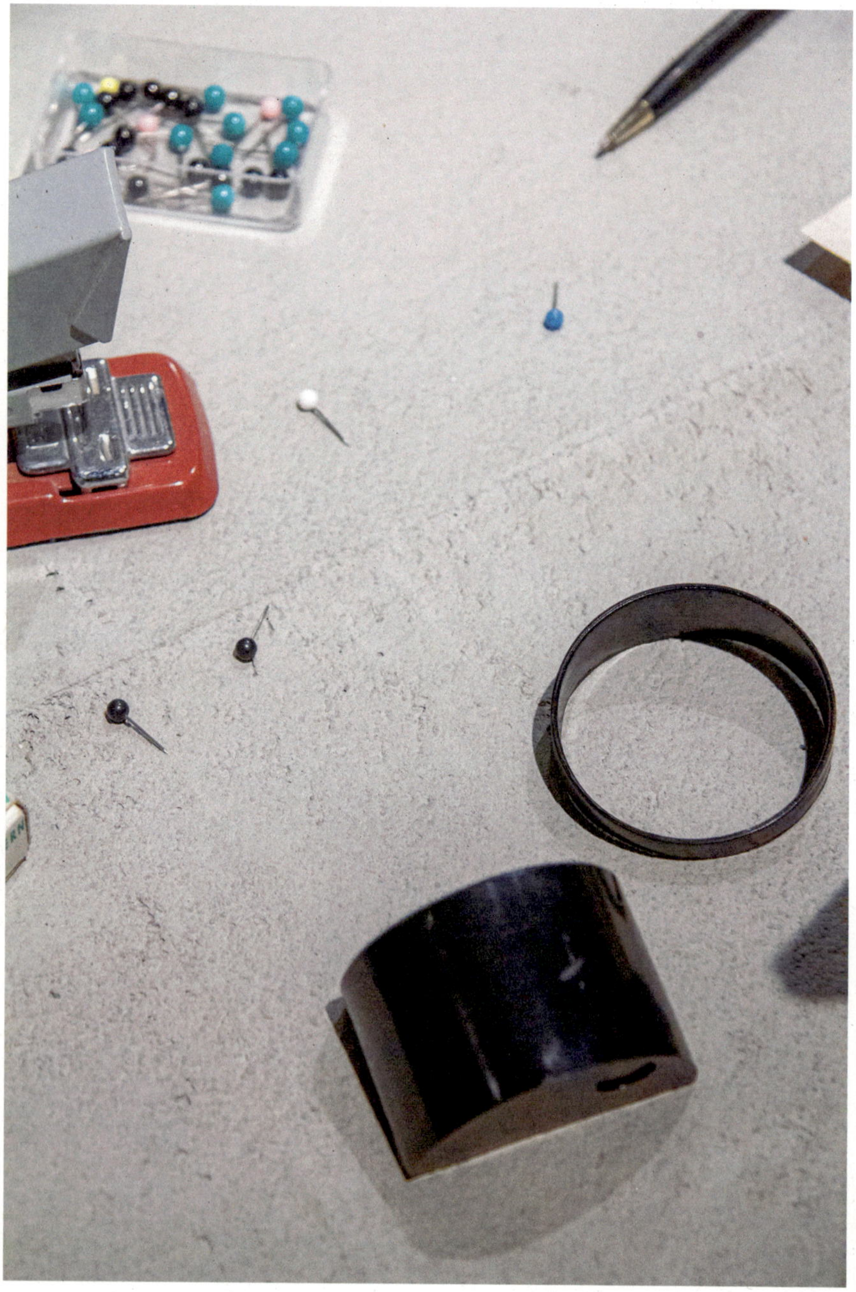

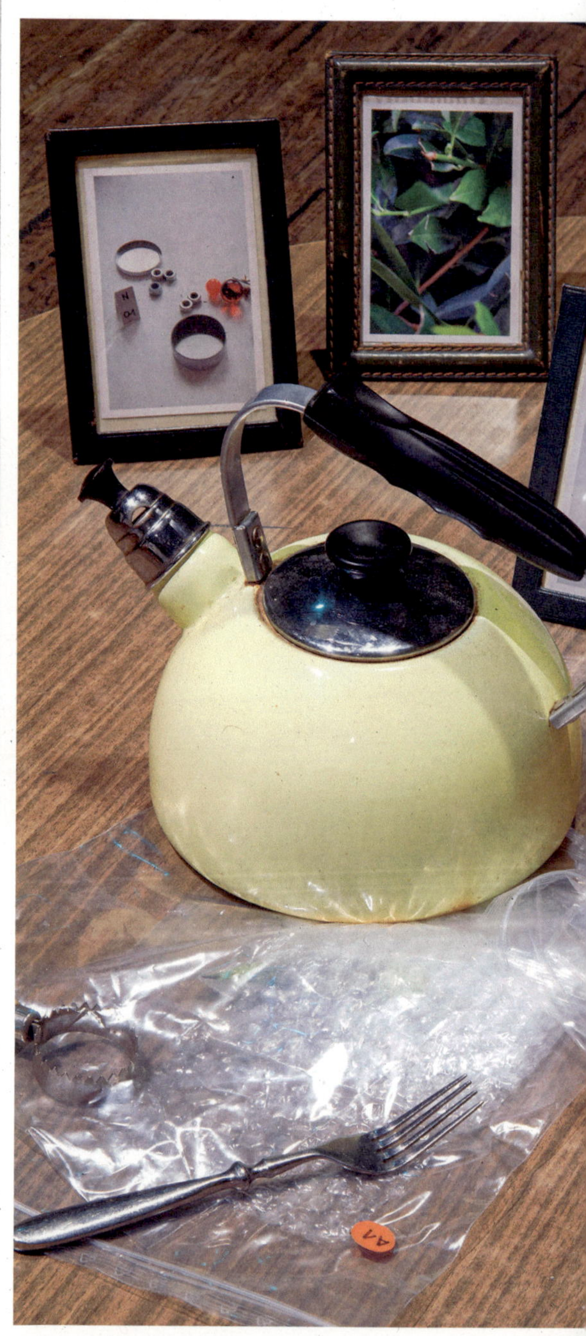

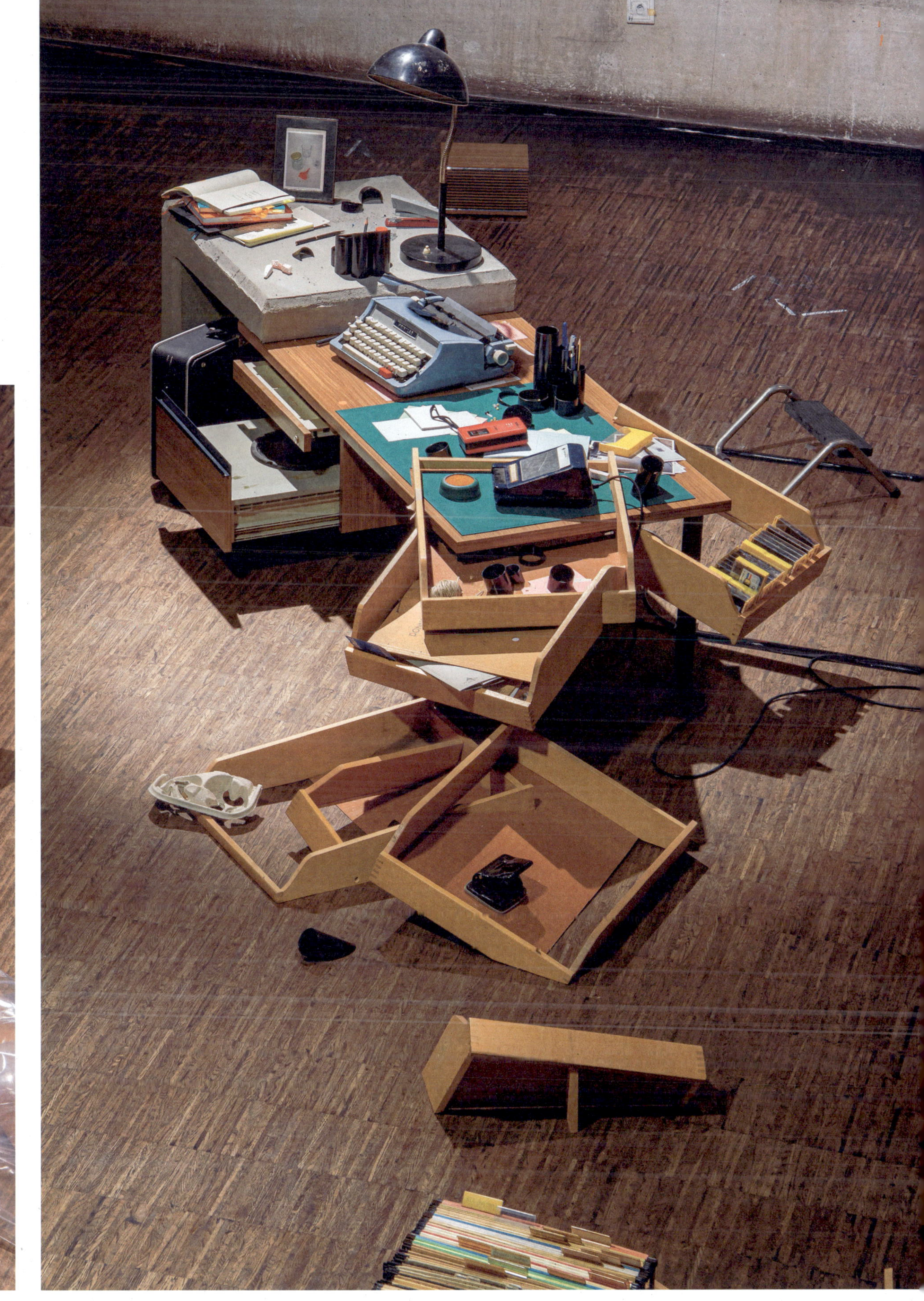

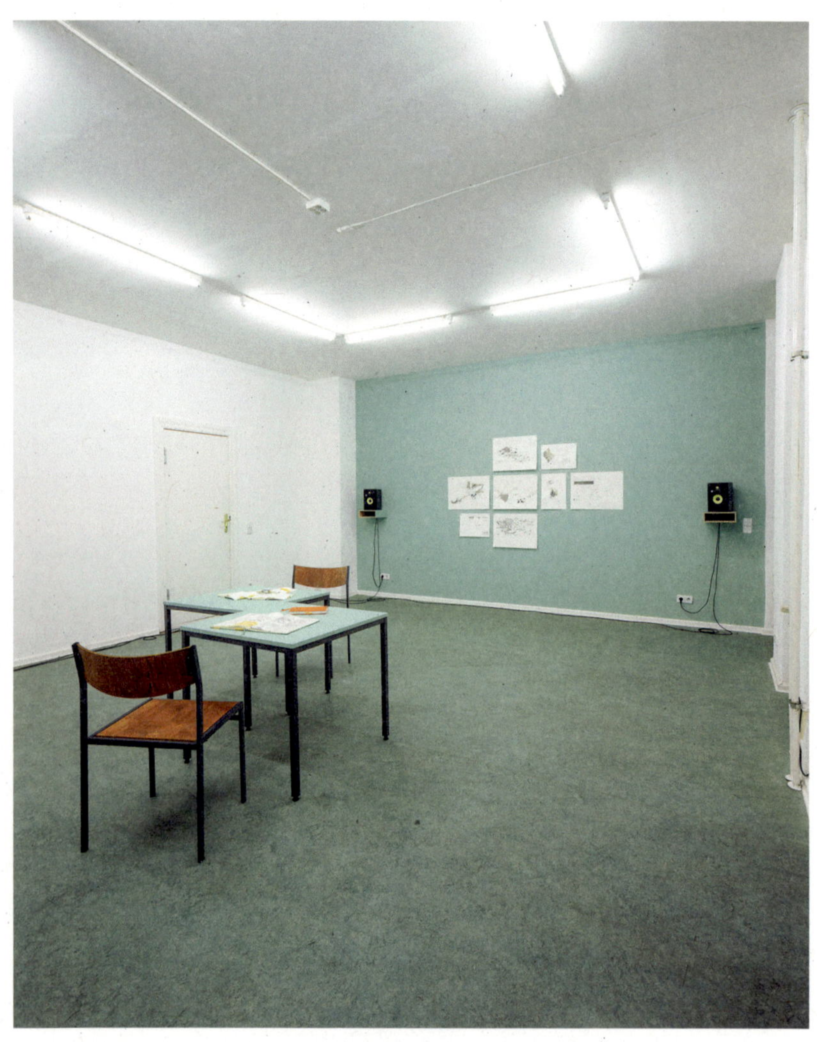

Traces—Of
(Chapter 2)

2022

ongoing artistic research project
**» Continuation of the Artistic
Investigations Into the Reconstruction
of an Electroacoustic Composition**

Material:
diverse notebooks with
written notes from the
interviews and notes on the
artistic process involved in
the piece, musical graphics
tables, chairs, wall consoles,
acrylic paint, magnets, active
loudspeakers, cables
and playback equipment **/**
600 x 400 x 250 cm
(set-up variable)

Sound :
4-channel acousmatic
composition **/** dynamic
audio-play-like arrangement **/**
recordings of the interviews,
presumably recognized
noises from the original
composition, which have
been re-enacted concretely
and recorded by the
experiment participants
during the interview,
everyday sound actions,
room recordings from offices
and public buildings, bars,
private apartments and
vehicle cabs during drives **/**
loop (46:09) **/** CD 1 — track 6

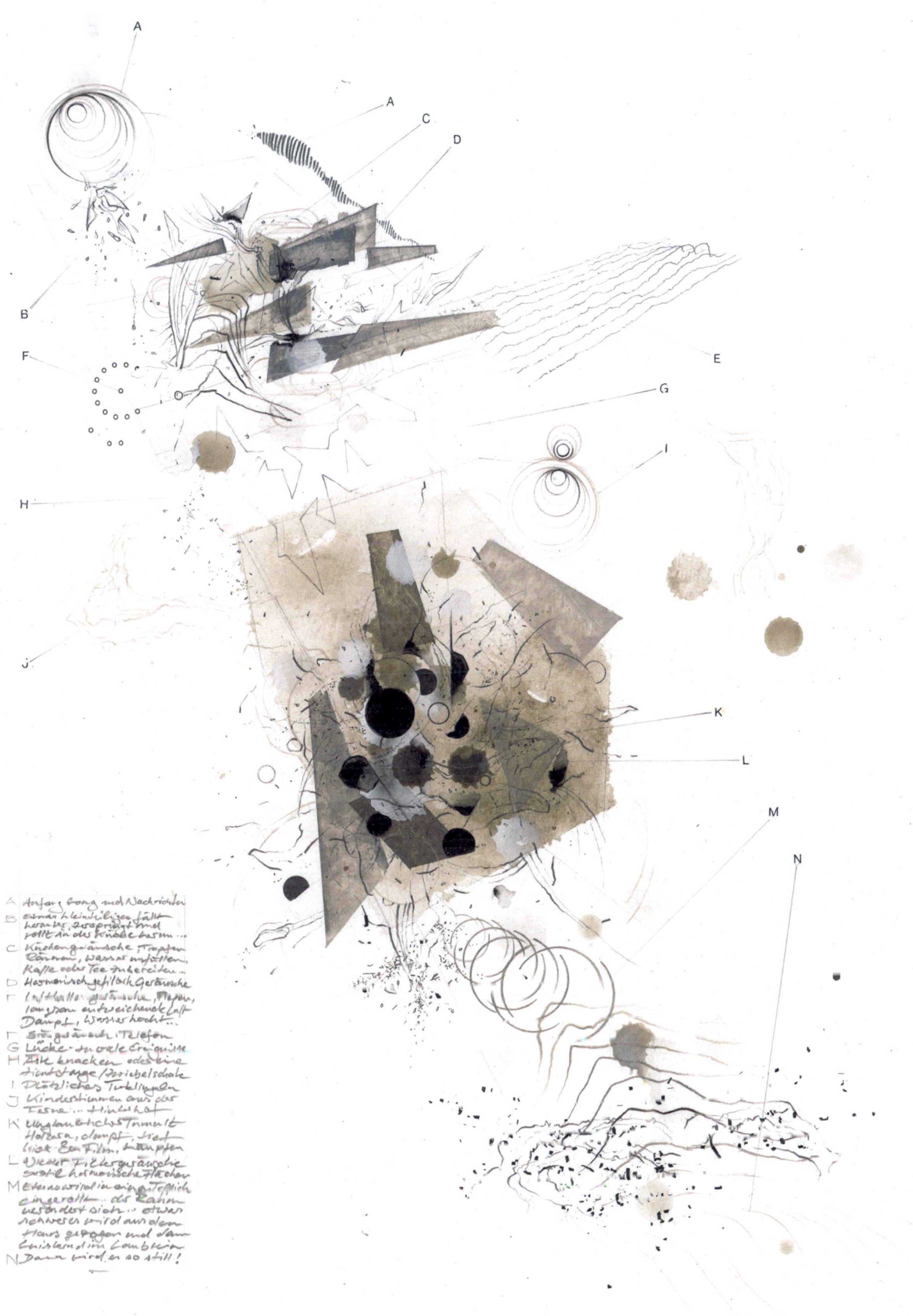
A Anfang Gong und Nachrichten
B etwas Kleinteiliges fällt
   herunter, zerspringt und
   rollt in die Knochen herum …
C Küchengeräusche; Tropfen
   Rinnen, Wasser einfüllen,
   Kaffee oder Tee zubereiten …
D Harmonisch gefilterte Geräusche
E Luftballon geräusche, Maßen,
   langsam entweichende Luft
   Dampf, Wasser kocht …
F Stör geräusch, Telefon
G Lücke · zu viele Ereignisse
H Äste knacken oder eine
   Zündstange / Zwiebelschale
I Plötzliches Türklingeln
J Kinderstimmen aus der
   Ferne … Hintelhof
K unglaublicher Tumult
   Hafen, dampf, sied
   läuft Ein Film, abklopfen
L Viele Filtergeräusche
   exotil harmonische Flächen
M etwas wird in ein Tüllich
   eingerollt … der Rahmen
   verändert sich … etwas
   schweres wird aus dem
   Haus gezogen und dann
   Knistern, im Laub sein
N Dann wird es so still!

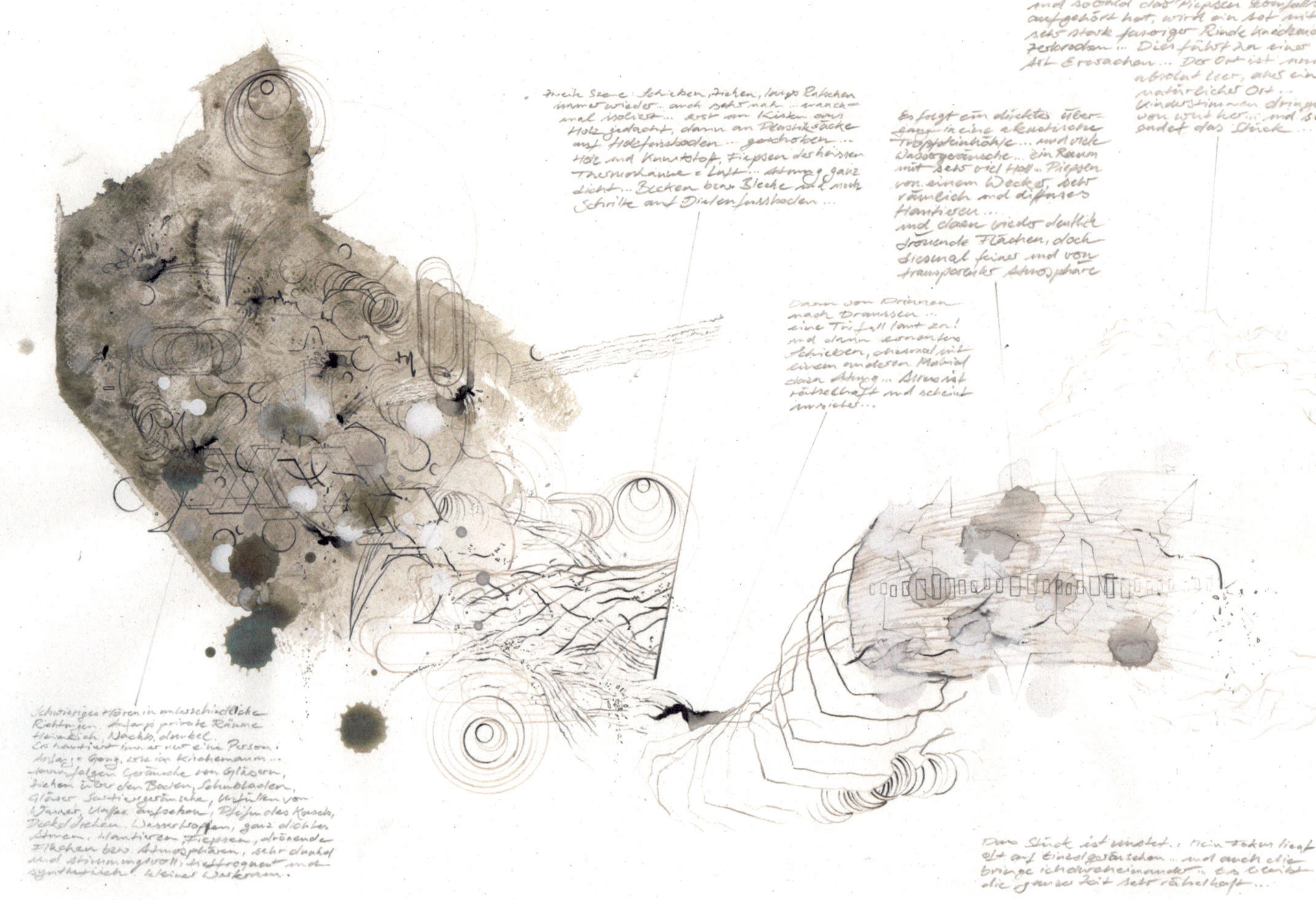

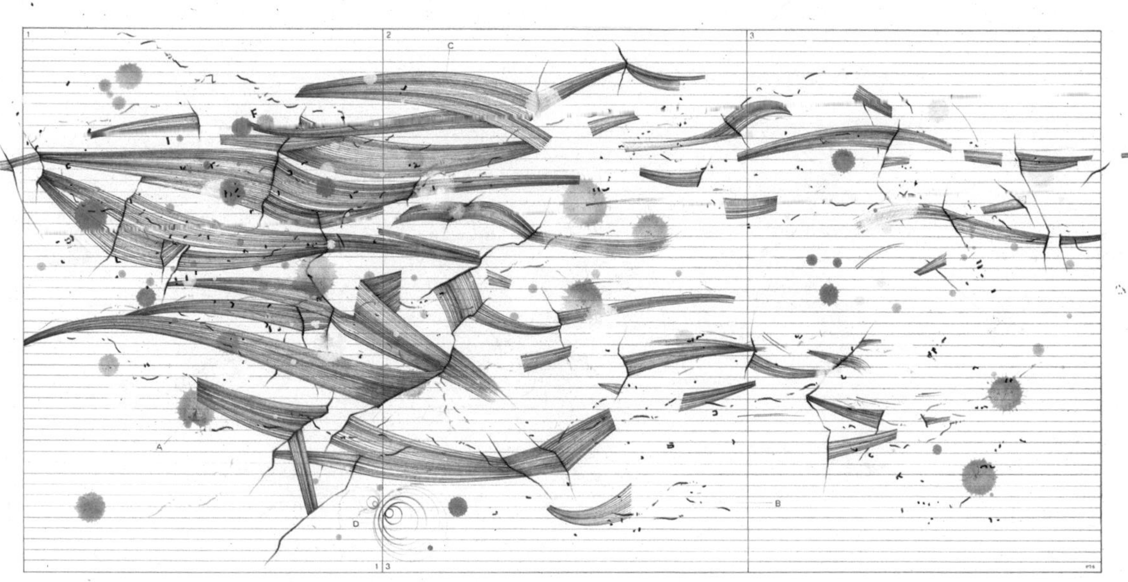

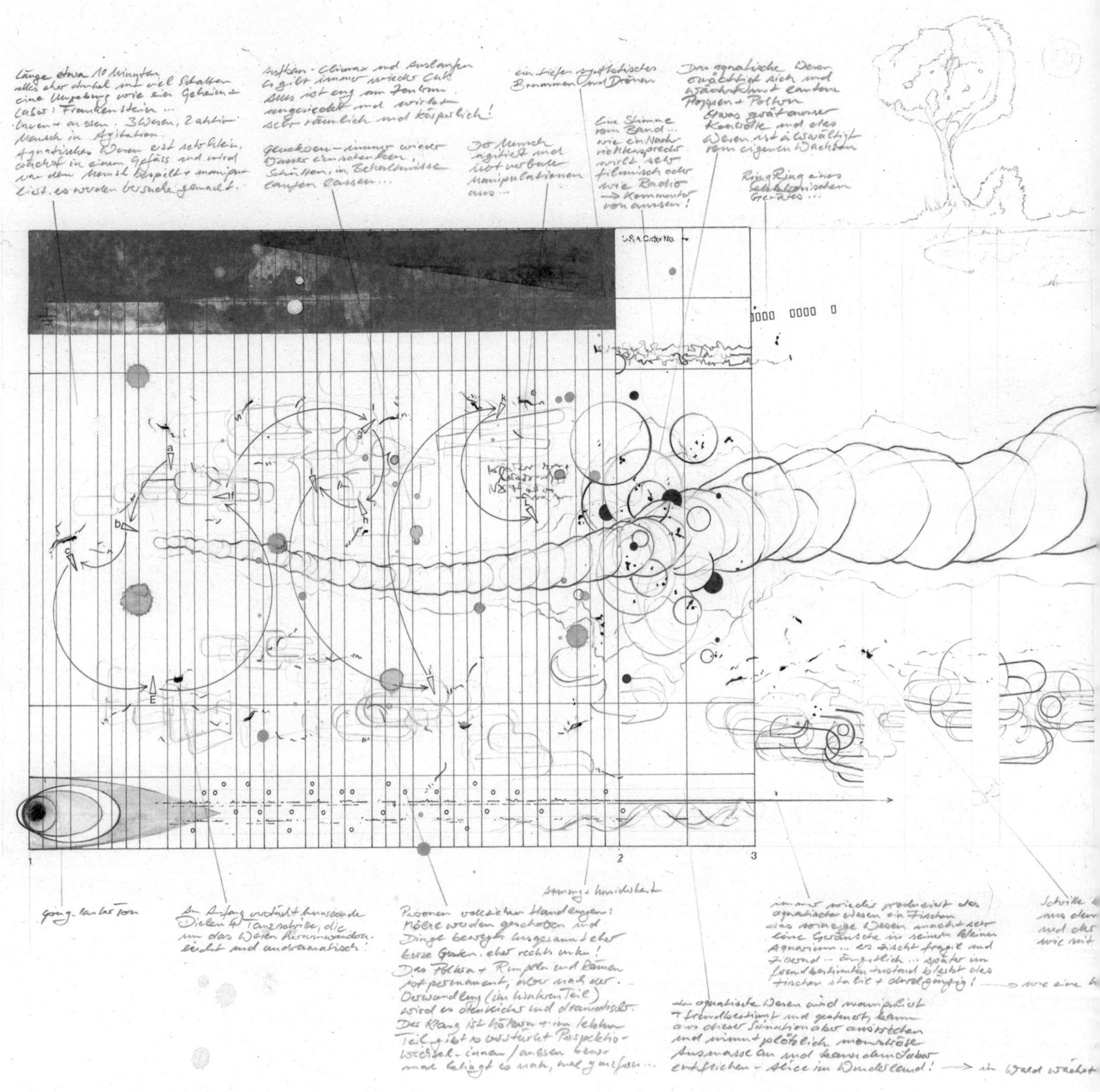

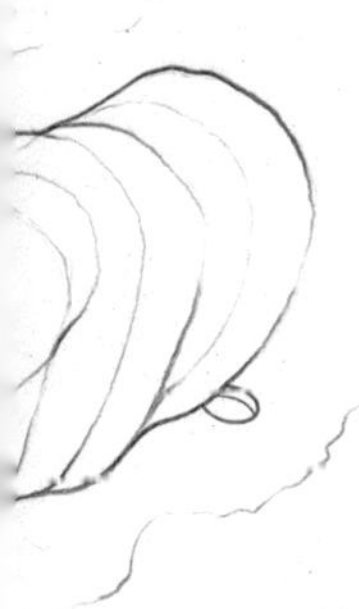

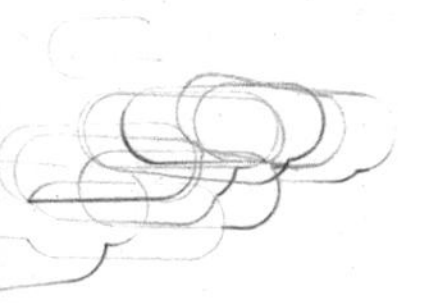

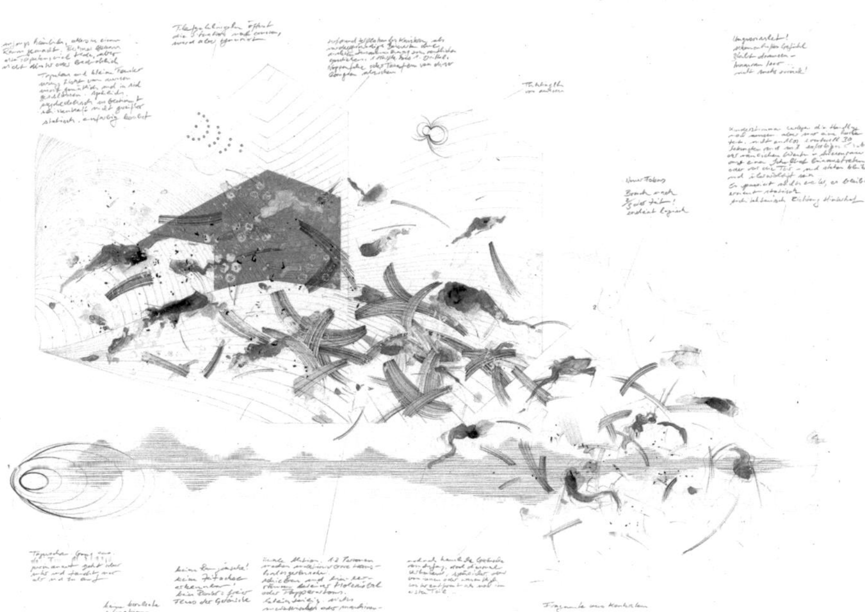

im Wald...

Monarch der
Entspannung und
des Surgleichs...

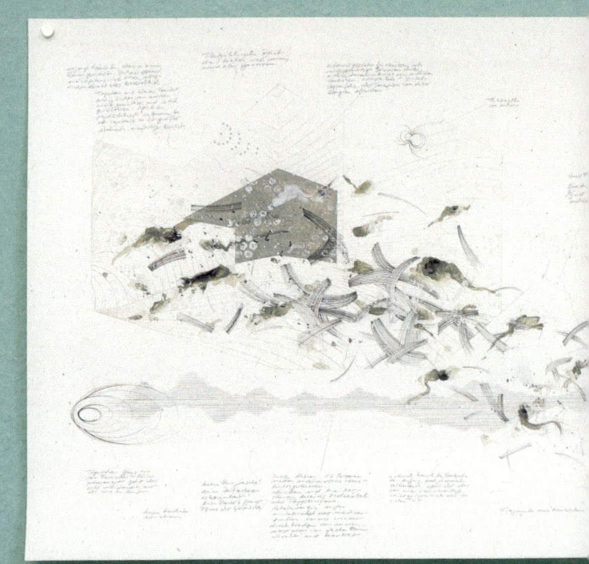

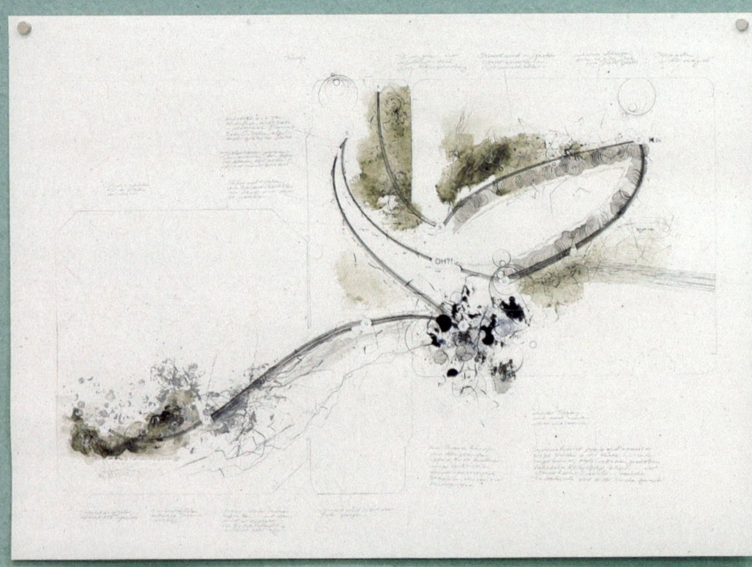

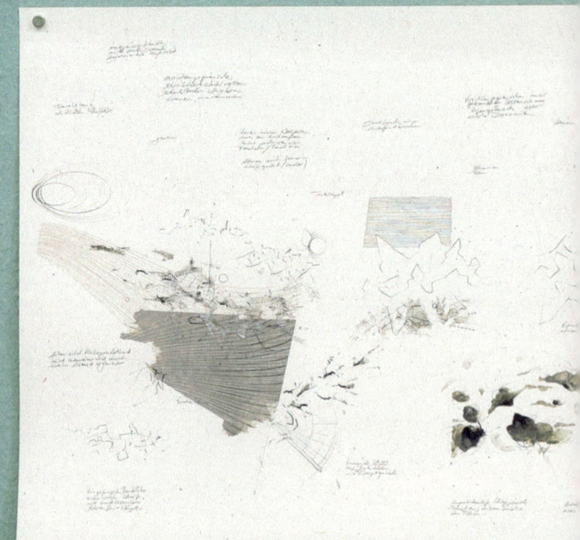

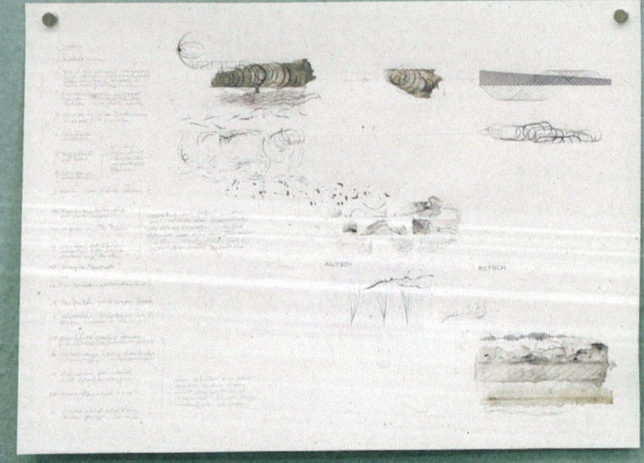

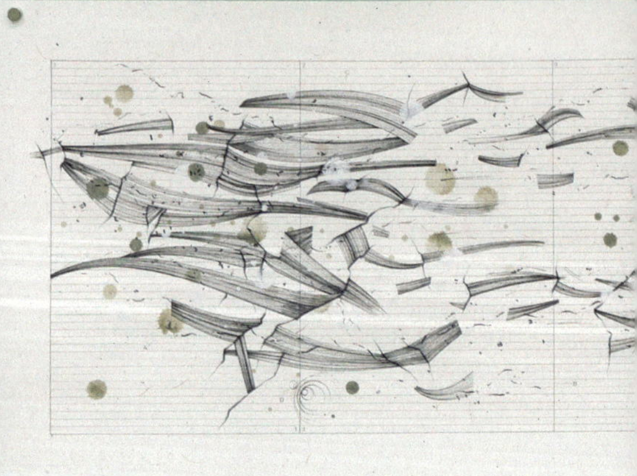

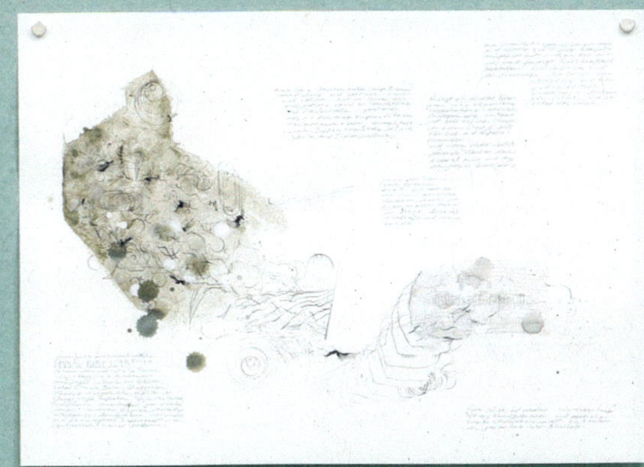

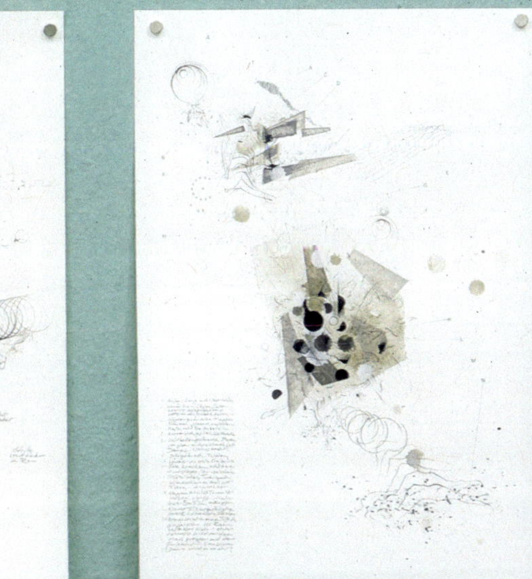

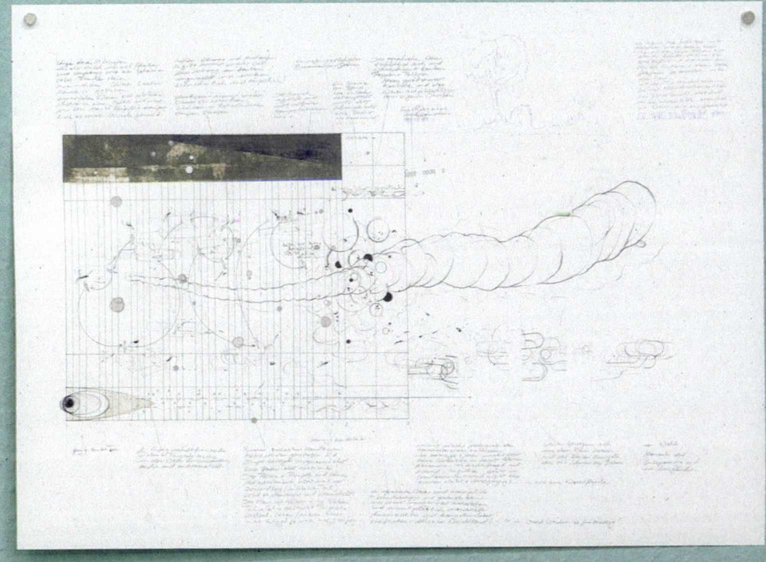

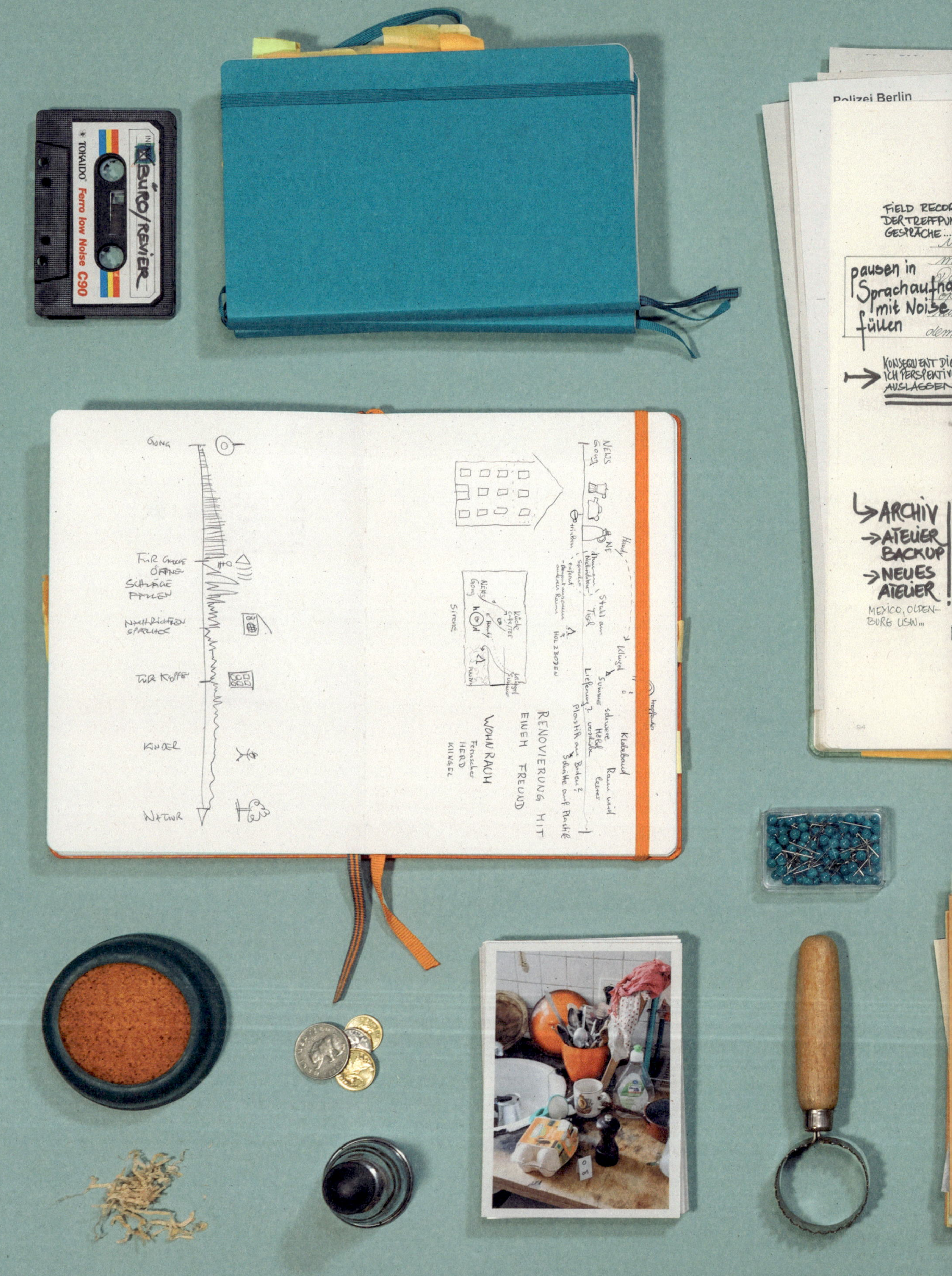

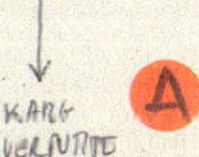
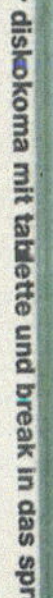
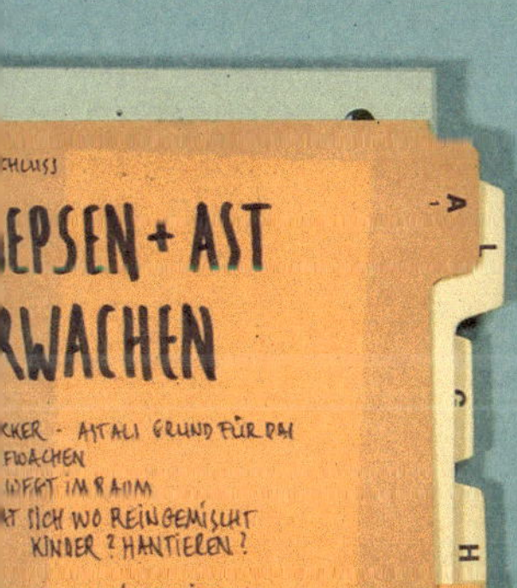
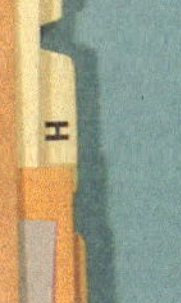
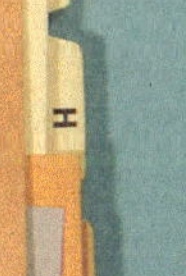
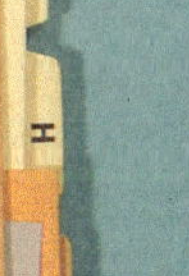
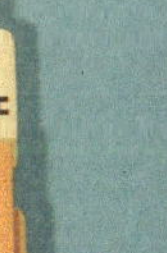
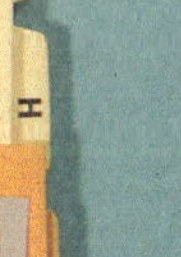
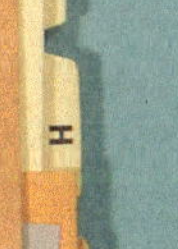
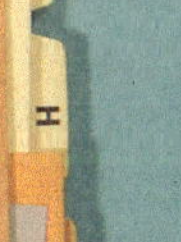
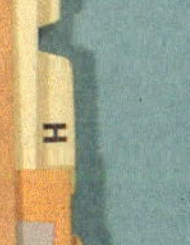
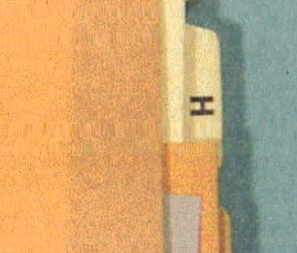
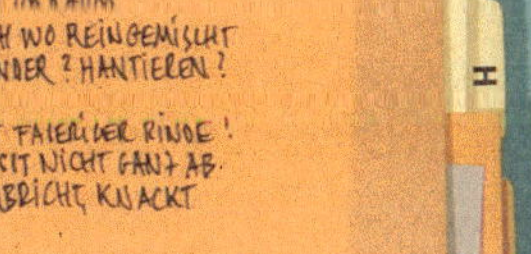
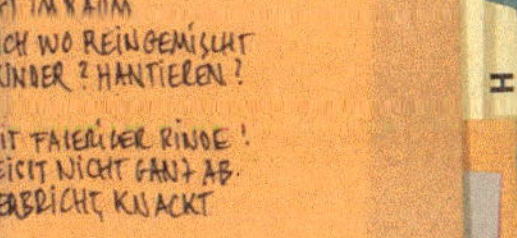
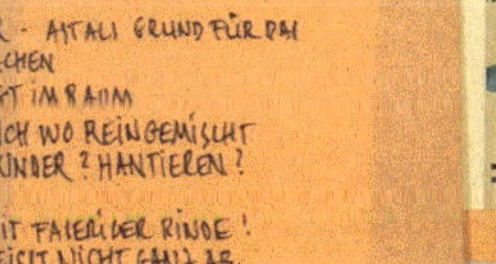

BERLIN

SURREALE COLLAGE

FIELD

DISCO

GEGENÜBER STELLUNG VON

ABER EVENTUELL DAS GLEICHE MIT BESTIMMTEN AUS SAGEN

übergeordnet

DRONES

BLACK OUT

wenn die phase des chaos ansetzt,
dann müssen sirenen kommen…
sirenen, die langsam verschwimmen

IDEEN FÜR
SOUNDS = FIELD REC.

STIMMEN

CUT UP COLLAGE KAKOPHONIE

DRONES
AUS STIMMEN GENERIERT UNTERLEGT

LEIERNDE TAPEAUFNAHMEN (AAB)
AUS VOCALTÖNEN

ZUM ENDE DEN SOUND DUMPFER?
DRONIGER ???

AUFZÄHLUNGEN
„„„„..

FOTOS MACHEN KLICKKLICK…

eine gegenüber stellung z.B
von 4 Kaffem aschinen!…
3 MÜCKEN os.

IDEE: AUFSTEHEN, BÜRO, DANN

übergang bar oder diskokoma mit tablette und break in das sprudeln...

TÜRKLOPFEN
2. BRUCH

HALL
LEERE

KARG
VERNUTZTE WÄNDE
NICHT GEMÜTLICH

GROBE DIELE

ALT

RAUE WÄNDE

NICHT LEER NICHT VOLL
NICHT/ENTWOHNT

EHER GESCHICHTE
JEMAND WIRD ÜBERWÄLTIGT UND GESCHLAGEN

VOM SOUND EHER SCHLÄGE AUF GEGENSTÄNDE, HART UND EI FEUCHTEN MENSCHLICHEN GERÄUSCHE WIE STÖHNEN ATMEN USW.

EHER MECHANISCH

KEIN GLAS ODER PORZELAN SONDERN KISTEN + HOLZ

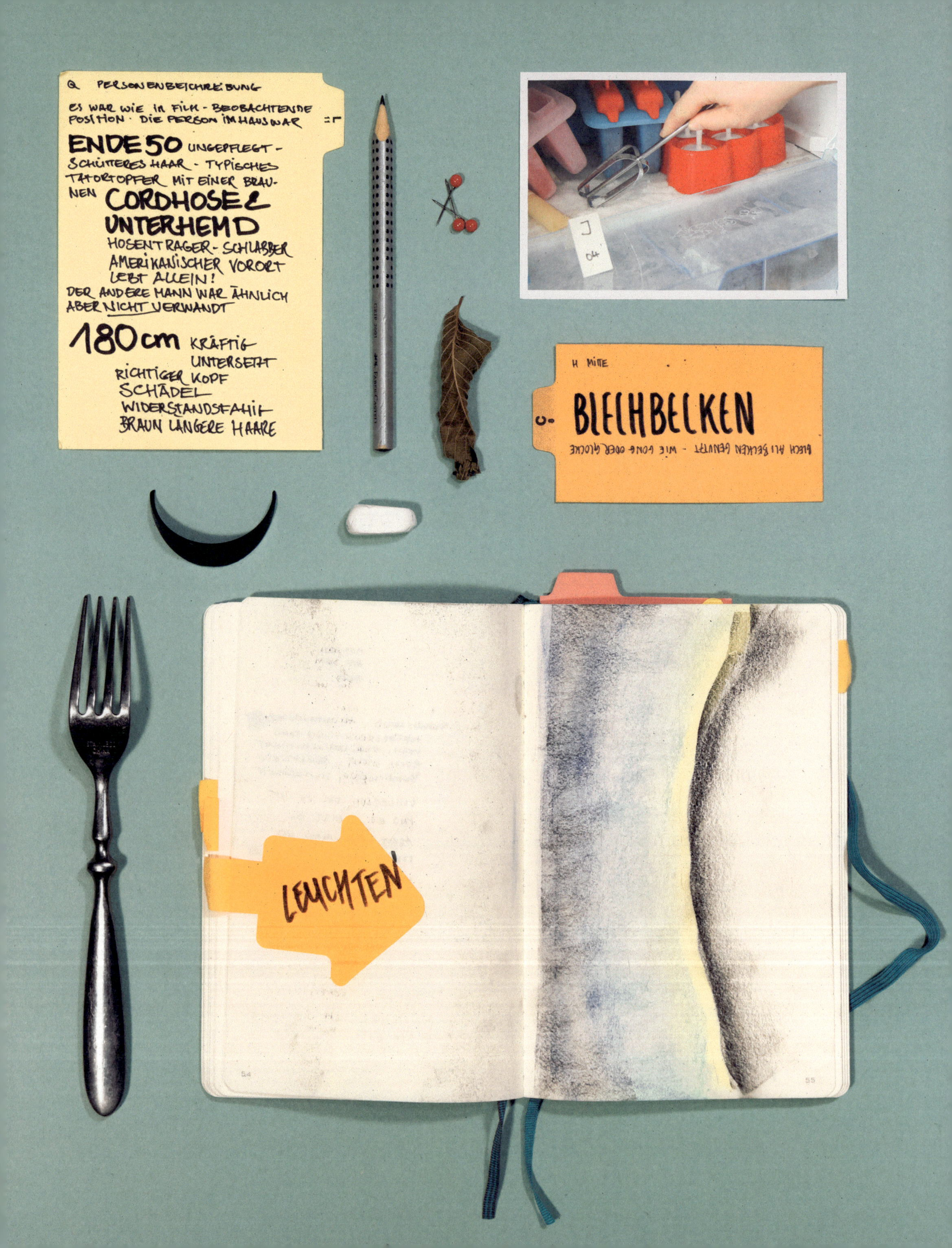

Q   PERSONENBESCHREIBUNG

ES WAR WIE IN FILM - BEOBACHTENDE
POSITION · DIE PERSON IM HAUS WAR
ENDE 50 UNGEPFLEGT -
SCHÜTTERES HAAR - TYPISCHES
TATORTOPFER MIT EINER BRAU-
NEN CORDHOSE &
UNTERHEMD
HOSENTRÄGER - SCHLABBER
AMERIKANISCHER VORORT
LEBT ALLEIN !
DER ANDERE MANN WAR ÄHNLICH
ABER NICHT VERWANDT

180 cm KRÄFTIG
UNTERSETZT
RICHTIGER KOPF
SCHÄDEL
WIDERSTANDSFÄHIG
BRAUN LÄNGERE HAARE

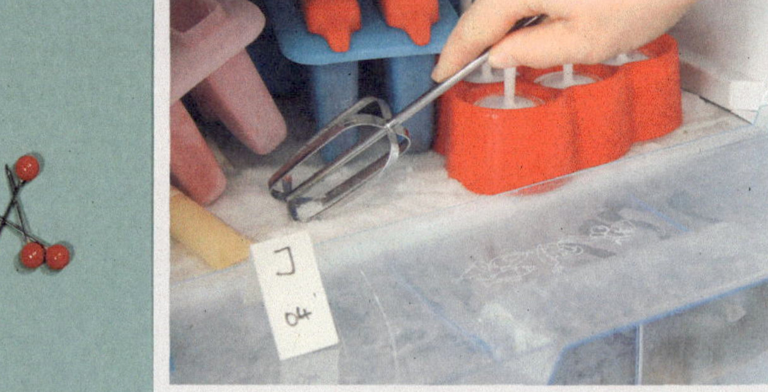
J
04

H MITTE

BLECHBECKEN
BLECH ALS BECKEN GENUTZT - WIE GONG ODER GLOCKE
C

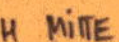
LEUCHTEN

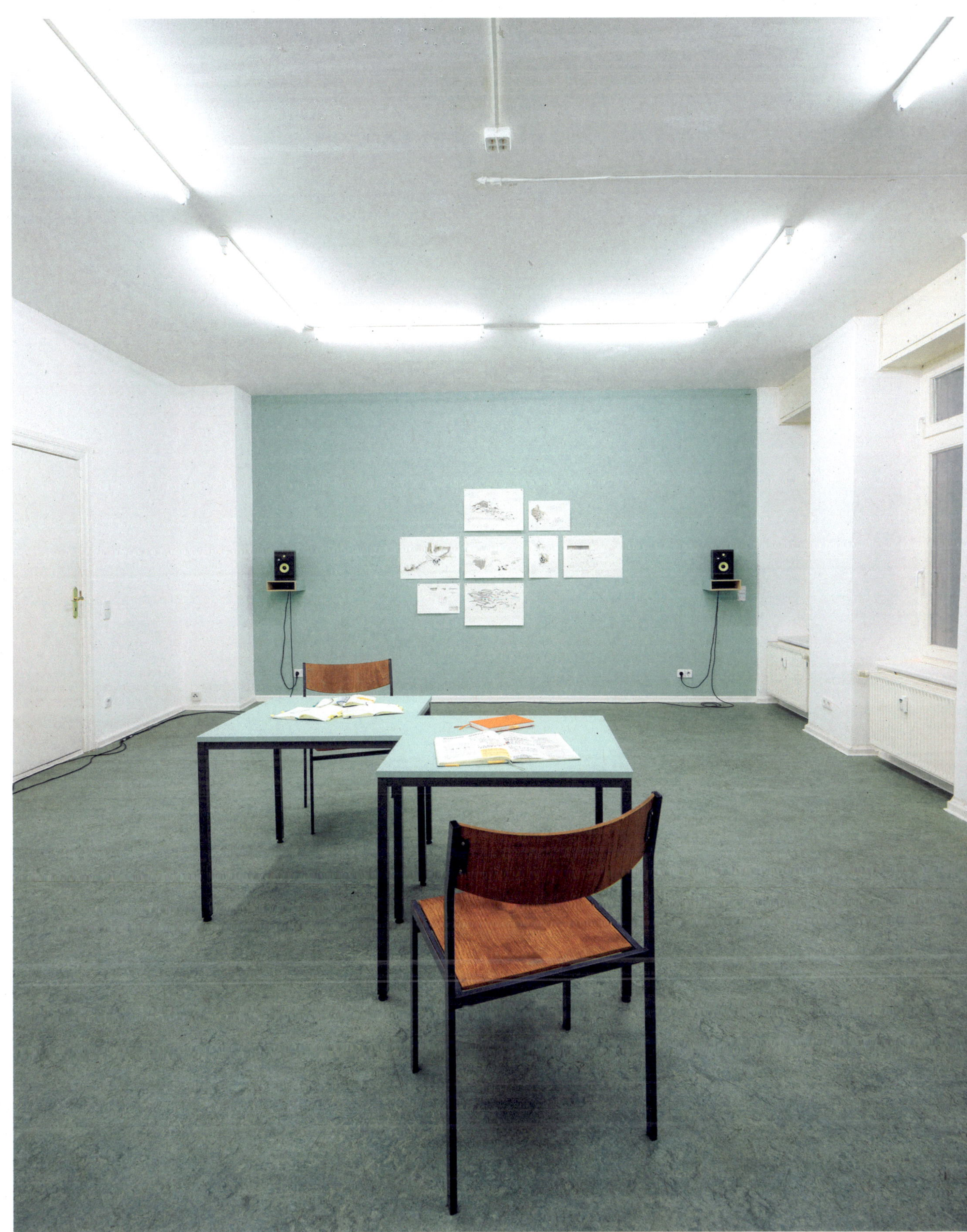

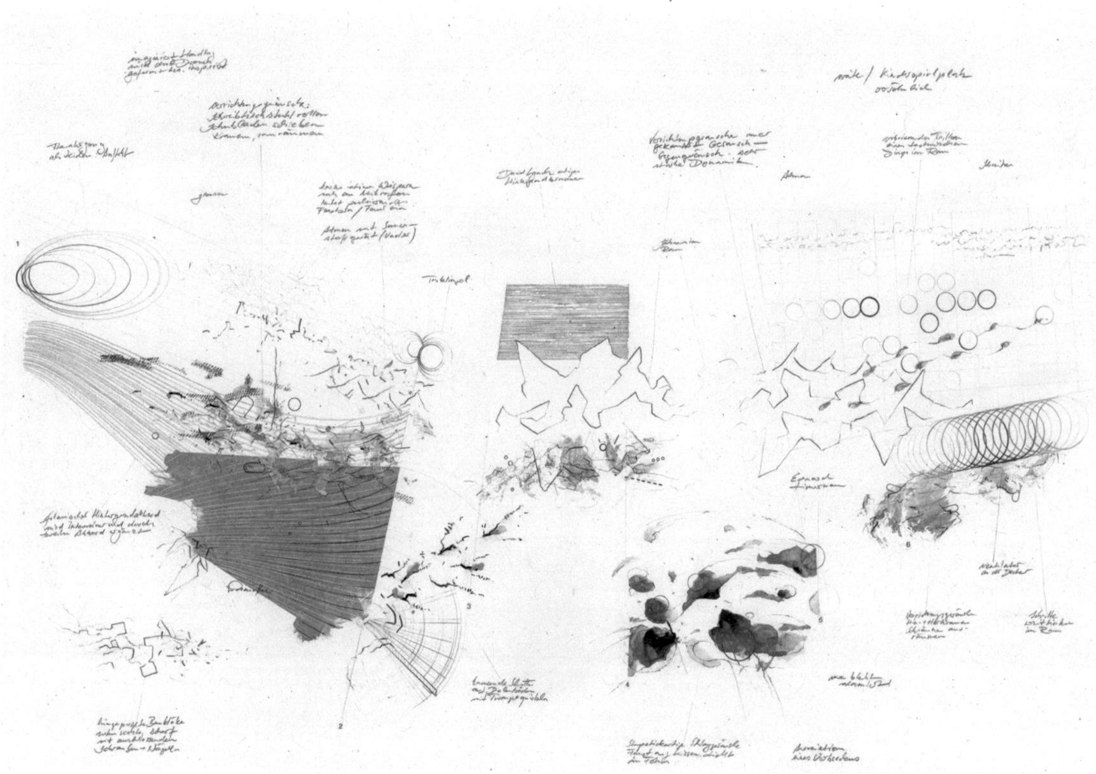

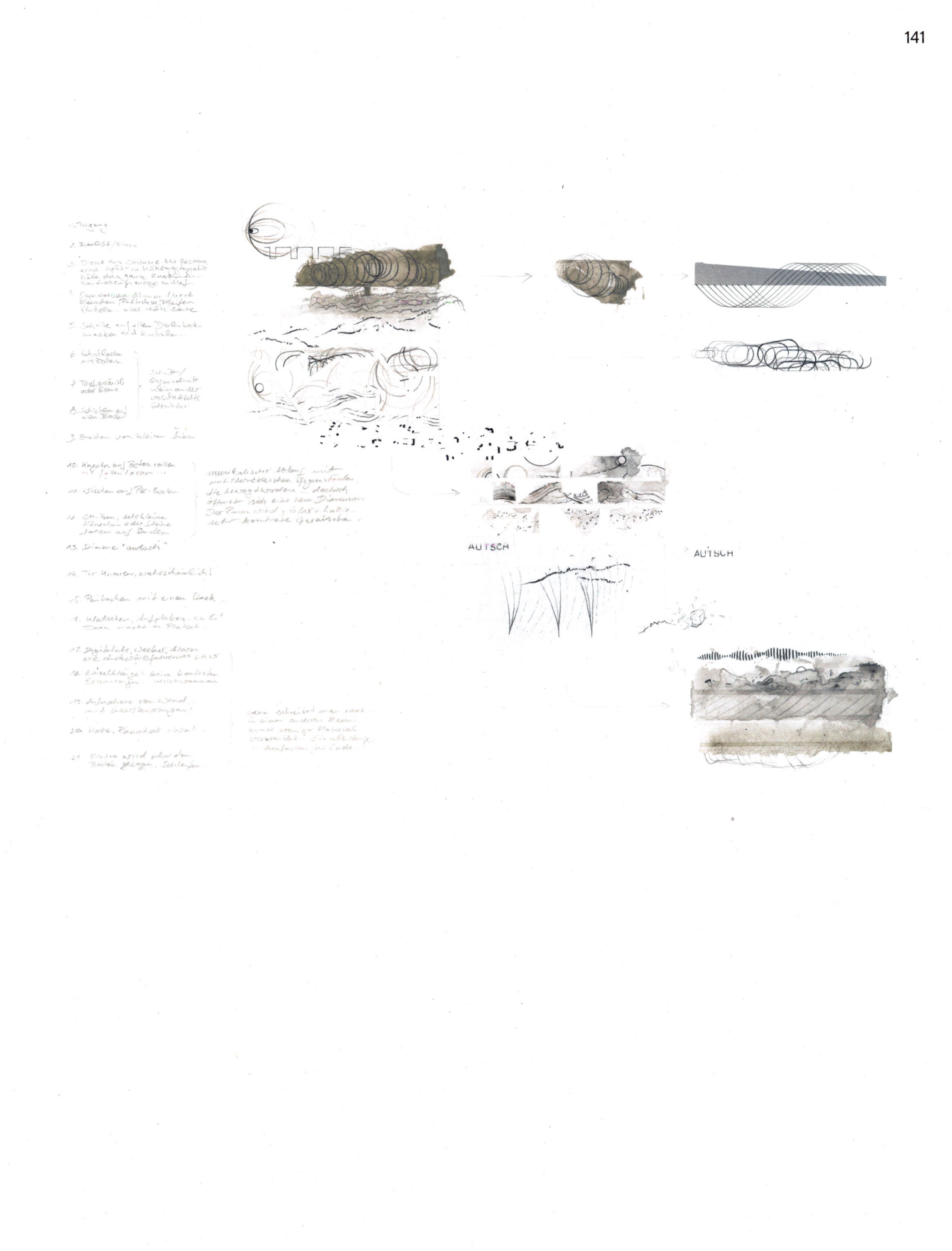

AUTSCH

AUTSCH

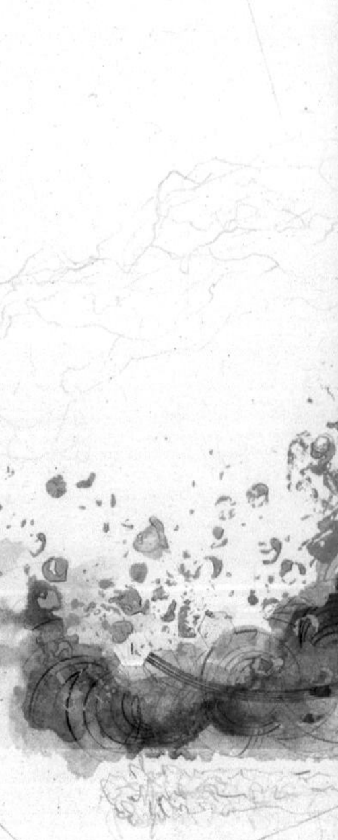
Kinder spielen
auf der Straße,
von weitem...

Tagesschausprecher
spricht ARD Tagesschau

Ein
erläu...
sel...

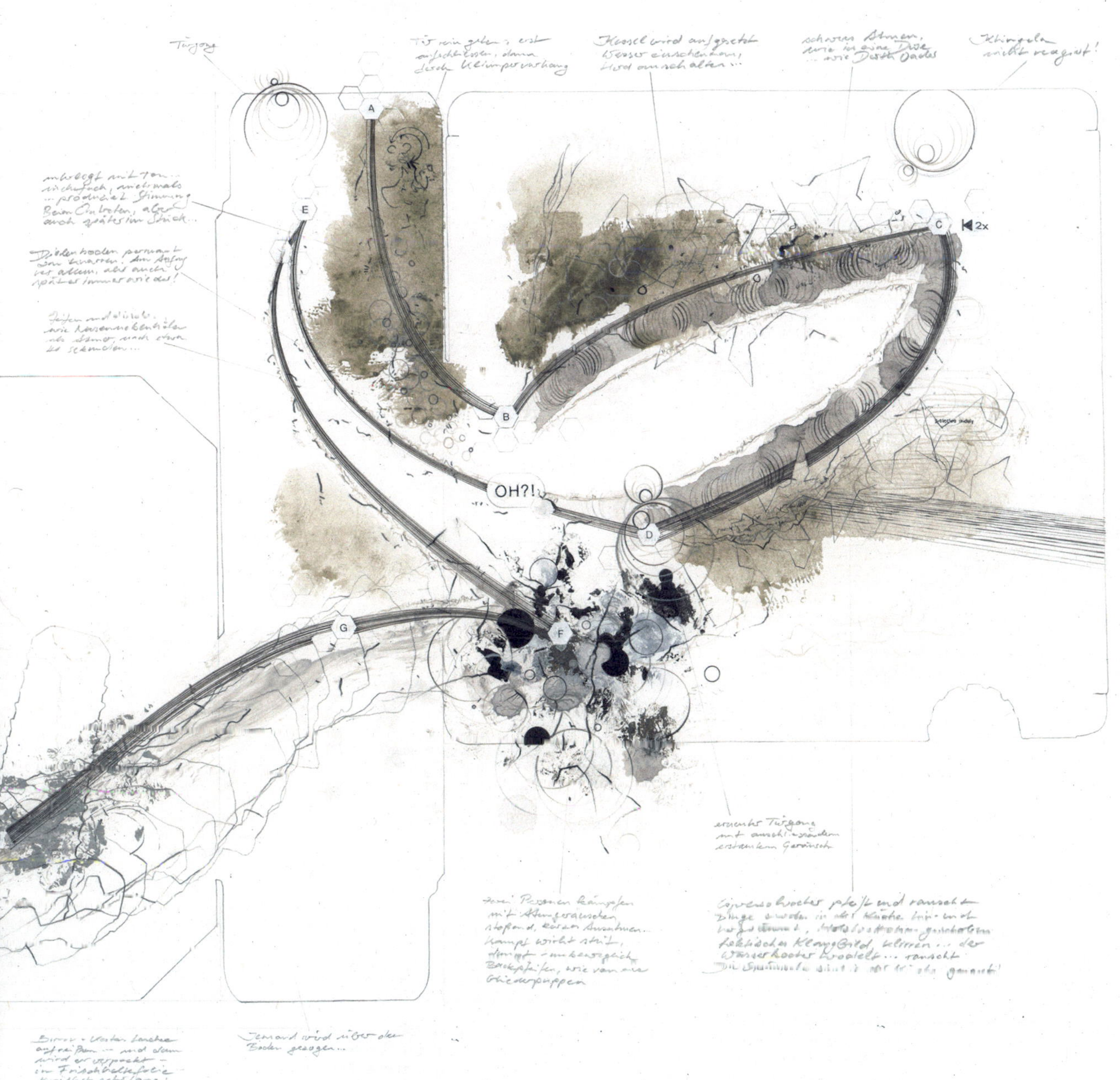

A
B
C
D
E
F
G
2x
OH?!